A TILTED GUIDE TO BEING A DEFENDANT

the tilted scales collective

combustion books

A Tilted Guide to Being a Defendant
Copyright 2017 The Tilted Scales Collective
TILTEDSCALESCOLLECTIVE.ORG

Published by Combustion Books
COMBUSTIONBOOKS.ORG

ISBN: 978-1-938660-18-4

Version 1.1

*For our imprisoned comrades in struggle
who have joined the ancestors*

CONTENTS

3
Acknowledgments

7
About Tilted Scales Collective

9
Introduction

15
Chapter 1
On Being a Defendant

39

Chapter 2

Setting and Balancing Personal, Political, and Legal Goals

83

Chapter 3

Common Legal Situations

109

Chapter 4

Working with Your Lawyer

135

Chapter 5

Working with Your Codefendants

153

Chapter 6

Working with Your Defense Committee

173

Chapter 7

Working with the Media

213

Chapter 8

Resolving Your Case

253

Chapter 9

Surviving in Prison

279

Conclusion

281

Appendix A

The Criminal Legal Process

291

Appendix B
Sample Joint Defense Agreement

299

Appendix C
Sample Attorney Retainer Agreement

303
Endnotes

ACKNOWLEDGMENTS

Jenny Esquivel

I would like to thank Kristian Williams for his merciless editing and his invaluable friendship; Combustion for always being down for the cause with the skills and abilities to make rad shit happen; all the current and former prisoners who participated in the making of this guide in one way or another, despite the potential to suffer serious retaliation for their contributions; the legal workers, support crew members, and lawyers who not only offered their invaluable experiences and insights to make this a better guide, but who also do amazing work every day to help free our imprisoned comrades; Denver ABC for hosting the amazing conference from which this guide grew; Betsy Raasch-Gilman for her amazing contributions—drafting, editing, and constant moral support! I would also like to thank Eric, because we did that shit together. I hope that our experiences and struggles will help those who find themselves reading these pages. And, of course, Jude, who has been a trusted confidant and comrade through many struggles—personal and political. His kick-ass organizing, support work, and writing are the foundation of the book you have in your hands.

Jude Ortiz

This book is the result of years of thinking/re-thinking, writing/re-writing, delays due to life, delays due to urgent prisoner support organizing, and continual support from friends and comrades who gently (and repeatedly) nudged us to finish the damn thing already. While two of us have our names on it, this is a book that could only come from a radical community spread across Turtle Island. I am proud to be a part of that struggle and to be connected to so many amazing people. I would especially like to thank the current prisoners who drastically shaped our thinking in this book, both by providing us with critical, honest feedback on our outline at the outset of this endeavor and by engaging in conversations about our ideas over the years. We have chosen to keep these prisoners anonymous to decrease the chances of retaliation against them for their involvement, such as by giving the state yet another reason to deny them parole. Yet they know who they are, and we hope they will see their ideas and contributions reflected in this book.

In addition to everyone who Jenny thanked, I would like to thank the Cleveland 4 defense committee, Daniel Regenscheit, Dennison Williams, Garrett Fitzgerald, Jihad Abdulmumit, John Viola, the late Ken Tilsen, Kevin Van Meter, Kris Hermes, Luce Guillén-Givins, Lynne Stewart, Maddy Pfeiffer, Maryam Khajavi, Megan Books, Molly Armour, Rachel White-Domain, Ralph Poynter, Red Bird Prison Abolition, Ryan Levitt, Sarah Shourd, Sharlyn Grace, Sterling Stutz, Tim Phillips, and Will R. Logan for their contributions. And especially Wopashitwe Mondo Eyen we Langa, who provided us with detailed feedback before he joined the ancestors in March 2016. If I neglected to name anyone, please know that your contributions were invaluable and the oversight was unintentional.

And, of course, many thanks go out to Combustion for helping us turn our ideas into a tangible resource for those engaged in struggle. Likewise, many thanks to Strangers in a Tangled Wilderness for the design work and timely feedback on both the chapter excerpt released as a zine earlier this year and the completed manuscript. Finally, I would like to thank Jenny for her dedication, perseverance, and consistent willingness to push forward with this work despite some of the biggest life challenges and changes one could imagine in a few short years. You are a dear friend, amazing collective member, and wonderful partner in (thought)crime.

ABOUT TILTED SCALES COLLECTIVE

TILTED SCALES COLLECTIVE IS A SMALL COLLECTIVE OF DEDI-cated legal support organizers who have spent years support-ing and fighting for political prisoners, prisoners of war, and politicized prisoners in the occupied lands of Turtle Island (i.e., the so-called United States). The collective formed out of conversations at an Anarchist Black Cross conference about the need to stop allowing the state to use criminal charges to dismantle, destroy, and neutralize radical movements. From those conversations was borne the idea for this guide for de-fendants. A companion guide for lawyers who are representing the kind of defendants we are talking about in this guide is forthcoming. As a collective, we seek to help radicals and revolutionaries figure out how to protect themselves and their comrades when faced with state repression, while strengthen-ing their movements and advancing the fight for liberation.

INTRODUCTION

IF THIS BOOK FOUND ITS WAY INTO YOUR HANDS, CHANCES are you are in dire need of it right now. Maybe the person who acted like your best friend was working for the cops the whole time. Or those FBI agents who have been harassing you for months put you in handcuffs this time, and now you are facing terrorism charges. Or you woke up a couple of days ago with an assault weapon pointed at your head and some Darth Vader dude shouting at you not to move. Or you went to a demonstration and suddenly the district attorney wants to make a felon out of you.

However it happened, rest assured that you are not the first one to be targeted by the state—and that help is here. Others have been in your situation before, and this guide is based on their experiences. While writing this book, we received feedback and insights from dozens of prisoners, former prisoners, legal workers, and lawyers to make sure we were able to provide you with the best advice possible. Who is "we"? The Tilted Scales Collective is a loose group of anarchist legal workers who decided to write this guide based on years of supporting anarchists (or people targeted for allegedly being anarchists) and others as they have dealt with serious criminal charges. We are not lawyers and nothing in this guide should be construed as legal advice.

We wrote this guide for people who are seriously entangled in the criminal legal system, whether they are facing federal felony accusations, conspiracy charges, terrorist enhancements, or potential years or decades in prison. Of necessity, we could not focus in-depth on state-level charges because they vary quite a bit from state to state. However, the basics of handling your case will largely be the same, regardless of which criminal legal system you find yourself confronting. We also did not write this guide to be specific to everyone scooped up in mass arrests at protests or spontaneous rebellions, although we hope it will be useful in those situations, particularly for those facing serious felony charges.

A word on the political framework guiding our thoughts and analyses in this book: in the broadest sense, we consider all criminal charges to be political. For example, people would not be in jail if private property and the state did not exist, and if racism, hetero-patriarchy, capitalism, and the like did not run our world. Mass incarceration is a defining part of the era we are in, and that institution is thoroughly racist, transphobic, and classist, to say the least. State repression of dissidents is also a real part of this historical era, and there are certain state processes that are adept in squashing revolutionary movements, including targeting individual dissidents. In this book, we assume you stood up to one or more of these unjust conditions in some form, and that is why you are in trouble today. We also assume you want to continue your struggle and have a commitment to your comrades, loved ones, and community.

Our advice in this book is based on the premises that you can and will defend the movement you are involved with as well as yourself, and strive to use your rotten situation to advance the struggles that threatened the state in the first place. We refuse to allow the state to succeed in its efforts to dismantle our revolutionary organizing through criminal charges and incarceration. The late Nelson Mandela, reflecting on his twenty-seven years in prison in South Africa, captured this sentiment clearly:

> I was now on the sidelines, but I also knew that I would not give up the fight…. We regarded the struggle in prison as a microcosm of the struggle as a whole. We would fight inside as we had fought outside. The racism and repression were the same; I would simply have to fight on different terms.[1]

These terms are complex and always stacked in the state's favor, but that does not guarantee the state victory or mean that you have to let them railroad you.

You have a lot of decisions in front of you, and possibly many years of legal hurry-up-and-wait maneuvers. You may want to put this whole episode behind you as fast as you can and get out from under the crush of the criminal legal system by accepting a plea agreement. There are lots of good arguments for taking this road, especially if you are a parent, trans / intersex / gender non-conforming / queer, undocumented, have health concerns, or have other factors that put you at more risk. Or you may want to take your case to a jury and use the system every last step of the way to get publicity for your cause, or to simply maintain your innocence in the face of false accusations.

This guide will try to help you weigh different strategies and anticipate how they will affect your life, relationships, and future. It will also offer you insights about selecting and working with your lawyer(s), working with a defense committee, conducting a media campaign, working with your codefendants (if any), and surviving prison, should it come to that. We will attempt to give you the knowledge you need to make decisions that are best for you, your comrades and loved ones, and your movement, without sacrificing one for the other. We cannot tell you exactly what to do, as each situation and person is different. Our aim is simply to see our social movements come out stronger because people handle their charges from a revolutionary perspective.

In basic terms, you have two options when you face charges: plead guilty or go to trial. Right now in the United States, about 95% of all criminal cases are settled with plea agreements.[2] Plea agreements save the prosecution and the courts time and money by avoiding lengthy pre-trial hearings and trials. The criminal legal system depends on people pleading guilty and prosecutors and judges are extremely adept at coercing pleas. The closer your trial date comes, the more intense the pressure will be on you to plead guilty, often in exchange for the potential of a reduced sentence.

This pressure often includes attempts by the prosecution to get you to cooperate against your comrades. We cannot stress this enough: in all aspects of handling your case, you must not jeopardize any of your comrades, indicted or not.

The criminal legal system always tries to divide and conquer defendants. To that end, you may be offered seemingly sweet deals if you provide information, and/or testify against someone else, and/or appear in front of a grand jury, and/or wear a wire for the cops. You should reject these offers out of hand, on principle—snitching should never be an option. Yet this is not to say that you should reject plea agreements out of principle, as sometimes pleading guilty is the best decision all around. If you decide to sign a plea agreement, consider the terms of your plea agreement from every possible angle to ensure it does not put someone else in danger with a careless word or phrase. Hopefully, your attorney will be alert for such things, but most attorneys are not used to working on criminal cases where solidarity is the first concern. You are ultimately responsible for being absolutely sure about what you are signing, saying, and doing. This guide will go into much more detail about your options for resolving your case.

No matter what the prosecutors tell you, your choices will not boil down to going to prison or betraying your supporters, comrades, or movement. There are many other possible outcomes. As one example, in the 1970s, the Wounded Knee Legal Defense/Offense Committee successfully turned the tables on the prosecution and put the FBI on trial instead of Dennis Banks and Russell Means, resulting in a hung jury.[3] A great deal can be done by coordinating a savvy legal strategy with an assertive political strategy, even if it cannot always give us exactly what we want. Read on to find out more!

We wrote this book with this question in mind: "How is my case part of the revolutionary struggle?" The idea for this book arose out of discussions at North American Anarchist Black Cross conferences because we realized a strategic need to fight back against serious criminal charges that ended in our comrades serving decades in prison, which demoralized our movements and diverted our resources into defensive projects rather than offensive revolutionary organizing. We hope this book will help you simultaneously fight your charges and strengthen your movement.

Chapter 1
ON BEING A DEFENDANT

THIS CHAPTER COVERS SOME BASICS ABOUT THE CRIMINAL LEGAL system and the challenges it typically creates for people, whether they are arrested because of their politics or because of the government's routine oppression of particular segments of society to maintain the ruling power structures. We also explore some basic aspects of facing serious felony charges that are specific, although not necessarily unique, to political defendants.

Defining Our Terms

In the broadest sense, we believe that all prisoners are political since the criminal legal system is one way the state keeps particular communities oppressed and downtrodden to benefit those with power. Historically, these communities have been poor, Indigenous, recently arrived immigrants, and/or people of color. This system is also designed to suppress dissent and punish those who work to protest against, subvert, and destroy the dominant social order and government. Thus, the criminal legal system is a political process and all those who are swept up in it are there for political reasons, whether explicitly or implicitly. While the state goes to great lengths to fool people into believing the myth that courts impartially deliver justice to the people, it is easy to see that every criminal charge is political in nature and thus being a prisoner is an inherently political condition.[4]

And state repression of political movements also exists. Thus, "political defendant" or "political prisoner" describes those who face criminal charges because of their political activity (e.g., protesting, direct action, civil disobedience, clandestine actions) or alleged political beliefs (e.g., the state often calls political defendants "anarchists" to smear them in court and in the media, even if these people do not self-identify as anarchists). "Politicized prisoner" is also often used to describe prisoners who are charged with crimes that are not generally considered to be political but who have a political analysis of their situations and the power structures within society that created the conditions they are in. "Prisoner of war" is chosen by some prisoners who do not recognize the legitimacy of the United States government to put them on trial. See, for example, many of the Puerto Rican independence fighters (*independentistas*[5]) and some members of the Black Liberation Army (BLA)[6], among others. Other prisoners will choose this term because they see their charges as part of class war or social war.

▬ ▬ ▬ ▬ ▬ ▬ ▬ ▬

We are using "political defendant" and "political prisoner" to refer to everyone the government targets as a threat to the ruling power structures and social orders. These people often find themselves facing charges through a number of distinct processes, including:

- *Arrested at a protest:* Often, activists are singled out at a protest and charged with felonies. Finding themselves stuck in jail unexpectedly, their lives can be turned upside down. They are often suddenly faced with the need to raise thousands of dollars to make bail, if they are eligible for bail at all. The cops and prosecutors also often smear them in the media as "violent anarchists" or "radicals" to justify police brutality and oppression in the streets, enormous expenditures on so-called security at protests, and laws being passed to restrict free speech and other rights in advance of the protests.

- *Charged with committing an illegal act:* At times, people are arrested for allegedly committing an illegal act that is political in nature or motivation, such as liberating animals, destroying property, or hacking websites. At other times, people are arrested because they fit a particular stereotype and happened to be in the vicinity of an alleged crime, were involved in a situation where the cops intervened and targeted them for arrest, or were selected to be the scapegoats for a crime when the state needs to get a conviction to avoid the embarrassment of the crime going unsolved.

- *Swept up in a campaign of state repression:* When the state focuses on particular groups, communities, or movements, people can be arrested and charged with serious crimes because of their alleged political associations and activities. Undercover cops and informants may gather evidence against them or snitches may give testimony about them. The Palmer raids, COINTELPRO, and the Green Scare are infamous examples of targeted state repression of political groups.[7]

- *Entrapment:* Increasingly, the FBI and local police across the country are relying on undercover agents, infiltrators, and informants to manufacture the elements of a crime in order to charge people. These defendants can be targeted as individuals or as a group. The FBI in particular has refined this approach by targeting Arabs and Muslims in the so-called "War on Terror."[8] When applying this tactic to domestic social movements, the FBI often targets activists who are new to these movements, on the fringes of them, or generally do not have a lot of connections or support.

- *Targeted while incarcerated:* Prisoners are often targeted and slapped with disciplinary infractions and new criminal charges because of their political speech and activity within the prison or because of their resistance to the brutal, oppressive, and dehumanizing conditions of incarceration.

This list is not exhaustive by any means and we hope that, regardless of how your charges came about or whether you would choose the term "political defendant/prisoner" for yourself or not, you will be better equipped to fight back against the oppressive criminal legal system after reading this book. Throughout this book, we will be urging you to consider yourself and your criminal charges to be part of a revolutionary movement in resistance to the dominant power structures ruling the world.

Never Alone

Part of understanding your charges as a piece of radical struggle and social movements is understanding that you are not alone in your ordeal. The criminal legal system and prison-industrial complex are designed to make you feel isolated. The people who maintain this system will mostly be treating you like a criminal, a threat, a monster to be feared and locked up. You will likely feel enormous pressure to consider only your own personal interests (e.g., getting off with the lightest punishment possible, no matter what you must do to achieve that). The judge will likely issue rulings to prevent you from talking about the political context of your charges at trial, thereby enforcing the myth that the charges are about criminal activity rather than political struggle. If you are incarcerated pending trial, you may be put in solitary or another form of restricted confinement to keep you physically and emotionally removed from your support base. All of these factors are used to make you believe that you are alone and your charges are unrelated to anything else going on.

This, of course, is all a lie. Understanding this truth helps you place yourself squarely in a political struggle.

When you are engaged in revolutionary struggle or social movements, you are likely to be in court at some point or another. Dealing with the criminal legal system is difficult, we are not going to lie. Even when the state has no evidence to substantiate the charges, prosecutors routinely scare people into pleading guilty by threatening them with years or decades in prison, using technical legal rulings to stack the deck in their favor at trial, and wearing the defendants down by dragging out the court process until they are emotionally and financially exhausted.[9]

But remember that many people have been through this before and have survived. Many have faced multiple life sentences and fought back to defeat the charges entirely or lost at trial but were sentenced to a fraction of the time they were threatened with originally. Many have found ways to get the charges thrown out before the case even went to trial or continued fighting after conviction to get the convictions overturned so they could be released. Many of our prisoners have suffered greatly while incarcerated, too many have died captives of the state, and they have all been held in cages for too long. While we do not want you or anyone else to be held captive, you should remember that you have peers in struggle whose experiences can help you figure out how to survive your own.

Many of these prisoners would likely say that fighting criminal charges is not the most inspiring political work they have ever done, much less their preferred battlefield in the struggle against the state and systemic oppression, but they have survived with their politics intact and have grown from their ordeals. As your case progresses, develop the habit of asking yourself this question: "How is my case part of the revolutionary struggle?" Considering this over and over may help you with important decisions and affect the way you portray your case to supporters, to the media, and in court. (See Chapter 2, "Setting and Balancing Personal, Political, and Legal Goals," for more on this topic.)

Power Concedes Nothing Without a Demand

Another part of understanding your charges as a piece of radical struggle is realizing that the criminal legal system will not do what is right or just or fair. This system will do whatever it can to maintain state control and the power of the elite. No judge or jury will deliver us justice. At best, our struggles will force the courts to take actions that correspond with our notions of justice, but the courts themselves do not give us justice—we must demand it and fight for it. Frederick Douglass's famous quote, "Power concedes nothing without a demand," is clearly true of the courts. So your legal defense, if you choose to use one, is a matter of making demands of this power in a system with largely unfathomable technicalities and procedures that are designed to disempower you and thwart your every effort. This particular form of struggle is inherently limited by the rules the court has laid out, and there are other factors to be considered in determining how to make your demands (again, see Chapter 2), but whatever legal maneuvers you take are about fighting back.

These legal struggles generally take way longer than we would like. Pre-trial proceedings can drag out for years, appeals and *habeas corpus*[10] petitions after conviction can take years or decades, and probation after release can keep people under the thumb of the criminal legal system for years after release—or even for the rest of their lives. The victories and tragedies are too numerous to name here, but a few examples seem warranted.

In March 2009, four animal rights activists were indicted under the Animal Enterprise Terrorism Act (AETA). The second count of the indictment alleged that Joseph Buddenberg,[11] Maryam Khajavi, Nathan Pope, and Adriana Stumpo—who came to be known as the AETA 4—had interfered with an animal enterprise and threatened animal researchers and their partners to the point that they feared for their safety. The first count alleged that they had all conspired to commit these acts. Both of these charges were labeled terrorism by the state. As the pre-trial proceedings progressed, it quickly became clear that the government's scant allegations were mostly about political activity that is supposedly protected by the First Amendment, including being present at protests, wearing bandannas at protests, chanting, and writing on sidewalks with chalk outside of the residences of animal researchers. The alleged actions that were clearly illegal, including a claim that a husband of one of the animal researchers was hit with a "dark, firm object," were not attributed to any of the defendants. The defense lawyers filed a motion to dismiss the indictment because it insufficiently specified the actions the defendants allegedly took. In July

2010, the judge found that the indictment was insufficient and dismissed the charges, although he gave the government the option to refile a sufficient indictment. As of the time of this writing, the government has not done so.[12]

Not all cases are resolved so easily, of course. For example, Dhoruba Bin Wahad, a leader of the Black Panthers at the time of his arrest in May 1971, was charged with attempted murder after two cops were shot at outside of the Manhattan district attorney's home. His first trial ended in a hung jury, the second in a mistrial, and the third with a conviction. He was sentenced to twenty-five years to life and served nineteen before his conviction was overturned due to evidence being withheld by the prosecution.[13] Bin Wahad, like many radicals of that era, was a target of COINTELPRO. Since his release, he has tirelessly organized to defend the oppressed and fight racism across the globe.

And sometimes, power does not concede until it is too late. Marilyn Buck, for example, was released from prison just three weeks before she died from cancer. She had served more than three decades in prison after being convicted of actions she took as a white, anti-imperialist ally to self-determination and national liberation struggles of oppressed peoples in the United States (namely the Puerto Rican and Black liberation movements). As is the rule in prisons, she had been denied medical care until her cancer was so advanced that treatment could not save her life.[14] Herman Wallace, one of the Angola 3, was released just three days before he too died of cancer. He became a Black Panther while in Louisiana State Penitentiary in Angola and was quickly targeted by the prison administration because of his radical political activity. He and two other Black Panthers, Albert Woodfox and Robert Hillary King, were falsely charged with murder and held in solitary confinement to prevent them from engaging in what one warden called "Black Pantherism." Herman spent forty-one years in solitary confinement before his conviction was overturned and he finally left prison. The state of Louisiana re-indicted him two days later and he passed away the day after that (although the state had not rearrested him and he was not in a cage at the time of his passing).[15] The passing of Marilyn and Herman sparked renewed calls for freedom for all political prisoners and prisoners of war, which is possibly the greatest honor that can be paid to these freedom fighters.

We do not offer these examples to depress or demoralize you, and we certainly hope that your case is resolved as quickly and painlessly as possible. Yet we do not want to sugarcoat the brutal reality of the enemy we are up against. We also point to these examples because they show how people have not fought alone—they were supported by loved ones and comrades for months, years, and decades to demand justice.[16]

Know Your Rights—And Use Them!

We offer this brief section as an overview of the rights the United States Constitution is supposed to guarantee to everyone within the political boundaries of the US, regardless of whether they have citizenship or not. In practice, these "rights" are not nearly as strong as people are generally led to believe and are routinely violated with impunity by the cops, prosecutors, and courts. These violations occur in the ways that other acts of oppression typically occur, i.e., they are much more common against poor people, people of color, trans / intersex / gender non-conforming / queer people, and people without legal status in the country. Much more powerful than any right a government can give us are our human rights to not cooperate with our oppressors and aid in our own oppression.

So what do these struggles look like on the ground? They start at the moment of arrest, so we will start there as well. First and foremost, remember: you have the right to remain silent. Use it! Invoke this right by saying, "I am going to remain silent." Then do so, no matter what the cops do to you or say to you to get you to give them information. If they take a softer approach, they may offer to help you out, improve the conditions of your incarceration, put in a good word for you with the prosecutor or judge, or other seemingly helpful things. They will almost certainly tell you that they already have everything they need to send you to prison for decades, your codefendants or others have already snitched on you, talking to them will help you save yourself, and other such lies. If they take a harsh approach, they may starve, beat, freeze, or otherwise torture you. These tactics are all meant to break you and force you to turn on yourself and your comrades. Even if you are held for days before going in front of a judge or seeing an attorney, keep your mouth shut and remember that silence is your greatest protection in this situation.

You also have the right to an attorney, so invoke that by saying, "I want to speak to a lawyer." Keep demanding this until you are able to speak with one. Again, hold firm on this even if you have to sit in jail for days before seeing an attorney. Do not sign documents or make legal decisions about your case until you are able to speak to an attorney. If you waived your right to see a lawyer under duress (i.e., you were pressured, scared, threatened, etc.), you can always re-invoke this right by saying those words. Once you secure an attorney, make a commitment to yourself that you will be an active participant in your case.

Revealing the Hollowness of So-called Constitutional Rights

In various Supreme Court rulings over the last several years, the Supreme Court has consistently ruled that people must explicitly state their rights to invoke them. For example, simply remaining silent may not constitute invoking your right to remain silent in the eyes of the law. Thus, it seems to be legally safest to invoke your rights clearly and then to stay silent. See *Salinas v. Texas*, 133 S. Ct. 2174, 186 L. Ed. 2D 376 (2013) and *Berghuis v. Thompkins*, 560 U.S. 370 (2010) for the rulings that remaining silent in and of itself is not sufficient to invoke your right to remain silent. See *Davis v. United States* (92-1949), 512 U.S. 452 (1994) for the ruling that people must explicitly and unambiguously invoke their right to a lawyer, such as by clearly stating, "I want to speak to a lawyer."

Remember that you are dealing with your enemies (friends do not keep you in a cage and guard you with guns, after all), so they never have your best interests in mind. In contrast, exercising these rights is always in your best interests—and in the best interests of your codefendants, if you have any, and everyone else you know. Overall, you might find it helpful to think of these less as "rights" and more as responsibilities to yourself, your communities, and your comrades. Keeping your wits about you and maintaining your focus on your responsibilities can be challenging, so be kind to and patient with yourself. You can always re-invoke your rights to silence and to having an attorney even if you have already answered questions or waived your rights previously. (We say this not to imply an endorsement of answering questions, as any time you cooperate, you could be putting yourself or others in danger. Rather, we are simply acknowledging how the pressure and fear that people often feel after being arrested can cause them to make bad decisions. Messing up once does not mean that you have to continue doing so or that you should no longer invoke your rights.)

Another piece of important advice is to avoid the temptation of thinking about your situation as a game that you need to play correctly to save yourself. The odds are against you and the cops have every conceivable advantage, so the only advantage you really have is your silence. Talking to the cops robs you of your power and gives them more power over you.

Acting from Solidarity, Not Fear

In a recent high-profile case involving multiple codefendants, several had close ties to each other while one did not. Fearing betrayal from the one with looser ties to the group, a couple of the defendants gave statements to the police after arrest in the hopes of protecting themselves and their closer comrades. While these defendants did not snitch on the other defendants or anyone else, the idea that talking to the cops can protect you or others is faulty.

Fortunately, these statements did not hurt anyone in court and the defendants were able to maintain solidarity, ultimately taking non-cooperating plea deals and serving their prison terms. Lucky breaks cannot be counted on, however—silence is our greatest weapon and strongest form of solidarity when we get arrested. One of the defendants later said, "Life would have been easier had neither of us given a statement and all of us should have focused on our solidarity during that first day, but they don't call it a trial by fire for nothing. So, as always, push on as a whole where possible, you will make it."

Another lesson this defendant points to is that people should support each other when they are arrested together. If you are arrested with other people and someone seems vulnerable to police manipulation or coercion, extend your support and solidarity immediately. Even simple gestures such as saying "we" and "us"

> when talking about your charges (without
> discussing the details of your case, unless you
> are meeting with your lawyers) can help peo-
> ple feel supported and protected. Supporting
> and caring for each other is another strong
> form of solidarity when we get arrested.

Be careful with how you speak about your case to people aside from cops, as well. A good general rule is to not speak to other prisoners about the details of your case (aside from your codefendants, of course). Jailhouse snitches are common, as the cops routinely coerce people into snitching on others for a chance at improving their own legal situations. Many people volunteer to do so because they are willing to hurt others to help themselves. Assume that all your conversations within jail or prison are being monitored and can be used against you. Do not set yourself or others up by speaking about the charges against you or the circumstances of your arrest. A good rule to follow is to only discuss the details of your case with your lawyer and other members of your legal team who are covered by attorney-client privilege[17] (if you do not know who that includes, be sure to ask your lawyer).[18]

Going to Court for Your First Hearing

At some point after your arrest, you will be going to court. The name of this hearing and what happens in it varies from jurisdiction to jurisdiction, so there is no one-size-fits-all ad-vice to be given about what to do in court. Appendix A has an explanation of the typical steps in a criminal prosecution in the federal criminal system as well as some of the terms you will need to learn when going through the court process. We offer this appendix as a good place to start to figure out what will likely be happening to you over the next several months, years, or decades.

When you first go to court, demand a public defender if you do not already have a lawyer representing you. Do this even if you want to hire a private attorney rather than sticking with a public defender. The court will have a process for determining who qualifies for a public defender based on income, but most courts have public defenders available to stand in with defendants at their first appearances, so demand that one is there with you. Chances are, you will not be able to talk at length with the public defender about your charges, but you should make clear that you are pleading not guilty and do not waive any of your rights in the trial or pre-trial process (e.g., you do not need to waive the right to a speedy trial even if you do not invoke that right explicitly). When you waive rights at this stage, they are generally waived for good.

Additionally, some courts allow you to postpone all the legal proceedings that would have happened at your first appearance so you can find a lawyer. You can ask the judge for a continuance until you can find your own lawyer; even if the court you are in does not allow this, the worst the judge can do at that point is to tell you "no."

When you are arraigned, the judge will read the charges against you and ask you whether you plead guilty, not guilty, or no contest (also known as "*nolo contendere*"). Plead not guilty or enter no plea. Doing so is the legally safest way to preserve your rights to a trial and ensure you have the time you need to explore the charges against you and examine the government's evidence as you determine how you want to handle your case (see Chapter 2 for an in-depth examination of aspects to consider when making this decision). Your situation may not be as bad as it first appears and you might be able to find ways of using the system's seemingly endless technicalities in your favor.

Pleading not guilty at your first appearance also lessens the chance that you will accidentally screw over others who are arrested on the same or related charges, as one person being convicted can often be used against others in court. Pleading guilty can also give the prosecutors more pressure to apply on the other defendants to force them to accept plea agreements. (See Chapter 3, "Common Legal Situations," for more information on common legal situations political defendants face.) Remember that you can always change your not guilty plea to guilty later on, but you generally cannot change a guilty plea back to not guilty.[19]

Talking About Your Charges

The heading for this section may be confusing, since we have already spent some time in this chapter urging you *not* to talk about your case. While that advice holds true, there are also important differences between talking about your charges in ways that are damaging to you or others and talking about them in politically and personally necessary ways. In this final section, we begin to explore some of the reasons you will want to talk about your charges and some good ways of doing so. We will explore these ideas more in Chapter 2, "Setting and Balancing Personal, Political, and Legal Goals, and Chapter 7, "Working with the Media."

You will likely want and need to talk about the charges you are facing with your loved ones, comrades, and supporters. When doing so, remember that any statements you make about the circumstances of your arrest (or about any other aspect of your life, yourself, your friends, family, etc.) can and will be brought against you and others in court. All phone calls from jail are recorded, many visiting rooms have microphones and cameras, and incoming and outgoing mail and email are often monitored and copied. There are too many examples of defendants' and supporters' words being used against the defendants in court to list, so suffice it to say that the state has many well-oiled machines for using us against ourselves and we do not need to help them.[20]

Also remember that there is a difference between talking about your charges and talking about all the details of the state's case against you, or all the evidence you have for your defense. Criminal indictments, criminal complaints, prosecution and defense motions, and judge's orders are generally public documents (what is public or not can vary based on jurisdiction, and some court documents can be sealed). Since they are public, you can technically share them with anyone. You may not always want to do so depending on your overall situation and your goals (again, see Chapter 2), but talking about what the state is alleging is most often necessary and beneficial to you. The state will generally benefit more from our silence about the charges we are facing than we will.

In contrast, there will be evidence that you receive from the state as part of discovery[21] that you may not be able to or want to talk about publicly. Likewise, there may be evidence that you collect for your defense that is protected by attorney work product privileges that you will not want to disclose to the prosecution by talking about it publicly. Even so, there may be times when you will want to take certain risks to talk about your case in ways that push up against standard criminal defense protocols because it is the best political move to make. Whatever you do, talking with your lawyer about it before you do it is a good idea.

Talking to Loved Ones

Talking to your loved ones about your situation can be particularly tricky, especially if they do not share your politics or were not fully aware of your political activity and associations prior to your arrest. People in your life who are not close political comrades (e.g., chosen or biological family, work friends, school friends, lovers) will generally want to be reassured that you did not do anything wrong or that the charges you are facing are total lies. Your definition of doing something "wrong" and theirs may not be the same and you may not be able to talk about the details of your case in the ways they want. However, you may find that this is a chance for you to explain your politics more clearly than you have before and educate them on the broader context of your charges. This is not to say that there will not be strained relationships or tense situations. The challenge will likely be to connect with them on a personal level while protecting yourself legally.

Being in custody pending trial can make it even harder to have these conversations since all your communications with people will be recorded and used against you. At times, you will need to wait to have these conversations until your legal case is done, even if this means waiting years. Having that kind of patience can seem impossible, but when your freedom and the strength of your movement is on the line, finding that patience within yourself will be in your best interest. You may also need to exercise strict discipline in limiting conversations to safer topics, even when doing so leads to awkward conversations, letters, or visits. Do not be afraid to cut people off if it seems that they are headed down a conversational path that might be damaging to you or others.

If you have the benefit of a defense committee or a close friend who understands your case and the politics, you can ask for people on the outside to talk with your loved ones for you. They may be able to help your loved ones understand your case in a way that eases tension and helps strengthen your relationships.

You and your supporters can also keep your loved ones informed about the progress of your case. Many times, people close to defendants have never dealt with the criminal legal system before or have never engaged with it to this extent. They may not understand the legal process and may be overwhelmed by the injustice of the so-called "justice system." Sometimes, they have to deal with all their illusions about this system being shattered on top of dealing with the emotional upheaval of you facing charges. This shattering of illusions can be incredibly difficult for some people, so you should be prepared to talk to them. While this can be a frustrating conversation at times, helping them through in this way might help them understand your politics even more. Also, they may not ask for updates on the progression of your case because they are worried about putting you in danger by asking, do not know what to ask, or do not want to pry. Do not take their silence on these issues as an indication that they do not care or do not want to know. Keeping them up-to-date on what is happening for you legally can help them better understand both your particular criminal case and the politics involved in it.

Another tricky aspect of interacting with loved ones, particularly biological family or parental figures, is that they may be incredibly generous about loaning or donating money for your defense. This financial support can often be a huge relief and one of the crucial factors influencing your situation. Many political defendants have found it necessary to have frank conversations with the people in their lives who are able to give money to reinforce that they need autonomy in setting their legal and political goals and strategies for their cases. That is, money does not necessarily get other people a seat at the negotiating table. If you value their opinions and want to seek their advice as you make your decisions, you should consult them to the extent that you can. However, if their money will create undue pressure on you or complicate your ability to make the best decisions for your case, then it may be better to refuse their money and tell your supporters why additional fundraising will be needed.

A Word on Media and Social Media

Some final thoughts on talking about your case are related to the media and social media. (Again, we cover these topics in more depth in Chapter 7.) You, your supporters, and your attorneys will need to be careful about what you say to the press. Prosecutors routinely monitor the media and will bring media reports into the courtroom to use against you. Many defendants and defense committees have found it useful to have clear talking points about the political issues involved in the case when talking to the media to keep the focus on what is really important and to avoid making damaging statements.

Yet media and social media are dangerous gambles. The FBI, cops, and prosecutors all use social media accounts when gathering evidence to use against defendants. Social media is dangerous not only because it can capture incriminating statements, photographs, videos, and other such things, but because it maps our social and political networks. This map helps the state figure out ways to attack, destroy, and neutralize us. If you have social media accounts open when you are arrested, you would do well to shut them down immediately. If you are in custody, give your lawyer your passwords so they can shut down your accounts, or have them contact the social media platforms to have your accounts shut down. Taking this action will not prevent social media companies from handing over records of your accounts to the prosecution, as the data in your accounts is never truly deleted and the companies routinely hand over this data at the government's mere request, not even bothering with the formality of a subpoena. However, shutting down your accounts after you are arrested can serve as a tourniquet, stopping the bleeding before more damage is done even if it will not heal the wound itself. For example, if you have Facebook and your account remains open, other Facebook accounts (whether from real people or not) can post damaging things on your wall that could then be used against you in court.

There is also a difference between using social media personally and using it to help spread the word about your case. Some of the authors of this book feel strongly that, as a revolutionary movement, we should not use corporate social media outlets because of the ways they are used to map and destroy our movements, so we are loathe to encourage anyone to do so. Yet social media is a prevalent force that only seems to be growing stronger and is undeniably a convenient way to connect with a large number of people almost instantaneously and with little effort.

This convenience can come at a high price, however, and should be considered a risk to be taken wisely. Make sure that you and your supporters do not make incriminating or otherwise damaging statements about your case over social media, as the prosecution will undoubtedly see them and use them against you and others in court. Even so-called "private" messages over social media are not private, as the companies will provide them to the government with little to no hesitation. Creating accounts that are not linked to particular individuals to help disseminate information about your case can help mitigate these risks, but do not be fooled into thinking that any use of social media is safe or anonymous.

Final Thoughts

Overall, it is important to realize that there is a difference between talking about your *case* and talking about the *issues* involved in your case. The state generally wants to argue that the only issues involved in a criminal case are related to laws being broken. On one hand, they argue that the social and political context is irrelevant and on the other they try to use people's alleged politics and political associations to demonize them in court and to justify the charges. We must not play this game. You and your supporters can talk about your political struggles, broader problems facing society and the world, state repression, capitalism, imperialism, various intersecting forms of oppression, and any other issues you find relevant to show the actual context of your charges and how they fit into revolutionary struggle. We should not allow criminal charges to gag us completely. While we need to be smart, strategic, and honest about what we say when facing charges, we should not allow the state to dictate the terms of our discourse.

Chapter 2
SETTING AND BALANCING PERSONAL, POLITICAL, AND LEGAL GOALS

As a political defendant, you will be dealing with the criminal legal system on its own turf. The political level of your situation includes largely unfathomable technicalities and procedures that are designed to disempower you and make it necessary to hire an expert (i.e., a lawyer). You can also approach your predicament on a political level, which may be more familiar ground to you and your supporters. A political defense may be less limited by the court's rules, ranging from complete disregard of those rules to calculated rebellions against the court's authority while attempting not to jeopardize your case entirely. Regardless of the balance you strike between political and legal defenses, you will also need to think about the personal level: what *you* want to achieve and what *you* are willing to endure.

This chapter is meant to help you think about your charges in broad, strategic terms. We explore three goal areas in this chapter: personal, political, and legal. These goal areas overlap a lot, but we have broken them down to facilitate their exploration. We also offer thoughts on ways to effectively balance these goal areas, although we do not presume to be able to tell anyone how they should handle their case. Rather, we encourage all defendants to consider the different ways in which their decisions affect them and others before committing to a course of action. Our social movements do not need more prisoners, yet when people are thrust into these situations, our movements do need dedicated, smart, and informed defendants who hold strong in the face of terrible consequences.

We must begin with examining one of the premises we bring to this chapter: criminal charges can be addressed with both a legal defense and a political defense. When we say "legal defense," we refer to the legal process itself: pleading not guilty, filing pre-trial motions to dismiss charges and suppress evidence, going through all the stages of trial (from jury selection to the verdict), being acquitted, or being sentenced and mounting appeals. If your legal team sees an opportunity to create social change through your case, or at least to limit the most outrageous abuses of the criminal legal system, your legal defenses may be creative, push the boundaries of the established rules and procedures in court, and/or attempt to inject the politics of the case into the legal record through oral arguments and written motions.

When we say "political defense," we refer to a much broader set of strategies and tactics. A political defense can take many forms, including talking about the politics of the case in the media, pressuring elected officials to drop the charges before the trial starts, seizing on opportunities within the legal proceedings to talk about the politics of the case, disrupting trial proceedings to make political points, or completely refusing to engage in the legal process at all. Many defendants have blended legal and political defenses, using the legal procedures and processes when doing so could be beneficial or strategic, and blatantly flouting them when doing so was necessary to make their political points.

While blending legal and political approaches can be powerful and effective, they can be incompatible in some ways. For example, the courtroom drama may actually be more important to you than an acquittal, if your primary goal is to further your political cause. Many political activists have used the court as their stage, not caring or not believing that they can get justice there. That perspective might lead them to make statements that are self-incriminating, so that they look guilty in the eyes of the law (though not necessarily in the eyes of the public or supporters). A legal goal, in contrast, would be to stay out of jail or off probation, which may not be achievable while arguing a political point in the courtroom. This is a frequent spot for friction between political defendants and their lawyers, as well as between defendants and their loved ones or supporters.

There are other instances in which a legal defense strategy and a political defense strategy may rub against one other. The differences may show up around use of the media, protests targeting the prosecutor, and attitudes about informers and *agents provocateur*. The battle outside the court affects the battle inside it at all stages, including in the sentencing phase. For example, if a judge receives lots of letters supporting a convicted felon because the battle for public opinion has been conducted well, the defendant's sentence may be lighter. Alternatively, the sentence may be higher if the judge took offense to any content of the letters or felt they were conveying disrespect for the law or the authority of the court. The consequences of mixing a political defense and a legal defense are not easy to predict, and they undeniably affect one another in powerful ways.

The courts would like you to believe the criminal legal system is a sacrosanct process unto itself that ensures law and order are upheld and justice is done. This myth says that once someone has been charged, the court process will proceed in a fair and impartial fashion so that the truth will be revealed. Furthermore, the myth continues, the case is about the alleged crimes alone, devoid of any context other than the legal one.

Now for a reality check: this system has nothing to do with justice and everything to do with maintaining state control and the existing power structures in society. This system is political through and through, from the way political dissidents are targeted to the way oppressed communities are routinely terrorized.

And the system has teeth. Prosecutors and judges are both skilled in and well prepared for hitting us hard when we buck their system. They will try everything in their power to get us to snitch on each other and betray ourselves. Thus, we must find strength in our solidarity and in our role in our movements to withstand these incredible pressures and avoid contributing to our own and others' repression.

The Potential Power of Political Defenses

CeCe McDonald is an African-American trans woman who was charged with second degree murder for the stabbing death of a white supremacist. The man was one of three white people who attacked her and her friends one night in June 2011 outside of a bar in Minneapolis, Minnesota. CeCe and her friends were all African-American, most of them queer. Community members quickly flocked to her support, countering the legal assault by accusing the county attorney of continuing the racist, transphobic attack on her that could have easily led to her death. (Many queer/ trans people do not survive attacks like the one she endured.) The county attorney (an elected politician who is straight) wanted people to believe that he was sensitive to the needs and experiences of gay people, both in his employment practices and through his prosecutions. Thus, the defense committee applied political pressure to expose the hollowness of this claim and make the prosecution of CeCe politically undesirable.

While the county attorney did not much care what a group of radical queers and allies thought of him, the defense committee was able to make enough noise about her case that the mainstream media eventually covered it. A particularly beneficial news piece came out a month before her trial, which embarrassed the county attorney's office and increased the pressure. In the final month before trial, the political campaign picked up steam and, during jury selection, the prosecutors offered a plea agreement to second degree manslaughter with a sentence of just over three years—significantly lower than the two decades they had been threatening. Nothing substantial about the legal situation had changed; indeed, the prosecution had the advantageous position since the judge had issued pre-trial orders limiting the scope of the defense. In the minds of many supporters, the political pressure campaign determined the legal outcome of CeCe's case.[22]

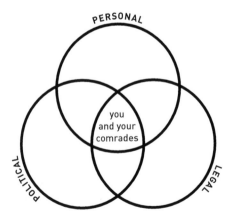

Personal Goals

Personal goals invariably have a significant effect on the other goal areas. Few people intend to catch serious charges or go to prison, so most are faced with figuring out how they want this unwelcome development to be a part of their lives overall (or how much disruption they are willing to tolerate).

Some activists have chosen to leave the country or go underground (or further underground) to avoid ever being put through the trial process once they got wind of potential charges or grand jury subpoenas coming their way. These people clearly prioritized their personal goals above either legal or political goals, trying to avoid any entanglement with the criminal legal system at all. These people decided to handle their (potential) legal situations more on their own terms—although uprooting oneself from one's life due to the threat of incarceration by the state is clearly a coerced decision.

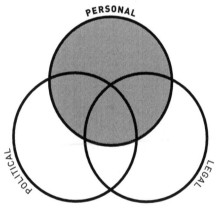

Avoiding capture becomes the overriding consideration in life for an activist who is underground, sometimes neutralizing their political activities. Moreover, the cat and mouse game with the government never ends, since the state rarely forgets about a political defendant who is underground. For example, Sarah Jane Olson (formerly known as Kathleen Soliah) evaded law enforcement for twenty-three years but was eventually captured and convicted for her involvement in two attempted pipe bombings and a bank robbery carried out by the Symbionese Liberation Army.[23]

In general, however, people lack the advance notice it would take to go underground and have no choice about dealing with the legal cases against them. Obviously, this guide assumes that you will be engaging with the criminal legal system. Determining your personal goals for your case is the first step in devising the rest of your strategy.

The most fundamental question is whether you will fight your charges or resolve your case as quickly as possible. There are many perfectly valid personal reasons to opt for a quick resolution, including the general state of your health, your commitments to children and other people you care for, your particular role in your movement, and your financial situation. A conviction may complicate your immigration status, domestic and international travel, child custody, access to hormones, and access to other necessary medical treatments. Taking your case all the way to trial puts you at risk of receiving harsh penalties, while negotiating a settlement quickly may soften those penalties (although this is not guaranteed!). Not to mention that resolving your case quickly reduces the uncertainty of the waiting game.

This guide explicitly emphasizes the value of fighting charges and getting some kind of victory out of the fight. We take inspiration from the many political prisoners and prisoners of war who have continued to engage in and contribute to their struggles despite the state's best efforts to break their wills and isolate them from their communities and movements. Stories from our captured comrades are spread throughout this guide to show how much their struggles

in court and in prison have s
movements. Their strength, r
people can figure out ways
dignity, integrity, and a comr
that made them targets of s
Life is not over, and our co
not end, when we catch ch

If, however, you are not
for several years and risk even more you
would likely be better for your supporters, comrades, and co
defendants if you were honest about that from the beginning
and set your political and legal goals accordingly. Likewise,
being certain that you are willing to fight your charges no
matter how long the process takes will likely help you make
good political and legal decisions.

"Resolving your case as quickly as possible" means pleading guilty to something. Often, this is something you either
did not do, or did and feel justified in having done. Consider
carefully whether you can live with a guilty plea. For example, if you are innocent or feel like your actions were justified,
how would pleading guilty affect your emotional well-being
and sense of integrity? Similarly, if you do not recognize the
authority of the state, would pleading guilty legitimize the
state in ways that you cannot live with?

You should not make your personal decisions at the expense of others. The most critical part of setting personal
goals is making your decisions with everyone's best interests
in mind: your codefendants (if any), unindicted comrades,
the movement you care about, and your loved ones. There
likely will not be ideal options and many may make you
feel disgusted, but it is important to remember that radical

revolutionary activity will inevitably be met
pression and stiff punishments. While you may
unfairly singled out to suffer these consequenc-
hat should not have happened, you now must make
ions that are in both your own and the movement's best
erests, striving not to sacrifice one for the other. And you
must be absolutely certain that you do not make personal
decisions at the expense of others.

The most common way that defendants make personal
decisions at the expense of others is to snitch—they provide
information to the prosecution about former comrades in exchange for the promise of a lighter punishment and a quick
end to their ordeal. You can expect that the prosecution will
try to enlist your active help in going after your political comrades as a condition of reducing your charges and settling
your case right away. In order to withstand this pressure and
not snitch, what are you willing to risk, suffer, or lose? What
do you need from your comrades when you protect them
from prosecution? You owe it to yourself to answer these
questions honestly. Be honest with yourself, whatever your
answers *are*—not what you think other people want or expect
them to be. Prepare yourself to make decisions in your case
accordingly, own the consequences as necessary (including
years in prison), and insist on the support you need. While
it is your responsibility to defend your movement and protect your comrades, it is their responsibility to appreciate and
support you through ongoing and active solidarity.

If you cannot fight the charges against you indefinitely,
you will be reaching a plea agreement sooner than others who
might have been charged with you, and/or sooner than comrades who might still be under investigation. Be extremely

careful about this plea agreement! A plea agreement contains a statement of facts, and your statement of facts can help the state prosecute others. Similarly, if you give a sentencing statement in court, be sure not to incriminate others or compromise their legal situations. See Chapter 8, "Resolving Your Case," for much more about plea agreements.

The Serious Consequences of Snitching

We must constantly be on guard against the pressures and manipulations of the cops and prosecutors to get us to snitch on others and incriminate ourselves. When you are under indictment or investigation, keep yourself and your comrades safe. Never speak to cops, prosecutors, prosecution investigators, and other people you do not know and trust who are asking about your case, associations, or activities. Snitching destroys our movements and communities much more effectively and quickly than all the state's repressive actions combined. We can come together to defend ourselves and our movements when attacked by our enemies, but not if we turn on each other when faced with consequences for our radical organizing.

Despite what prosecutors like to promise to cooperating defendants, snitches do not always receive dramatically lighter sentences than those who stand strong in the face of state repression. While some snitches have gotten lighter sentences, many have served more-or-less equivalent sentences as those who did not cooperate. In the case of the Cleveland 4[24], for example, the fifth person arrested in that case cooperated after being held for only a couple months. He originally negotiated a sentence of no more than fifteen years when all the defendants were facing life sentences. After testifying against his former codefendants (who were sentenced to between eight and eleven years), he withdrew his plea agreement and petitioned the court for a lighter sentence so he would not serve more time than the ones who did not snitch. The judge subsequently sentenced him to six years with lifetime supervised release, just two years less prison time than the non-co-operating defendant who received the lightest sentence. (All of the defendants received lifetime supervised release). At the time of this writing, the cooperating defendant is still serving his time without any support or solidarity from other activists.

The pressure to cooperate with the state is particularly difficult if you regret an action you carried out years ago, if you had a fall-ing-out with your former friends and com-rades, if your political thinking has changed dramatically, or if you now have people relying on you (such as children) when you did not before. Nevertheless, the safety of others (former comrades and newer radicals alike) and the success of the movement you were once a part of depend on your non-cooperation. We urge you to hold out for a plea agreement that does not require you to incriminate others; see Chapter 8, "Resolving Your Case," for more about negotiating those agreements.

For snitches, their cooperation and betrayal of their comrades and principles has always entailed a loss of dignity for themselves and support from the movement, which makes a raw deal from the state even worse. Staying in solidarity with your codefendants and sticking to your revolutionary principles can often help you set clear legal goals and make smart decisions to achieve them. And doing so always helps you retain your dignity in the dehumanizing machines called the criminal legal system and prison-industrial complex.

If you cannot accept pleading guilty to something you did not do or to something you feel was justified, you could join the ranks of other revolutionaries who have fought their charges through a jury trial and the appeals process, regardless of the costs or consequences of doing so, because their integrity and dignity required that resistance. Resistance has inherent value, and resistance is always met with repression, so the risks should not be taken lightly—yet there are many times when they must be taken. Our principles and the ways we strive to live up to them make us dangerous to our enemies, so we must draw on the strength of those principles when put to the test. One of the most important goals of this guide is to help defendants fight their charges and win something for themselves and their movements.

Even if you fight your charges vigorously and well, victory will usually not come as complete vindication. As we have already mentioned, most defendants either plead guilty to at least one charge (often on the eve of trial) or are convicted at trial of at least one charge. The criminal legal system is designed to force plea agreements and send people to prison, not to reveal the truth about crimes committed or to ensure that only the people who are actually guilty of committing a crime are punished.

Drawing Your Lines

> Bomani Shakur (aka Keith LaMar) is one of the Lucasville 5, five prisoners who were at the Southern Ohio Correctional Facility in 1993 when a riot broke out. The rebellion was a result of the deplorable prison conditions and the warden's refusal to provide Muslim prisoners with a tuberculosis test that did not require the injection of alcohol into their skin. These five were singled out as leaders and variously charged with the murders of

nine prisoners and a guard; another prisoner snitched on them and the five were sentenced to death. During his sentencing statement, Bomani said:

> "Throughout the whole trial it's been said, repeatedly said by the prosecutor that every man must be held accountable for his actions. I agree with that. In 1988, I was caught stealing some jewelry at a jewelry store. Because of my actions I pleaded guilty and was sentenced to two years' imprisonment. In 1989, I killed a man... and because of my actions, I pleaded guilty and I was sentenced to a term of eighteen years to life imprisonment. In 1994, I was charged with nine counts of aggravated murder with death penalty specifications. But because of my actions, I pleaded not guilty and I placed my life in the hands of uncaring people, man....
>
> "I could beg you not to kill me. My faith ain't gonna allow me to do that. You know, I don't wanna sound like I'm disrespecting anyone or even disrespecting myself, but I understand, you know, the result, the conclusion of this outrage. And I just want the record to reflect that I stand unmoved by your threats and promises of death. Death is a gift. It's inevitable. All of us must face it, but all of us aren't gonna face it the same

> or under the same circumstances. I just
> want the record to reflect that my faith is
> in He who created me. I'm not going to be
> governed by man-made laws, laws where
> it's left me to live death my whole life, been
> living the death my whole life. But within
> the confines of the prison I found myself
> and I'm not willing to sacrifice myself or
> belittle myself or bow to something I don't
> believe in. I don't believe in what took place
> in this courtroom."[25]

- - - - - - - - - - - -

A final word on setting your personal goals—it is of the utmost importance that you confront your own fears. Do you want to stay out of prison more than anything else? Prison is a terrible place that is designed to destroy people's characters, hearts, minds, and souls. Being afraid of prison is healthy! Whatever your fears, try to acknowledge and appreciate them rather than letting them make you feel ashamed or inadequate. Also weigh them carefully as you determine what you are willing to risk, suffer, or lose. Only the state benefits from your will collapsing because you did not adequately prepare yourself for potential consequences of your politics and political activity. You do not need to be alone in this preparation—reach out to those you trust and find strength in their support and solidarity. (Chapter 9, "Surviving in Prison," contains stories and advice from radicals who have spent time behind bars.)

Necessary Consequences

After the resolution of the RNC 8 case, which involved felony conspiracy charges for organizing resistance to the 2008 Republican National Convention, codefendant Luce Guillén-Givens wrote:

> "Is a movement of people unwilling to risk felonies and short prison sentences a movement strong enough to win? I hoped we would see acquittals at trial but, more importantly, I hoped that even if we saw convictions we would have had the opportunity to show that while we are not yet strong enough to end state repression, we can support and care for those who stand up to it. In my mind, this is part of laying the groundwork for a truly revolutionary movement.
>
> "I'm not suggesting that we should ignore the real impact of felony convictions and incarceration on individuals and movements, or that we should charge forward with reckless disregard for consequences. But I am saying that as long as mere felony convictions—which a few million people in this society manage to live with every single day—deter people, we're cheating ourselves out of the potential to win."[26]

Political Goals

When setting your political goals for your case, ask yourself, "How do I want to position myself and my charges in relation to revolutionary struggle?" The most important premise at the foundation of any answer to this question is that cooperation with the state is never an option. Another important premise for any answer to this question is that, regardless of how you wound up facing charges, you are in your position in part because of the way the government perceives your politics and because they are waging campaigns against dissidents to protect their own power. Whether you have been an active part of revolutionary organizing for decades or whether your first exposure to radical organizing entailed being

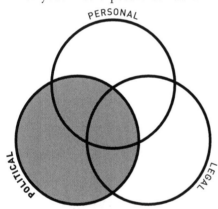

entrapped by an informant, your case is part of a broad campaign of state repression, not an isolated incident or a legal matter that only concerns you (although you are clearly the most affected).

The particulars of your case will weigh heavily as you set your political goals. For example, if you are one of the first people in your state or at the federal level to be charged under a new law, could beating the charges discourage future prosecutions? Even if you were convicted, would there be an opportunity to appeal and have the law struck down by a higher court? Would going to trial force the government to disclose information about surveillance, informants, broader investigations, or other information that would be valuable to the movement? Could your case result in some unfavorable publicity for the criminal legal system itself, or for the government overall? Could you discredit evidence handling or entrapment techniques? Could your trial set some helpful legal precedents or favorable political conditions that would affect other cases or organizing campaigns?

Using your trial to achieve such a goal could mean consequences for you, including incarceration; that is why we urge you to carefully evaluate your personal situation as you set your legal and political goals and strategies. Examining how your case fits into an intricate web of resistance and repression is one way to keep your case in perspective and to clarify what you want to happen as a result.

Another important question to ask yourself is whether your case carries serious liabilities for your movement. Chances are, the government already knows more about your organizing than you would like through surveillance, seizing computers and documents, and maybe even through others snitching. In your gloomiest moments, you might imagine that the state knows everything. That is seldom true, however, and it is a good idea to carefully consider the additional information the government may be able to gain through the pre-trial and trial proceedings. What are the chances that your case could result in some repressive precedents if you are convicted? The outcome of a trial is never a certainty and always entails risks, many of which cannot be predicted.

Consider which of the political points you want to make are the best suited for a legal proceeding. This system inherently limits what we are able to talk about, as the judge has the final say over what evidence can be admitted and can restrict the arguments you or your lawyers can present in the courtroom. At times, these limitations prevent you from achieving the political wins you want from your charges, and you might make greater progress in the court of public opinion.

The Smith Act Prosecutions

In 1940, Congress passed a law against teaching about, advocating for, or encouraging the overthrow of the United States government through force and violence. The first activists arrested under this law (called the Smith Act) were Trotskyist trade unionists, mostly involved in the Teamsters' union in Minneapolis. When eighteen of them went to trial in 1943, they defended themselves by arguing the case for Marxism in the courtroom. Their centerpiece 8-hour lecture did not seem to convert even one juror, and it certainly did not win acquittal for any of the accused.

Five years later, eleven top leaders of the Communist Party USA were indicted under the Smith Act. They argued that (1) they did not advocate force and violence, but rather a peaceful transition to a new order, and (2) that their speech should be protected because they spoke on behalf of a political party. In other words, they attempted to defend Marxism, as well as appealing to the First Amendment. A jury convicted them anyway, and an appeal to the Supreme Court (*Dennis v. United States*, 1951) upheld the jury's verdict.

More than one hundred prosecutions followed. As these wore on, defendants relied more heavily on the First Amendment defense and less on the fine points of Marxism. This defense gained traction, even though the country was in the grips of anti-communist hysteria. Finally, in 1957, the Supreme Court split some hairs and decided (*Yates v. United States*) that defendants could not be prosecuted on the basis of their *beliefs* in revolution, only on the basis of their *actions* towards overthrowing the government forcefully. Grudgingly, the criminal legal system allowed people to criticize the state because to do less would be hypocritical, based on its own Constitution. This limited victory came about as political defendants gained skills at using the system's rules against it, rather than arguing the correctness of their political position in the courtrooms.[27]

- - - - - - - - - - - - - - - -

Working towards political goals through the criminal legal system also runs the risk of diverting attention away from the political issues you care about. Additionally, some supporters may find the legal battle more compelling than the political battle you were fighting before being charged. It is easy to fall into the trap of adjusting the narrative of the case to get the most sympathy and support possible. For example, if you were charged with felonies as a result of a public organizing campaign against an animal testing facility or fracking pipeline that involved using sidewalk chalk to write slogans, you might find it tempting to frame your case as one about free speech instead of the original issues. Free speech issues can often appeal to more people than any particular campaign, as people from a variety of political persuasions may agree that you should be able to express your views even if they do not care about your views or the issues.

Finally, remember that criminal charges are inherently in the state's domain. Prosecutors start out with the upper hand in a system designed to give them the advantage and ensure convictions. At times, they outmatch us and the most strategic move is to cut our losses and push our struggles forward in other ways. Additionally, since this is their game, prosecutors and judges are highly skilled in ensuring the harshest sentences for those who resist and attempt to push the boundaries of the system.

These considerations are in no way intended to discourage you from making a political defense, or from blending a political defense with a more traditional legal defense at trial. Many times, the most important way to protect and advance our movements is to fight back within this system and accept the risks and possible consequences of doing so. Once you have a clear political understanding of your charges, there are several other areas you should consider as you set your political goals. These can roughly be broken down into framing your case and evaluating the potential political implications of going to trial and being convicted.

Framing Your Case

How do you consider yourself in relation to the charges the state has levied against you? Do you want to describe yourself as a "political prisoner"? The term carries some implications—the most obvious being that you have been targeted for some sort of political philosophy, politically motivated action, or political associations. People are going to want to know what that philosophy is and you might run the risk of some activists withholding solidarity if you are not exactly aligned with their politics. Likewise, the government and the media are going to be watching your response and that of your defense committee, if you have one. You, your supporters, and your lawyer need to decide the best approach. You might see this as a wonderful opportunity to talk about the issues that are important to you. Someone else might fear that talking too much about their political beliefs would increase the chances of spending decades in prison. There is no right answer here. Yet if you identify publicly as a political prisoner, it is important to anticipate the questions and to have a strategy in place for dealing with them.

Alternately, do you consider yourself a "Prisoner of War" (POW)? Historically, radicals and revolutionaries who have chosen this term have rejected the authority of the United States government and all state governments to bring charges against them. Some New Afrikan revolutionaries, for example, declared the government illegitimate and refused to recognize the legitimacy of the courts in trying Black people.[28] Many Puerto Rican independence fighters (*independentistas*) rejected the authority of the government to try Puerto Ricans because colonialism is illegal under international law; some of these revolutionaries demanded that their trials be moved to international courts (which, of course, did not happen).[29] People who have taken this approach have historically refused to participate in any trial proceedings, which often resulted in prosecutors steamrolling them at trial and locking them away for decades. Yet the revolutionary example they set through their fierce refusal to bow to illegitimate authority strengthened their movements in many ways, inspired others to take action, and helped motivate people to support them for decades as they were held hostage by the state.

Political Prisoner or Prisoner of War?

One of the seditious conspiracy cases against alleged members of the Fuerzas armadas de liberación nacional (FALN, or Armed Forces of National Liberation) illustrates the ways that a prisoner of war (POW) approach can co-exist with a legal defense approach. The FALN was a clandestine Puerto Rican independence group based in the United States. Alejandrina Torres, Edwin Cortes, Alberto Rodriguez, and Jose Rodriguez were arrested in July 1983. Jose Rodriguez decided to take a legal defense whereas the others took a POW approach, as the revolutionaries indicted on seditious conspiracy before them had done. They were all convicted; Jose was

> given probation and the others were sen-
> tenced to thirty-five years in prison. While
> these different approaches were clearly able
> to co-exist during the legal proceedings, the
> consequences varied drastically, to say the
> least. We offer this example to highlight how
> unpredictable the consequences of any given
> approach can be, not to argue for the value of
> one approach over the other.

You and your supporters will likely be talking about your case in the public realm to a greater or lesser extent at some point. The state will most definitely describe your case in the worst possible terms to demonize you and bolster their myths about protecting society, maintaining law and order, and so on. How do you fight back against their narrative?

First, talking openly and honestly about your case is not the same as discussing the details of the allegations against you, any pieces of evidence, or your legal strategy. As a hypothetical example, you could talk about being targeted as a prominent environmental activist without discussing what happened or who else was present the night you were arrested at a pipeline construction site.

Second, you have the responsibility to come up with framing that is both honest and aligns with your political goals, values, and ethics. For example, imagine that you are charged with conspiracy to commit property damage at a protest, and you maintain you neither planned nor committed any property damage. You could decry your arrest as a sign that the government is trying to criminalize you simply because of your political beliefs and associations (i.e., a political witch hunt). Alternatively, you could bring attention to the necessity of revolutionary struggle through a diversity of tactics while still asserting your own innocence. Then again, you could point out how often the state completely manufactures the conditions for their prosecutions in order to neutralize an organization or movement. Whatever framing you use, being honest in your narrative of your case will ultimately be the best approach to advancing your goals.

Please note: we cannot stress enough the difference between being honest in the way you frame your case and talking about the facts of your case—particularly those that could incriminate you or others. In the example above, you should not say anything about what you or others actually did that could be prosecuted as a crime (either one you are charged with already or another one). Thus, if you were in fact guilty of conspiring to damage property, then your framing should not include a denial of those actions. However, your framing could focus on the hypocrisy of the government criminalizing property damage at a protest while giving defense firms lucrative contracts to destroy entire countries abroad. This framing would satisfy the joint criteria of being an honest presentation of your case and not being incriminating.

- - - - - - - - - - - - - - - - - -
Revolutionary Honesty and Integrity

We want to emphasize the importance of honesty in framing political cases because we have seen prisoners lose support unnecessarily because they were not honest about their cases. We cannot stress enough the importance of not presenting untrue, exaggerated, or politically opportunistic reasons for being targeted. You may be involved in the criminal legal system for several years or decades, and supporters will have many opportunities to hear accusations against you. If you make your stand on solid ground from the beginning, the accusations will fall flat, at least in the minds of your supporters. And you need your supporters for the long haul! Also, if the support you receive helps you slog through the criminal legal system long enough to beat the charges at trial or have them thrown out through legal maneuvering, you will want to be able to walk away knowing you took a principled stand and that people supported you for it.

Third, remember that accountability with your supporters flows both ways. Your supporters must be clear about why they support you. Perhaps they whole-heartedly agree with your tactics; perhaps they agree with your right to say what you think, and not with the content of your thoughts; perhaps they have reservations about your tactics but greater reservations about the repressive measures the state has employed against you. All of these are legitimate reasons. Pay attention to the limits and conditions of their support. You, in turn, must be accountable to them because they are putting in their time, energy, and labor to help you fight your charges and win your freedom.

Here are some additional pitfalls that should be avoided when discussing legal charges:

- *Do not distort the reasons why you are being charged:* Do not say that you have been targeted for reasons unrelated to the allegations. For example, if you are a member of a revolutionary organization that is being investigated by the government, you are in a stronger position if you just say so. If you claim that you are being targeted because you work with youth or community gardens, or because of some aspects of your identity, later on you will have to explain that you are also a revolutionary and that this is the actual reason why you were targeted.

- *Do not falsely claim that charges are a fishing expedition or witch hunt:* Often, people quickly call investigations, grand jury subpoenas, and criminal charges fishing expeditions or witch hunts when the reality is not so clear cut. Granted, the state will seize every opportunity to persecute political dissidents and collect intelligence on revolutionary communities and organizations. Law enforcement agencies will also set up sting operations and entrap people. However, the state gathering additional information through subpoenas, house raids, and interrogations after an incident occurs is different than the state simply trying to gather intelligence without much direction (i.e., a fishing expedition). Likewise, the state gathering additional information after an incident is different than the state casting a particular political group as the enemy and seeking individuals to take the fall (i.e., a witch hunt). All of these actions and motivations should be decried and resisted, of course. What is important is calling things what they are as best we can, even though we rarely know exactly what the state is trying to do.

- *Do not promise to go to trial "no matter what":* Many defendants come out strong when charged, vowing to fight the charges to the bitter end. As the pre-trial proceedings get underway and they learn more about their legal situations, however, these stances can change. There is nothing inherently wrong in accepting a non-cooperating plea agreement—doing so could be the most strategic move just as easily as it can be a capitulation to the state. However, leading supporters to think they should stand in solidarity with you because of your dedication to going to trial, as opposed to the fact that you are being charged at all, can set you up for going back on your word should you ever decide to take a plea agreement.

- *Do not say that you know nothing about an alleged crime when there is evidence that you do:* Many times, defendants will claim that they know nothing about an alleged crime when there will be evidence (e.g., computer or cell phone records) that prove or suggest that they do. People choosing to break the law as part of revolutionary struggle should be supported, of course, and guilt or innocence should not be important for solidarity anyway. In these situations, defendants should clearly be careful not to admit guilt unless they are pleading guilty and should not talk about the details of the case in ways that could harm them or others. Yet there is a difference between talking about, for example, the illegitimacy of the laws being used to bring charges against you, the political motivations of the charges, or your rejection of the state's authority to impose laws and telling your supporters something that the state knows to not be true.

- *Do not hide what you are being charged with:* In a handful of cases, defendants have chosen to go public with being charged but have not specified what the charges are or what the alleged incidents were that led to the charges. This is a disadvantageous approach since the state is left knowing more about the situation than the people being asked to extend solidarity. An important reality of legal charges to keep in mind is that most court documents (e.g., indictments, motions, court transcripts) are public documents, so many of the state's allegations and evidence against you are made public even if you do not go to trial. There is a difference between talking publicly about the state's allegations and talking about information related to the charges that are best kept secret for your and others' safety and security.

- *Do not make statements that damage yourself or others:* Some defendants have made damaging or incriminating statements about their charges, whether online, to the media, during phone calls or visits in jail, or in court. Consider all statements thoroughly before making them, particularly when you have codefendants or when other people could be charged with related crimes.

Evaluating the Political Implications of Trial and Convictions

As you set your political goals, you would be well served to consider the myriad implications of going to trial. Subjecting your political organizing and actions to public scrutiny through the criminal legal system presents dangers as well as opportunities. You clearly did not have any say about whether you were charged or not. You also cannot be sure whether the jury will side with you if you go to trial. You will have limited say, if any, about the charges you plead guilty to if you decide to take a plea agreement. Even so, your charges and the outcome of your case have many implications for you, your comrades, and the movement as a whole. Thus, the decisions you make about your case, no matter how limited in scope they are allowed to be, will have implications for others. This aspect of your political goals overlaps greatly with your legal goals for your case.

Consequently, you must consider the political implications of putting information on the record in court—that is, of providing the state with information. Often, people in radical movements draw a hard line against providing information to the state. This is clearly an important principle in general and it should be adhered to rigorously whenever someone is questioned by law enforcement or prosecution investigators. When going to trial, though, you will need to present some information in court and, at times, the prosecution might not know this information in advance. As a result, you will need to consider the political implications of this information and ensure it does not incriminate yourself or others, or otherwise damage your movement or others' organizing.

A lot of information about cases is presented in pre-trial proceedings, as these typically set the terms and scope of the trial—and in many ways the range of political topics that can be brought up in your case. Thus, it is important to make convincing arguments about the evidence to be introduced, the specific charges to be considered, the expert witnesses to be called, and the judge's instructions to the jury. That is, your lawyer (or you, if you are *pro se*) must present information to the court—some of which the prosecution may not know. Typically, judges favor the prosecution in determining what is and is not allowed to be put on the record in trial, which might mean that the state can put a lot of damaging information about you and your comrades onto the record at trial while you cannot put much out there about them. Additionally, to argue your pre-trial motions successfully, you may be forced to divulge information the government has not already picked up through its investigations. Similarly, some of your pre-trial motions may require testimony from other activists, which could put them in the position of revealing information that the state does not know and that it would be best for them *not* to know. The state can also subpoena your comrades to testify against you. If they refuse to answer questions, they could be charged with contempt of court and handed jail time of their own.[30] While we do not want to discourage you from going to trial and taking these risks, we do want to remind you that the deck is always stacked against you in the criminal legal system.

Nevertheless, the state runs similar risks by going to trial, as prosecutors may be forced to disclose information they would prefer not be made public in order to effectively argue their pre-trial motions. There is no way to predict what will happen in the lead-up to trial or during trial, and thus these proceedings inherently carry both a lot of potential and risk.

- - - - - - - - - - - - - - - - - -
Maneuver for Your Own Advantage

In 2006, radical environmental activists Daniel McGowan, Jonathan Paul, Nathan Block, and Joyanna Zacher[31] faced serious prison time as a result of a series of arsons carried out by members of the Earth Liberation Front (ELF). A former comrade set them up for prosecution by engaging them in "reminiscing" about ELF actions while taping their conversations. To make matters worse, some of their codefendants snitched. Their legal situation looked terrible and prosecutors threatened the four defendants with the harshest possible sentences.

McGowan's attorney filed a motion to reveal any National Security Agency (NSA) spying in his case, as unconstitutional spying could potentially have led to his case and other "Operation Backfire" cases being thrown out. The judge ordered the government to reveal whether the NSA had been involved in any surveillance in the case. Shortly thereafter, McGowan's attorney withdrew the motion and McGowan and his codefendants accepted plea agreements that explicitly stated that they would not have to provide information on any other activists. It seems that this defense motion was a turning point in the case, and this creative legal maneuvering helped the defendants negotiate better sentences for themselves, as well as protect their comrades. As journalist Will Potter wrote, "While this agreement impedes investigation into other ELF crimes, the government avoids a national security investigation."[32]

The same is even truer of trial, as trials tend to expose more to the light than pre-trial proceedings. Both sides have incentive to put evidence on the record during trial to argue their positions and set themselves up for strong appeals. Additionally, prosecutors are often adept at getting evidence on the record in one trial that will help them in future prosecutions. If you testify on your own behalf, the prosecution may be able to ask for information that damages you, your unindicted comrades, and/or your movement during cross-examination. The same goes for your comrades—they could be called on to testify against you. If someone refuses to answer questions from the prosecution, they could be held in contempt of court (which could entail being held in jail until the trial is over and/or facing criminal charges for contempt). And, of course, no matter how much you prepare, you never know what will be revealed during someone's testimony.

We also must not forget that going to trial involves a high risk of being convicted. How would a conviction affect your movement? Your comrades? Your future organizing? Your life?

For example, would a conviction on hacking charges prevent you from using computers after you are released? Would probation or parole after incarceration prevent you from associating with your closest comrades and loved ones? At times, these consequences are necessary to bear so we can advance our struggles. These risks should always be taken with full knowledge and consent, of course.

In contrast, could the public and your support base believe you acted in the right, even if a jury finds you guilty? Or that you are innocent in moral terms even if you are guilty in legal ones? A legal defeat in this kind of situation may be a political victory, as it could lead to opportunities to challenge laws and the powers you are struggling against in your organizing.

Another important question to ask yourself is, "If I decide against going to trial, would pleading guilty discredit my action, movement, and/or comrades?" For example, if you are charged with terrorism for nonviolent civil disobedience, would pleading guilty to terrorism (as opposed to a lesser charge of trespassing, property destruction, etc.) bolster the state's demonization of your movement and facilitate future prosecutions against your comrades under those same laws? If you are charged with conspiracy, would your guilty plea be used against your codefendants, either at trial or to pressure them into taking plea agreements as well? Whether you plead guilty to lesser charges or are convicted at trial, how would you discuss your case to counteract any possible discrediting with supporters or the general public?

Alternately, would pleading guilty bolster your movement or express pride in your choice of tactics? For example, the Tinley Park 5 (Alex Stuck, Cody Sutherlin, Dylan Sutherlin,

Jason Sutherlin, and John Tucker) are anti-racist and anti-fascist activists who were arrested after an attack on a white supremacist gathering in May 2012 at a restaurant in Tinley Park, a suburb of Chicago. A number of anti-fascists broke up the meeting with physical force. Ten of the white supremacists were injured, and three of them required hospitalization. In January 2013, the defendants all took non-cooperating plea agreements with sentences ranging from three to six years. Early into his prison sentence, Jason wrote, "It's time to ask yourself some hard questions when thinking about taking direct action. Are you prepared to be locked up? Are you willing to stay locked up to protect your comrades and community? Solidarity is a gift and a responsibility."[33] While the tactics were controversial and all the defendants received prison sentences, they stood in solidarity with each other and owned their actions.

- - - - - - - - - - - - - - -
The Wounded Knee Trials

A notable example of successful outcomes from a political trial is the case against Dennis Banks and Russell Means, who were charged as leaders in the seventy-one-day siege of Wounded Knee in 1973. After an eight-month trial in which the defendants rested their case after only a few days of defense testimony, the jury stalled in their deliberations after one juror was hospitalized. The prosecution refused to accept a verdict from only eleven of the twelve chosen jurors and, rather than calling for a mistrial, the judge dismissed the charges against the defendants. Later, most of the jurors formed a group and advocated that the government dismiss the charges against other people arrested during the siege of Wounded Knee, even writing a letter to the attorney general urging him to drop the charges and talking with Justice Department officials in Washington, DC.

The prosecution appealed the dismissal of the charges but the appellate court upheld the decision, so the alleged leaders of the Wounded Knee siege walked free. This trial also exposed the military's presence on the reservation (a blatantly illegal use of the military), an FBI informant who had infiltrated the American Indian Movement (AIM), and extensive FBI misconduct during the siege and afterwards. Additionally, the extensive publicity about the trial helped AIM talk about treaty rights and the abhorrent conditions Indians faced on the reservations. The victory for AIM was mixed, though, as some other Indian rights activists were convicted subsequently on Wounded Knee charges and the extraordinarily long and intensive trial sucked up a lot of the organization's resources, energy, and momentum for their broader struggles against imperialism and genocide.[34]

Legal Goals

Facing criminal charges necessarily requires defendants to set legal goals. These goals often cover areas such as not admitting guilt to a crime you did not commit, minimizing or avoiding prison time, not paying restitution, or not having a felony on your record. Some defendants may set a legal goal of resolving their cases in ways that require them to serve prison sentences without probation afterwards so they can move on, whereas others may set a legal goal of avoiding prison time in favor of probation. Of course, rarely will there be times when

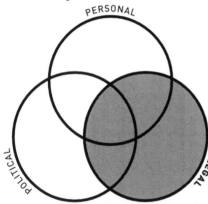

a defendant will be able to negotiate the most ideal plea agreement or have a smooth road to acquittal at trial so they can walk free.

Setting your legal goals is in many ways figuring out how to make the best of a bad situation, even if the best means years or decades in prison. There are also many other considerations that tie in to your personal goals, as criminal convictions and press coverage of high-profile charges (regardless of whether you are convicted on them or not) can have drastic impacts on your life. Similarly, the legal consequences you are willing to accept will likely influence the political goals you set for your case.

Whatever decisions you make for your case, you should be absolutely certain that you do not directly or indirectly implicate other people. Despite what prosecutors like to promise to cooperating defendants, they do not always receive drastically lighter sentences than those who stand strong in the face of state repression. While some snitches have gotten lighter sentences (particularly in contrast to draconian sentences such as those meted out to Eric McDavid[35] and Marius Mason), many have served more-or-less equivalent sentences as their non-cooperating former codefendants.

With non-cooperation as a given, your task will be to determine the consequences you are facing, the options available to you, and the support and resources you have available. The consequences in large part depend on the crimes you are charged with and your life situation as a whole, as some people are in better positions than others to cope with a lengthy pre-trial incarceration or years of prison.

Your options in large part depend on legal matters such as lesser-included charges (or other lower-level crimes) that you might be able to present to the jury at the close of your trial or plead guilty to, the sentencing guidelines for the charges you are facing (if any exist), mandatory minimum sentences for your charges (if any exist), the judge's history of handling cases like yours or other serious cases, and any number of other factors that are impossible to predict. Talking with your lawyer about your full range of options is one of the most valuable benefits of working with a lawyer. Of course, not all of these options will actually be available to you even if they are theoretically available, so various legal maneuvers might be necessary for you to get the option you want. Various political efforts might be necessary as well since political pressure can be successfully applied to the criminal legal system through a variety of means (see Chapter 6, "Working with Your Defense Committee," for more ideas on this topic).

In terms of support and resources, ideally you will have a solid lawyer who understands your politics and a strong defense committee that will support you through everything. Even if you do not feel you have everything set up ideally the moment you are slapped with the charges, do not give in to the pressure from the cops or prosecutors. In summer 2012, Occupy activists in both Cleveland and Chicago were entrapped and charged as terrorists. The Cleveland 4 were entrapped by an FBI informant and thus faced federal charges with terrorism enhancements at sentencing, whereas the NATO 3[36] were entrapped by two undercover Chicago cops and charged with terrorism, conspiracy, and possession of incendiary devices under the Illinois state version of the USA Patriot Act. In both cases, the activists were largely new to radical politics and did not have the strongest support bases at the outset. Yet other activists came together to form defense committees to support them and help them through their legal processes and incarcerations. Even if you do not have resources such as this, non-cooperation should be your guiding principle, as snitching on others will inevitably lead to you losing any potential support and being faced with weathering all your ordeals with neither support nor your integrity.

While every person's situations will be different, there are some general legal considerations that many defendants may find useful and that may not be immediately obvious when setting legal goals and making decisions about cases. Unfortunately, the vast majority of people who are charged end up pleading guilty to or being convicted at trial of at least some charges. All charges carry some consequences, some of which you might find tolerable whereas some would be devastating to your life and political organizing. The consequences that come to mind most readily for most people are lengthy prison sentences, long and strict probation terms, and exorbitant fines and restitution. After all, everyone knows how devastating a felony conviction can be for one's abilities to find a job, housing, education loans, and other necessities. These consequences are legitimate causes of concern and should be evaluated carefully as you make your legal decisions in your case.

There are also many consequences that are less obvious, such as how convictions on certain crimes can prevent you from finding future work in specific fields whereas a conviction on another crime at the same level (e.g., felony, gross misdemeanor) may not. As a hypothetical, if you were planning on working in health care, would a conviction on a charge of violence against people prevent you from entering that field but not a conviction on a charge of property destruction? Talk with your lawyer about whether lesser-included charges may be a possibility for your jury to consider when you go to trial to hedge your bets. Alternately, if you are able to gain leverage in your case to negotiate a plea agreement to a charge that would not have as many collateral consequences, that may be the legal goal you set for yourself.

Other considerations include implications for immigration status, domestic and international travel, child custody, access to hormones, and access to other necessary medical treatments. Another potential consequence to consider is whether an admission of guilt to a particular crime could set you up for future legal actions such as civil suits for defamation, copyright infringement, and other such civil legal situations. The range of potential scenarios and their likelihoods of coming to pass are impossible to predict, of course, but talking with your lawyer about these potentialities can help you make the most informed legal decisions about your case.

Balancing Your Goals

Balancing your personal, political, and legal goals is no easy task. There are no formulas to follow, no simple answers, no magical solutions. Nevertheless, working through these clearly and in depth will help you make the best decisions for your case—the best for you, your comrades, and your movement. Taking this approach will make you much more likely to come out of the experience with something you and your comrades can consider in some degree a victory. As you decide upon the overall weight of each of these goal areas, you would benefit from keeping your focus on how you want to conduct yourself in the revolutionary struggle. Answering this question will likely help you set your particular goals more easily.

Criminal legal charges are never of our choosing and are solely the result of the oppressive system that implements them. The state can take nearly everything away from us—our freedom, our agency, our loved ones, our health, our lives. Yet the state cannot take our dignity or our integrity; only we can give those away. No matter how your circumstances change as your case proceeds, no matter what else is going on in your life, these truths remain.

Working with Others to Achieve Your Goals

Out of necessity, you will be working with other people to achieve the goals you set. You will likely be working with your lawyer to advance your legal and personal goals, and hopefully your lawyer will take your political goals equally seriously. Have clear, open conversations with your lawyer about your political goals, and discuss ways to achieve them as you make your legal decisions. Whether your lawyer is one of your choosing or one appointed for you, ideally you will work together as comrades, or at least as peers. Remember that your attorney works for you, not the other way around. See Chapter 4, "Working with Your Lawyer," for much more about this critical relationship.

If you have codefendants, then you will also need to work with them in setting and achieving your goals. Advancing political goals in the criminal legal system can entail bucking that system in ways that lead to unpleasant consequences. Thus, everyone who could be affected by actions or choices should be able to participate in making decisions about them. Similarly, every defendant must be careful when taking actions, issuing statements, and making decisions not to negatively affect other defendants or make decisions for them. See Chapter 5, "Working with Your Codefendants," for more on this topic.

Your supporters, unindicted comrades, and loved ones will be your main help in achieving your goals. Fighting criminal charges requires a lot of organizing, emotional energy, and time. Talking with people you know and trust about your plans and decisions can be an invaluable asset as you weather the pre-trial and trial proceedings. See Chapter 6, "Working with Your Defense Committee," for more information on working with supporters.

Court battles necessarily disrupt our lives and divert resources from other projects to legal defense and support needs. However, they do not need to put an end to all organizing. Many political prisoners have urged people to keep on with their work to show that repression will not succeed in disrupting or destroying the movement. Joe Hill, renowned for his labor movement songs written while active in the Industrial Workers of the World (IWW), famously wrote before his execution, "Like a rebel I lived and like I rebel I will die. Don't mourn for me, organize."

Chapter 3
COMMON LEGAL SITUATIONS

WHILE EVERYONE WHO IS ARRESTED FACES THE SAME LABYrinth of a judicial system, radicals can often expect particular kinds of charges, behaviors, and maneuvers from the prosecution. The state knows which court tricks work best in any given situation for any particular group of people, and radicals and revolutionaries are no exception. We will start with some general advice, and then expand upon some of the legal tactics frequently used against radicals.

The courts, jails, and laws are meant to disempower and intimidate you. Demystifying and understanding the state's tactics are part of your struggle against them. The more you can remain actively engaged with your case, with opinions and a will of your own, the less you will feel like a victim and the fewer scars the experience will leave on you. The system has less power when people fear it less. Just as you may take heart from learning about radicals who have gone up against the criminal legal system and survived with their politics intact, so may others eventually take heart from your story.

Some General Advice

The prosecution's first moves will probably be designed to scare you into giving up quickly. Sometimes they pile on charges as soon as a person is arrested. Seeing a huge list of charges with your name next to them can be terrifying. In reality, they may not be sure they have any charges that will stick, so they hedge their bets, knowing they can drop the weaker ones later on—unless you take a plea agreement and they do not need to after all.

The prosecution may also add charges several months after your arrest. After dealing with the legal system for several months (often from jail), and knowing the kind of work it will take to prepare for trial, the thought of fighting even more charges can feel pretty daunting. Just remember that this is a common scare tactic and may be a political move designed to discredit you in the public eye.

The prosecution might also try to scare you into cooperation by lying to you about what is happening with your codefendants, if you have any. For example, they might tell you that someone is cooperating when they are not, or they might let one of you out on bail but keep the others locked up. There is a temptation to speculate as to why one defendant is free and the rest are still incarcerated. Do not jump to the conclusion that the free one is working with the state; look for evidence to support that and any other suspicion. As long as you are in custody, it is easy for law enforcement to use even vague details from other prisoners to manipulate you. ("Hey, guess what I heard about your codefendant?") Do not trust what other prisoners are saying about you, your case, or statements they claim they have heard from guards or other prisoners. If the state can divide you from your codefendants, it will have a much easier time disposing of your case, with the additional benefit of weakening the movement you care about with internal suspicion, accusations, and unfounded self-criticism. Be on the lookout for this kind of behavior and make sure you never trust information representatives of the state give you unless you can verify it with your lawyer and defense committee. Defense committees have the responsibility to check things out as best they can to help defendants make the best decisions.

Sometimes other prisoners may offer advice on how to settle your case, why you should take a plea deal, or other general legal advice. Again, this could be someone trying to give you what they think is sound, helpful, friendly tips. Or it could be someone who the state is leaning on in an effort to secure your cooperation. Never take legal advice from *anyone* except your lawyer, no matter how many years they have been locked up. Thank people for their thoughts then quietly file them in your mental trash can.

Surveillance will continue even after your arrest. The prosecution will gather evidence against you by talking to your comrades, employer, loved ones, and anyone else they can persuade or pressure into helping them. Statements made after an indictment is handed down will be used against you in court just as much as the evidence collected to issue the warrant for your arrest.

Legal cases can drag on for much longer than you expect. Court appointments can be scheduled and postponed at the last minute. Sometimes nothing may happen for a long time, but when it does you have to drop everything else to go to court. If you are in custody, you may be taken from your cell without any notice. Time can start to feel like your enemy, and your lack of control over things that so dramatically affect your life can be frustrating and painful. Prepare for things to change either in an instant—or not at all for a long time. This is just the "normal" functioning of the so-called "justice" system.

Delays and postponements do not necessarily mean anything is happening behind the scenes or going wrong with your case. More likely, a lawyer had a scheduling conflict, or the judge decided to take a vacation, or another trial has gone longer than expected, or something else happened that has nothing to do with you or your case. The state has little to lose by drawing things out and often a lot to gain. The longer they delay, the more attractive their plea offers may appear to you, especially if you are in jail the whole time. (Remember that time in jail now will likely be applied to any sentence you receive in the future.)

Grand Juries

Grand Juries are used at the federal level and in many states to secure indictments on felony charges. They are, in essence, how the state decides whether or not someone should be charged with a crime. In a grand jury, the jurors (usually sixteen to twenty-three people who are not screened for bias) only hear evidence presented by the prosecutor. The state claims that grand juries exist to prevent prosecutorial abuse by allowing a panel of citizens to review the evidence and decide whether or not to issue the indictments (rather than an individual prosecutor deciding these matters). The state also claims that grand juries are not investigative bodies that can search for evidence through questioning people; rather, they only determine whether there is probable cause to prosecute someone. In reality, prosecutors use grand juries to fish for information and get people to turn on each other. In political cases, they fish for information about individual radicals, radical communities and networks, groups and organizations, and ideologies. They also use grand juries to put pressure on potential "witnesses" whose testimony could enable the state to bring an indictment (whether or not there is real evidence that a person is guilty of a crime).

The unexpected nature of grand jury proceedings confuses witnesses. For starters, no judge is present. A witness is not allowed to bring a lawyer into the courtroom and often does not know whether they themselves are the object of the investigation. Questions come from the prosecutor and from the jurors, as the jurors are able to ask anything they want (including personal questions that have absolutely nothing to do with the charges under consideration). This situation makes it easy for the prosecution to frame so-called evidence in a way that implies guilt, thus convincing the jurors to bring an indictment.

If you have already been indicted on a felony charge, a grand jury may have been used, although this is not always true. You probably did not know that a grand jury was hearing evidence about your activities, and you may not even receive a record of their proceedings in the discovery documents the prosecutor gives your lawyer. Some of your friends and comrades might have been or could be subpoenaed to the grand jury if the prosecutors seek indictments against other people. If it seems that a grand jury has already investigated you, your lawyer can argue for the transcripts. The rules about which grand jury transcripts can be provided to the defense vary based on the jurisdiction, so you may not be guaranteed to receive them at all or may only receive partial or redacted transcripts. Records are almost always difficult to obtain because grand jury proceedings are sealed.[37] Your lawyer might be able to claim them as discovery through filing motion to demand the transcripts, such as a Giglio or Brady motion in a federal case.[38] Since grand juries serve for up to eighteen months and can be extended several times (perhaps indefinitely), there may be transcripts dating back months or years that might be useful for your defense.

Grand jury transcripts also may help you and your legal team raise claims of prosecutorial misconduct and/or problems with the indictment itself. For instance, does the indictment accurately reflect the testimony presented to the grand jury? If the prosecution indicates that they will call a witness at trial who already testified before the grand jury, the transcripts of their testimony before the grand jury should be made available to you in discovery. However, because the federal government wants to keep grand jury proceedings a secret, it rarely calls a grand jury witness as a trial witness. (However, cops often testify before a grand jury to obtain an indictment and later testify at trial, with their trial testimony usually being basically a repeat of their grand jury testimony.)

Resist Grand Juries!

If you suspect that a grand jury is still oper-
ating in your case, let your friends and family
know about it and ask them to prepare themselves to resist answering questions. They
must take immediate steps to put a support
network for themselves in place. Refusal
to testify before a grand jury could lead to
imprisonment on civil contempt charges, as
well as open them up to charges of criminal
contempt later on. Nevertheless, testifying
before a grand jury—particularly testifying
about other people—is not an option for people engaged in struggle.

Any information presented to a grand jury
can be used in a criminal trial. A subpoena to
appear before a grand jury may not give any
indication of the alleged crime being investigated or the names of the people who might
ultimately be indicted. So the best protection
for us and our movements is to refuse on
principle to testify to any grand jury—even if
you have no reason to think the investigation
might bear on your political activities. Law
enforcement might be looking for evidence in
a case that is years old, and you may have forgotten about your connection to it. Testifying
before a grand jury only aids the state in its
efforts to dismantle our movements and could

lead to the arrest and imprisonment of comrades on potentially serious charges.

This may sound like an invitation to spend months in jail on civil contempt charges. However, the workings of grand juries are not always predictable. In 2010, the FBI raided homes of anti-war and international solidarity activists in Minneapolis, Chicago, and Grand Rapids, searching for evidence of supposed "material support for terrorism." Over the next few months, twenty-three activists received subpoenas to a grand jury in a federal court in Chicago. Most of them issued statements of their refusal to cooperate and many made a public show of not going to Chicago to appear before the grand jury. At the time of this writing, none have yet been cited for contempt of court.

More information on grand juries and ways to resist them is available at GRANDJURYRESISTANCE. ORG. If you are being held pre-trial and cannot access the internet, ask your supporters to send you the information and resources that you need to understand everything going on in your case.

- -

Some of your friends and comrades could be subpoenaed to testify against you at trial too, whether or not they were subpoenaed to the grand jury. Non-cooperation during trial can also lead to them being imprisoned on civil contempt and/or charged with criminal contempt. However, trial testimony is different than grand jury testimony for a couple of reasons. First and foremost, grand jury testimony almost invariably results in charges being filed against someone.[39] If someone is testifying at trial, charges have already been filed. Another clear difference is that a defendant has more legal protections in place during trial testimony. Since the lawyer for the person subpoenaed is not allowed in the grand jury room, the prosecutor and grand jury members can ask any questions they want without objection. Additionally, since no judge is present to enforce procedural rules, prosecutors have an easy time of framing so-called evidence in a way that implies guilt. That is not as easy in a trial situation, in which a defense lawyer is actually present and able to challenge evidence (including testimony) and make objections. Further, in a trial, a judge is also present and can block inappropriate lines of questioning (though they may not).

Surveillance and Infiltration

Surveillance and infiltration are such integral components of the state's repression of activists today that it is hard to imagine a case in which they are not only present, but pervasive. The state has long used both of these to put people in jail, and to destabilize and destroy movements. One historical example can help illustrate the long history of these tactics. As the Industrial Workers of the World (IWW) gained strength and prominence in the 1910s, employers and the government devised networks of spies to keep tabs on and disrupt the workers' movements. This spying culminated in raids on

IWW offices around the country and the arrest of virtually all the leaders in 1917. In one mass trial in Chicago, nearly a hundred "Wobblies" received prison terms of ten to twenty years. Vigilante groups (often funded by employers) took this as a sign that they could raid IWW gathering places, and the government ignored (or aided) their activities for the next several years.[40]

Surveillance and infiltration leave a trail of distrust and betrayal among those whose groups were infiltrated—both those who have been arrested and those who remain on the outside. When someone you thought was a friend or comrade turns out to be working for the state, it can feel impossible to trust anyone. This difficult and heartbreaking experience can make it hard to think rationally about legal strategy afterwards. Of course, that is part of the state's reason for using these methods in the first place. We cannot let fear control us and the decisions we make.

The damage an informant or infiltrator does in a court of law can be substantial, but the movement can fight back with an honest account of what happened and the clues that might have shown that the informant had switched sides or that the infiltrator had made their way into our communities. We also must share any public information about the informants so others can protect themselves as well as possible. Additionally, defendants sometimes get more information about informants as the evidence in the case becomes available. They can then decide what to make public, even if this means running afoul of the court, going against the lawyer's advice, or doing something that is not in their best legal interests (i.e., they prioritize their and the movement's political interests over their own legal interests).

Surveillance and infiltration can produce mountains of evidence to sift through. Defendants often receive thousands of pages of computer records, transcriptions of recorded conversations, reports or summaries from FBI agents about interviews they have conducted (known as "302s"), photographs, and more. Unfortunately, you do not know at first what the prosecution will pull out of the morass to use against you, or what they might conveniently ignore because it helps your case instead of theirs. Rereading minutes of all your boring meetings and mundane conversations with friends can be a major chore. But doing so is absolutely necessary. The needle in the haystack could potentially be a key component to your defense. You (and possibly members of your defense committee) can assist your lawyer in this tedious job. In fact, you are probably the person best suited for this task since you might know or remember things that you said or did, or things that the informant said or did, which might be helpful. If you figure that these conversations have been recorded, but they do not show up in discovery, demand that the prosecution turn over the evidence they are withholding. Also, sometimes you know of a conversation that seems immaterial to the hurried eyes of your lawyer, but might actually be crucial to your defense. Have these things in mind when digging through the discovery in your case.

Furthermore, consider hiring an investigator who can look into the informant's past.[41] Most paid informants have their own criminal records. In fact, they may have become an informant in an effort to get reduced charges or lighter sentences for themselves. Finding out their criminal history and using this information to discredit them publicly and in the courtroom can be easier than you might imagine. Even if an informant does not have a criminal history, learning about their past can be beneficial to your case. Did they have an agenda when deciding to work for the state? Are they attempting to achieve some sort of personal gain from your arrest/conviction (personally, professionally, etc.)? All of this information could be helpful when building your case and when questioning the informant, if they take the stand at trial.

If your case goes to trial, the informant's testimony will more than likely play a key role in the government's presentation. Plan ways to counter the narrative they create on the stand, either through evidence or through witnesses of your own. Talk to other people who knew or interacted with the informant so you can get a more complete picture of who they are (or who they pretended to be). What kind of behavior did they participate in that you and your codefendants might not know about? Have your investigator interview people who also knew and interacted with the informant. Sometimes, you can find out if the informant has been involved in similar cases. If they have, track down the people who were prosecuted and ask them for any information they might have gathered on the informant. Additionally, the government may present "evidence" that can only be corroborated by the informant (because, for example, the most incriminating things the government claims you have said conveniently occurred when the informant was *not* recording).

While the state often depends on infiltration and surveillance to make their cases, these tactics do not play so well with the public in general, and especially not with liberal and radical supporters. You can often build your case against the informant through your political defense much more effectively than you can through your legal defense, where the judge gets to determine what is problematic or not.

Most potential supporters can see that informants and infiltrators have a strong incentive to come up with outrageous and less-than-factual information. That is what they are paid to do and, if they give their bosses what they want, they will keep receiving a paycheck. Remind the public (and potentially the jury) that almost any casual remark can be interpreted in a sinister way, almost any statement can be taken out of context and twisted. Transcripts do not convey sarcasm or our sensationally biting wit and humor. The state will point to these moments as evidence of someone's intent, character, or predisposition. Present your side of the story, either with supporters through statements you put out, the media, or your defense (some of these avenues carry risks to your legal case and goals, of course). Unfortunately, while telling your side may make a difference in the court of public opinion, they do not always make much difference in a court of law. Paid informants are used routinely in the so-called War on Drugs and War on Terror. Defense attorneys generally have a hard time proving that their reports lack credibility because the rules in criminal courts are designed to protect these and other police tactics.

That said, there are some legal strategies to fight this particular brand of government repression. Ask the judge to bar certain kinds of surveillance from evidence. Were the proper warrants issued? Was the surveillance happening somewhere it is not technically legal to have cameras or recording equipment? Does the surveillance footage show signs of being tampered with? If your lawyer needs help figuring out what kinds of motions might be beneficial in these circumstances, they should contact other lawyers who have fought similar cases.

━ ━ ━ ━ ━ ━ ━ ━ ━ ━ ━

Smoke and Mirrors

In 2004, Conor Cash was on trial for charges of arson related to Earth Liberation Front actions in the Northeast. During the trial, the prosecution showed still pictures taken from a videotape. While they deliberated, the jurors asked for the entire videotape. Upon seeing the video for the first time, Conor's lawyer noticed "major discrepancies between the video about to be shown to the jury, the stills entered as evidence, and the video provided in the discovery phase."[42] Because the tape had obviously been doctored, the judge threw out the tape and the jury voted to acquit.

━ ━ ━ ━ ━ ━ ━ ━ ━ ━ ━ ━ ━

Different law enforcement agencies may have conducted surveillance on you and your friends, and although the prosecution is legally required to turn over evidence accumulated by all the agencies, they do not always do so. Think about who might have been involved in the investigation at any point in time: the FBI, local police, highway patrol, Homeland Security, the Secret Service, the Drug Enforcement Agency. Sometimes the state does not want to turn over evidence because doing so might disclose "illegal"[43] spying or other evidence of wrongdoing on the part of the government. File motions to uncover evidence such as this, as it could be incredibly useful in high-profile cases. You also might benefit from having your lawyer file a Freedom of Information Act (FOIA)[44] request for you and any groups you might have been a part of or associated with. Documents often appear in FOIA files that do not get turned over in discovery, although the timeline for getting these documents often means they are not seen until cases are in the appeal stage.

When you are already buried in discovery documents, videotapes, and tape recordings, it seems counterintuitive to ask for more. However, the evidence the government holds back (or denies the existence of) may be the key to successfully resolving your case. Although sifting through tapes and recordings means much more work for you and your legal team, remember that there could be evidence that points to your innocence or reveals a technicality that can work in your favor in court.

Conspiracy Charges

Conspiracy charges are nasty. They are also some of the most common charges brought against targets of state repression because they are by nature broad in reach and loosely defined. Conspiracy charges are strikingly similar to what has become known as "thoughtcrime,"[45] as it is not necessary for any actions to be carried out for a person to be found guilty. Even if they did not know everyone allegedly involved in the conspiracy, even if they misunderstood what was allegedly planned, even if they did nothing to advance the conspiracy, defendants can still be convicted of conspiracy. Simple association with others charged with conspiracy seems to be sufficient to convince a jury of guilt (and is often enough to force a guilty plea).

Conspiracy laws are different from state to state, but under federal law the government needs to establish that only one—not all—of the alleged conspirators committed an "overt act" in furtherance of the conspiracy. One "conspirator" must have taken at least one step toward enacting the alleged plan. The overt act does not have to be illegal. In fact, it usually is not. Buying a book, picking up a pamphlet, purchasing something at Walmart, buying gasoline, and doing an internet search have all been successfully presented as overt acts furthering a conspiracy.[46] When the prosecution can claim almost anything as an "overt act," it is easy to understand why conspiracy charges are a favorite tool of the state.

Conspiracy, by its very nature, assumes more than one person is involved. (In a federal case, a government informant cannot be the only co-conspirator.) When several people are charged with conspiracy, it often makes sense for them to have a joint legal defense. Many practical and political considerations may point toward joint defenses. With several trials, defendants often cannot afford everything they want at each trial (e.g., expert witnesses, defense witnesses, investigators). One big trial also demonstrates your solidarity and builds a feeling of fighting the charges together. There are some potential drawbacks to a joint defense, though. The jury might hear evidence about every defendant—positive or negative—that they might not hear if the defendants had separate trials. Joint defenses can also be tricky when the defendants never really got along or did not know each other well before their arrests (see Chapter 5, "Working with Your Codefendants" for more on this). Weigh all these considerations with your lawyers before deciding which choice is best for each of you and for the group. In general, we believe that joint defenses offer the best position from which to fight charges and build solidarity.

For defendants to consolidate their cases, the defense attorneys must file a motion to consolidate. (Joint defense agreements are helpful, if not required, in these situations; see Appendix B for a sample.) Usually, this is a formality since the judge prefers one trial to several, and many cases involving codefendants are handled from the get-go as if they will be consolidated. However, the prosecution may object to consolidating trials, claiming that when several people are tried together, one individual's innocence may be hidden by their codefendant's guilt. In reality, the prosecutors may be more afraid that one person's obvious innocence will persuade a jury that all the defendants are innocent. In this sense, consolidating trials can sometimes give all the defendants an advantage, although this result is by no means guaranteed.

Perhaps the most important thing to remember about conspiracy charges is that they dramatically up the ante on any potential plea agreement. In any criminal case, for someone to plead guilty, they must admit to all the elements of the crime for which they are charged. With conspiracy charges that means admitting that: (1) there was a conspiracy; (2) at least one step was taken to further that conspiracy; and (3) you personally participated in the conspiracy. The remaining codefendants may then be placed in the position of having to prove that either (1) there was in fact no conspiracy (even though someone else already admitted to it); or (2) it existed but they were not involved in it. Again, conspiracy charges require that there be at least two co-conspirators, neither of whom can be the informant. So by pleading guilty, a person automatically admits that at least one other person is guilty— whether or not they name that other person. The informants' testimony, the statement of facts from the plea deal, and any testimony from cooperating codefendants will likely "prove" a conspiracy in the eyes of the law. So, unfortunately, one guilty plea in a conspiracy case could potentially seal the deal for all the remaining codefendants. At the minimum, one guilty plea provides the prosecution with more pressure to apply on the remaining defendants to force them to take plea agreements.

The prosecution is acutely aware of the above reality and will employ underhanded tactics to divide and conquer you and your codefendants. Be vigilant. And if one of your codefendants truly does flip and signs a cooperating plea agreement, the court documents proving this fact should be posted online immediately.

Entrapment

When people hear the word "entrapment," they often think of a cop or informant tricking people into committing a crime. For example, they may consider entrapment to be an informant or undercover cop drawing people into a dependent relationship of some sort (often providing them with money, housing, drugs, etc.), creating a "crime," and pushing them into it. But the legal definition of entrapment is not this clear and simple. Understanding the differences between the legal and popular definitions of entrapment is of the utmost importance.

While the law varies from state·to state, most cases in the federal system will have jury instructions with language similar to: "The government has the burden of proving beyond a reasonable doubt that the defendant was not entrapped. The government must prove the following: (1)

the defendant was predisposed to commit the crime before being contacted by government agents; or (2) the defendant was not induced by the government agents to commit the crime. Where a person, independent of and before government contact, is predisposed to commit the crime, it is not entrapment if government agents merely provide an opportunity to commit the crime."[47] This instruction leaves the government and the defense to argue over a defendant's "predisposition" to commit a crime without government involvement and whether or not the defendant was "induced" to commit a crime.

Regarding predisposition, how do you "prove" a person's will or intent? The government usually proves this predisposition by introducing a defendant's politics, reading habits, written words, and lifestyle as "evidence" against them. In order to do so, prosecutors have to introduce materials and testimony as evidence, which provides defense attorneys with the opportunity to ask questions that can show how this evidence does not prove predisposition. Defense attorneys also have the opportunity to inject the politics of the case into the trial through their questions. This countering can be done both in the courtroom and in the media.

The other important element is "inducement." According to an oft-cited legal precedent, "Inducement can be any government conduct creating a substantial risk that an otherwise law-abiding citizen would commit an offense, including persuasion, fraudulent representations, threats, coercive tactics, harassment, promises of reward, or pleas based on need, sympathy or friendship."[48] Although these elements are always present in entrapment cases, the courts almost never find any "evidence" of inducement.

In the world at large, entrapment is a powerful political defense. In court, an entrapment defense requires some tricky legal maneuvering that intersects with the political defense. A person who has been entrapped cannot claim "innocence" in the traditional sense. They are essentially admitting that they have done something the state defines as illegal, but that they only did so after being coerced by an *agent provocateur*. They would not have done so (and were not predisposed to do so) without government involvement. This legal defense requires a much different trial strategy than most cases, as well as a different approach in the media and even with supporters. If you are defending yourself legally by arguing entrapment, anyone who speaks publicly about your case should be careful not to use a framework that relies on guilt or innocence. The focus could instead be on things such as the government creating crime where none previously existed or the targeting of particular groups, movements, or people for their politics, religion, or identities.

As in the case of infiltration, hiring an investigator can be essential to a sound defense. The *provocateur's* history and background should be thoroughly explored. While the government is supposed to hand over any evidence they have about the *provocateur's* past, they often will not do so without a fight. The same applies if undercover cops or FBI agents acted as *provocateurs* in your case. If you do not have a good investigator and are relying on the government to turn over information, you may have less power in negotiating a plea agreement and will likely be in a more difficult place if the case goes to trial.

Since 9/11, no one has successfully used the entrapment defense in a federal case (or any state cases we know of) targeting radicals or Arab Muslims caught up in the "War on Terror."[49] However, the trial of one of the Texas 2 defendants ended in a hung jury (although that defendant took a plea deal before his re-trial).[50] Jurors in Eric McDavid's trial said that they would have issued a different verdict if the judge had given them the correct instructions about the *agent provocateur* during their deliberations.[51] And, in Miami in 2007 to 2008, the state needed three separate trials to get convictions in a terrorism case because there were strong indications of entrapment in the government's behavior. The first two trials ended in hung juries. One of the seven defendants was ultimately acquitted, charges against another defendant were dropped, and the other five were convicted on some of the charges in the third trial. Although the Liberty City 7, as the defendants were known, did not use an entrapment defense, the very smell of entrapment twice kept the jury from convicting.[52] All of these facts suggest that an entrapment defense may be difficult and nuanced, but we should not discount it too easily.

Unfortunately, if you have been entrapped, you may have a hard time thinking about your case legally, politically, or even sensibly. Being kidnapped by the state and thrown in jail is always isolating and scary. For people who have been entrapped, that isolation can take on a particularly painful edge. Informants and undercover cops who entrap activists often spend a fair amount of time detaching their targets from others before a "crime" is committed so that the informant can coerce them into going along with the plot. Upon arrest, the defendants might not have strong ties to the communities that can offer them support. To further compound this problem, all too often other activists in the same or similar movements react publicly with alarm and condemnation when a "plot" is exposed and the targets of entrapment are arrested. This reaction creates fallout in the press and divides potential supporters. Lawyers and defense committees need to be quick and smart about creating narratives that undercut the government's version of events. (See Chapter 7, "Working with the Media," for more on this.)

Meanwhile, sitting in jail, you may feel doomed because the person who acted like your best friend betrayed you. All the pressure is on you to plead guilty and cooperate with the system, and other activists are denouncing you. So why not go along with the prosecution and get some leniency for yourself? This line of thinking only aids the state in repressing you and your comrades. Focus on remaining in solidarity with your codefendants (if you have them) and other comrades. Solidarity puts you in a position to fight back. Sometimes, it takes a while for the dust to settle after an arrest. Even if you cannot see it right away, folks outside will likely help you and work hard to defend you, as long as you do not cooperate with the state. Being in custody makes it even harder to see this potential because communication with the outside world can be so difficult. If you are considering taking a plea, ask somebody to get a defense committee together before you do so. Your situation will look better when you have support. Folks who have been through this already can be essential members of your defense committee. They can also help you understand the political and legal nuances of the entrapment defense. Someday, when your own ordeal is done, you may be able to return the favor to another activist who is singled out for outrageous treatment by the government.

Terrorism Charges

Since 2001, the use of the word "terrorism" to describe any sort of action taken by activists has dramatically increased. The label "terrorist" divides movements and convinces many people that they are better off living in a police state than engaging in struggle to change it. As in the McCarthy Era, it is easy to throw around a word and work the public into a frenzy. If you are facing terrorism charges or your charges include a terrorism enhancement at sentencing, you must take command of the narrative that is playing out both in the media and courtroom.

By calling a defendant a terrorist, the government aims not only to scare them into submission, but also to scare the entire movement of which they are a part and to deny them public support. That is not a new tactic. Red Scares from 1919 onward intimidated radicals, progressives, and liberals with the Communist ("red") accusation. The threat from the state was real. In the Palmer Raids of 1919 and 1920, the Attorney General rounded up and deported over 500 people because of their supposed leftist leanings. In the 1940s and 1950s, the House Committee on Un-American Activities investigated hundreds of people for allegations that they were Communists, often causing them to lose their jobs and standing in their communities. In the 1960s and 1970s, the FBI's COINTELPRO program used surveillance, infiltration, propaganda, and assassination to discredit and destroy individuals and movements. In the 1980s, the "War on Drugs" labeled predominately people of color and poor people as dangerous to society and led to a proliferation of anti-gang measures, laws, and propaganda that serve to isolate and destroy entire communities.[53] When the state can so thoroughly demonize people in the eyes of the public at large (e.g., by labeling them a "gang member," a "communist," an "anarchist," a "junkie," a "terrorist"), their job in the courtroom becomes easier. For your own sake and for that of your comrades, it is necessary to fight back against this vilification.

Because terrorism charges require a vigorous political defense alongside the legal defense, a defense committee is practically essential. Your defense committee can help you craft a political strategy that will redefine these terms and their application to you in the mind of the public. Defense committees are often much better situated to take on these kinds of fights than a defendant—or even a lawyer—might be. (For more on this, see Chapter 6, "Working with Your Defense Committee.")

The accusation of terrorism can enter in two ways: terrorism-specific laws and terrorism enhancements added to other felony charges. There are varieties of both of these at both the federal and state levels. Many states passed some version of the USA Patriot Act after 9/11, some of which include specific terrorism statutes. Most of the state terrorism-specific laws have never been used to prosecute anyone, whereas the federal ones have been used with increasing frequency, predominately against Arab Muslims. Your legal defense will necessarily be based on the court you find yourself in. Because state charges have been used less frequently, your legal team may have trouble navigating or predicting the legal ins and outs. The flip side is that these statutes might be ripe for constitutionality challenges or other legal attacks. Additionally, their terms may not be crafted as carefully as the federal statutes, which could either work in your favor or against you. The result of legal challenges is never a certainty, of course.

Activism has been codified into law as "terrorism" in the federal Animal Enterprise Terrorism Act (AETA) and many similar state statutes. The AETA, which was signed in 2006, is an expansion of the 1992 law called the Animal Enterprise Protection Act (AEPA). These laws were written to specifically target animal rights activists and label them as terrorists. The language of the AETA criminalizes "damaging or interfering with the operations of an animal enterprise."[54] But these terms are so broadly and loosely defined (if defined at all) that they could potentially include acts such as vandalism, blocking roads, or even running a website.[55]

Even if you are not charged with "terrorism," you can still face a "terrorism enhancement" at your sentencing. This enhancement could add years to your sentence. To apply the enhancement in a federal case, the government must argue at sentencing that your offense was "calculated to influence or affect the conduct of the government by intimidation or coercion, or to retaliate against government conduct." Knowing this, it would be wise for an attorney to weave counterarguments to this line of reasoning into all of the court proceedings, especially trial. This remains true even if you accept a plea agreement at some point, as the judge will still need to evaluate your case to determine whether the enhancement should apply. Having evidence on record that the enhancement should not apply could prove helpful in appeals as well.

Often, terrorism charges go hand-in-hand with conspiracy charges. Likewise, these two charges often involve heavy amounts of surveillance and the use of *provocateurs*. Talking about how the state creates these cases—and the supposed "crime" with which people are charged—can be an incredibly powerful strategy for your political fight.

A Parting Reminder

Despite our focus on common legal situations in this chapter, defendants must keep in mind that there are only trends and generalities in types of charges. Each individual case is different, and the approach taken to fight the charges must therefore be unique. This fact means that you must figure out the best way to handle your case. We hope this chapter and guide as a whole help you in this struggle.

Chapter 4
WORKING WITH YOUR LAWYER

WHEN MOST PEOPLE ARE ARRESTED, THEIR FIRST THOUGHT is, "I need a lawyer!" Likewise, the first question people usually ask them is, "Do you have a lawyer?" If you are reading this chapter, you have likely decided that you want to include a legal defense in your approach to handling your charges and that you want to work with a lawyer. This chapter is designed to help you figure out how to work with your attorney as you approach this situation as a radical or revolutionary. We hope that the advice within this chapter will be useful whether you are working with a "movement lawyer," a private attorney, a public defender, or another court-appointed lawyer. We have also included a sample attorney retainer agreement (see Appendix C), which can be a useful part of structuring your relationship with your attorney.

Hurry Up and Wait

All too often, court cases drag on and on. Sometimes unforeseen circumstances can cause legitimate delays, and sometimes it might make sense strategically to postpone the proceedings. The judge's and prosecutor's whims and schedules mostly dictate the pace, or your attorney may be the source of delays, or sometimes your needs will require the proceedings to be delayed (although judges are less inclined to adjust the schedule for you). Basically, you and your attorney are likely to work together for quite some time.

While a defense attorney is usually aware of the toll that waiting takes on a defendant, especially inside a jail cell, ask your attorney up front for an honest and accurate estimate of how long they will need to prepare for trial. An attorney with any experience should be able to provide a fairly good guess. Clarifying from the beginning how long you expect to be in this relationship may help you make some limited plans for your life and will hopefully help your attorney live up to their word. Your supporters can also use this estimate to develop timetables for fundraising and to clear space in their lives to attend court appearances.

- - - - - - - - - - - - - - - - - - - -
Time Commitments in Politicized Cases

In politicized cases, both the prosecution and defendant may behave in ways that an attorney is not familiar with or cannot understand. An attorney who does not have experience with political cases may be surprised by the prosecution's vehemence, as well as the inordinate amount of resources and attention the government often dedicates to political cases. This lack of understanding and experience can lead your attorney to underestimate the amount of time your defense will take—particularly if you are fully dedicated to going to trial. If you can provide your attorney with examples of political cases similar to yours, they may be better able to create realistic estimates of their time commitments.

The US Constitution says that you have a right to a speedy trial and, technically, you can instruct your attorney to insist on that from the beginning. Pragmatically, though, there can be good reasons to waive this right. The amount of discovery in a political case is a strong factor. Properly digging through the volumes of evidence you receive may take months. Rushing through this process and possibly missing important evidence could be detrimental in the long run.

Sometimes, there might be strategic reasons for delays. For example, Conor Cash was the first person to be charged as a "domestic terrorist" after the September 11, 2001 attacks.[56] Defending himself against charges of terrorism—in New York—so close to 9/11 could have had terrible implications for his case. Thus, his legal team successfully delayed his trial for three years, until May 2004. His trial ended after two weeks, and he was acquitted of all the charges against him.

Even if you are not in custody pre-trial, delays are stressful since almost everything in your life is on hold until your case is settled. Dealing with the uncertainty can make pleading guilty to a reduced charge attractive. This resolution, of course, is exactly what the prosecution wants. Pleading guilty may not always work out for the best, as sometimes taking a plea means spending years in prison with virtually no appeal rights. If your personal circumstances or goals require you to go to trial quickly, instruct your attorney to insist on a speedy trial and be sure they are able to prepare adequately on an accelerated schedule. Similarly, if you decide that pleading guilty is the best decision, you may benefit from working out a plea agreement sooner rather than later. But remember that the judge ultimately determines what "speedy" means if you demand a speedy trial, and being granted this right may not make much of a difference in the long run. Likewise, pleading guilty does not guarantee that you will be able to enter your guilty plea, be sentenced, and be transferred to a prison quickly (this process can still take months).

Finding an Attorney

Finding a competent attorney who can work with you on both the political and legal aspects of your case is no easy task. You should always request a public defender,[57] at least for the short term. Once you have a defense committee, they can help you look for candidates for the permanent position and even pre-screen them, if you are still in custody. An attorney may hesitate to talk to your defense committee about your case. If so, and if your lawyer will talk with your family and if your family (biological or chosen) is supportive, try having someone from your defense committee join your family in a visit with the lawyer to ask questions. You, of course, are entitled to interview any possible attorneys, even if you are in jail.

Much of what makes attorneys useful is not what they learn in law school, but what they learn in court. Understanding the nuances of the law, how it is applied, how particular judges or prosecutors work, how to examine witnesses, or how to really get through to a jury—all of these are lessons that only come with experience. Many attorneys have taken numerous cases or practiced law for a long time and have rarely gone to trial. This kind of attorney may be able to get you a good plea agreement, and yet may be unable or unwilling to adequately represent you at trial. Make sure you find out whether your attorney has trial experience, and what *kind* of experience. For example, if your lawyer has only represented defendants on misdemeanor charges for protesting, they may not be well equipped to defend you against felony conspiracy charges.

- - - - - - - - - - - - - - - - - - - -
Protecting Yourself in Court and Jail

If you have special legal/political vulnerabilities, be sure your lawyer knows something about those challenges. For instance, if your citizenship status is complicated, if you are trans / intersex / gender-nonconforming, if you are a single parent in a custody dispute, or if you have some other extra risk in the legal system, be sure your lawyer understands the implications. Not only may you be treated unfairly by the courts and prosecution (indeed, you may have been targeted in the first place because of your race, gender presentation, or other aspects of your identity), you

> may also be targeted by staff and prisoners
> inside the jail. You could be placed in a "pro-
> tective custody" unit (which often means sol-
> itary confinement), which carries its own set
> of complications. Just because a lawyer might
> be sympathetic to these difficulties does not
> mean that they have experience helping their
> clients navigate them. If your lawyer seems
> inexperienced in these areas, point them to
> resources that could help them understand
> and more effectively advocate for you.

If you anticipate that your case will be consolidated with others, ask how your attorney feels about working with your codefendant's lawyers as part of a defense team. While teamwork can be difficult and complicated, it also has numerous advantages, such as the ability to share resources (which can help cut costs), the chance to prepare a more unified and powerful strategy, and the obvious benefit that two (or more) heads are better than one.

Your attorney must also understand, accept, and respect your total unwillingness to cooperate or ever provide any information about other people. More than likely, you will need to reiterate your principled stand to your attorney throughout your case. Most criminal cases are resolved through plea bargains, and many plea bargains involve giving the government information about other people. Attorneys often pressure their clients to cooperate with the state, either directly or indirectly. Remember that your lawyer, no matter how well-intentioned, was trained in a system that puts the individual welfare of the client above any notion of solidarity. Grassroots movements are often the prosecution's ultimate target, with your case a stepping stone along the way, so your case does not exist in a vacuum. Additionally, you do not want to harm your movements. This is a fundamental difference of perspective and, depending on how radical your lawyer is, it may take time for them to grasp it.

It is hard enough to resist the pressure to provide information on others in exchange for a reduced charge when you are free awaiting trial. When you are in jail, it can be even worse. Ask your defense committee to reinforce with your lawyer your opposition to snitching on other activists. At the very least, your defense committee can clarify that fundraising for the attorney's fees will grind to a halt if the attorney pressures you to take a plea that involves cooperation. It will be impossible to get donations if your supporters have reason to believe that you will provide information to the state.

Although it is rare, attorneys have sometimes advised their political clients to cut off contact with other activists. This advice may come from a fear that the prosecution will build a case of guilt-by-association against you. Do not agree to this further restriction on your freedom! You and your attorney will have to figure out a way to defend you that does not require your isolation from your supporters and loved ones. Again, you may find that reminding your lawyer of your values, goals for your case, benefits of having a defense committee, and source of money to pay for their representation can be helpful.

Public Defenders and Court-Appointed Attorneys

Whether you are inside or outside, if you cannot afford an attorney, you should request a public defender. Many public defenders are highly skilled lawyers who can adequately represent you in court. Additionally, public defenders often have the essential qualification of hours in the courtroom. Mostly, they are drawn to this low-paying, difficult, demanding area of law by their zeal for justice. They also sometimes have access to free resources that a private attorney might have to pay for (which often translates into you having to pay for them). For example, a public defender or court-appointed attorney may get the state to pay for investigators, psychologists, or other expert witnesses. In short, do not assume the worst if you cannot afford a private attorney.

Even so, be aware that public defenders often cannot pay as much attention to your case as they might like to because they typically have outrageously heavy caseloads. They also might not have any political context from which to understand your case, your politics, or your goals. Thus, you might need to do a lot more education for your lawyer and advocacy for yourself as a defendant than you would with a movement attorney.[58] That is not necessarily a bad thing, and may smooth the way for someone else later on. If your attorney needs help understanding cases like yours, you or your defense committee can help them talk to lawyers with experience in political cases and point them to similar cases that might offer legal precedents or other helpful ideas and strategies.

As soon as you are appointed a lawyer, find out their qualifications, politics, experience, and other information that might affect how they represent you. Additionally, you and your defense committee can explore your networks to find lawyers who might be willing to talk to you about your public defender. Other lawyers can be good sources of information.

Of course, sometimes they will not speak poorly (or honestly) about their colleagues, so do not rely solely on their advice. Further, you can research the other cases your public defender has been involved in, what they have said in the media, complaints against them filed with the local bar association or American Bar Association, and so on. And, of course, you can interview your public defender, just as you would a private attorney. This is not a job interview, technically, since they are already "hired," but asking about their work history is perfectly reasonable.

If the public defender's office has a conflict, such as representing one of your codefendants, then an attorney outside the public defender's office will be appointed by the court if you qualify for this assistance. Sometimes, you can request that a certain attorney be appointed. Court-appointed "panel" attorneys come from a pool of private attorneys who have been approved to represent people when the public defender's office cannot. At times, they may have more experience with cases like yours than a public defender.

If you do not feel that your attorney is providing you with adequate representation, you might be able to fire the attorney. Some courts will grant you another free attorney, though firing your counsel might mean that you have to represent yourself (known as going *pro se*) or pay for a private attorney. Be sure to research your options for future representation and carefully weigh the pros and cons of starting over again with a different lawyer. Your defense committee can help you pull all the options together, especially if you are in custody.

In both federal and state jurisdictions, the court must approve your request to hire a new court-appointed attorney/ public defender. Usually you will need to provide the judge with sound arguments about *why* you need to change attorneys. Did your attorney fail to communicate with you about case strategy? Did communication between the two of you completely break down? Did the lawyer push you to take a plea agreement against your will? If you are thinking of applying for new counsel, document specific instances in which such things happened to show to the court, if necessary.

If you are unable to work with your public defender or appointed counsel, you can also ask the attorney to withdraw from the case and make a motion for the judge to replace them. Your attorney might be eager to do so, or might refuse because their reputation, paycheck, or status in the court's eyes could be affected or put in jeopardy. If your attorney puts in this request, though, the judge might agree; they sometimes do so, although they do not have to. During this proceeding or through the documents that are filed, remember to state clearly that you need a new court-appointed attorney, as the judge might otherwise take this motion to mean that you are hiring a private attorney.

- - - - - - - - - - - - - - - - - - - -

Magic Formula for Being Appointed a Different Attorney?

Each jurisdiction and judge will be different in terms of how likely you are to be appointed a different attorney if you cannot work with the first one who was assigned to you. No matter what your chances seem to be, you can create a document trail to help support your request for a new attorney. Generally, you will need to demonstrate how your attorney has inadequately represented you, not simply state that you do not like them.

Some specific steps to take to create this document trail include:

- Keep a log of all your phone calls, visits, and correspondence with your attorney.
- Note each time your attorney neglected to return your call, canceled a meeting or phone call at the last minute or simply did not show up, promised to do something for your case but did not, or disregarded your request for an action to be taken in your defense.
- Send your attorney a fax or letter saying that, through a difficult decision-making process, you have decided that they are not representing your best interests and using due diligence to defend you. Thus, you are asking them to immediately file a motion to withdraw and allow another lawyer to be appointed. List all the ways your attorney has failed to properly represent you.
- As soon as you fax or mail this letter, leave your attorney a message saying that they need to call and put the request to be removed on the docket today or, after two days, you will submit a request to the court to have your attorney removed and a new one appointed.

▪ Draft a letter or motion to your judge to
send if your lawyer does not submit the
request to be removed. (Find out what is
required for your judge, as some may accept letters or in-court statements, whereas others may require a formal motion.)
In this letter or motion, be clear about the
ways your lawyer has not represented you,
request that your attorney be removed,
and request that a new lawyer be appointed. Do not exaggerate; rather, be concise,
factual, and professional.

The court may be less likely to grant a third appointment
than a second, so be sure about your decision to fire your
public defender or appointed counsel. Again, the level of dif-
ficulty will vary based on the jurisdiction and even the particular judge presiding over your case.

If you feel that you need to keep your lawyer but are un-
happy with their representation, go back to your own goals
for the legal aspects of your case. Sometimes, people in your
defense committee can help you figure out how to get what
you want and need from your lawyer. Be careful, however,
not to violate attorney-client privileges when discussing with
them how you feel about your lawyer, as it might be impossible to keep some information private once those boundaries have been violated. Be sure not to talk about things you
would not want the prosecution to know about, such as what
you and your attorney are working on ("attorney work product"). Instead, focus on the things your lawyer has or has

not done that make you consider their representation to be inadequate.

Private Attorneys

If you have access to the necessary resources, you can hire a private attorney. That is often incredibly expensive, although sometimes lower rates or flat fees can be negotiated. In smaller cases that require less time, or in cases that appeal to attorneys for their own reasons, you might be able to secure free representation (*pro bono* representation). In general, finding qualified attorneys to represent you *pro bono* in a complex criminal case is difficult because the amount of time and work involved can be all-consuming.

Be upfront with your lawyer about money from the beginning. If you have limited resources, let the lawyer know that—and if those resources come from the movement itself, be sure the lawyer understands that. Also make sure your lawyer is upfront with *you* about money. Signed representation agreements that clearly spell out the amount and terms of payment can go a long way towards alleviating many of these pressures.

You do not have to accept the first offer of representation you get, nor the first price quote. In fact, sometimes it is best to interview several different candidates. Most likely, you can go back to the first one you interviewed if you decide they were the best. You might be tempted to take the first attorney who seems qualified, especially when you are in jail and are trying desperately to get out. As your lawyer is potentially one of your strongest allies, you want to make sure you are getting the best you can.

Start your search for a private attorney by contacting the National Lawyers Guild[59] for a referral. You can also try groups that are more local or regional, such as the Civil Liberties Defense Center[60] based in Eugene, Oregon and the People's Law Office[61] based in Chicago. If you are not in custody, you can search for newspaper articles about similar cases and find out who the attorneys were, or look at local attorney's websites. If you are in custody, ask your supporters to do this for you.

Look for an attorney who has experience with political prisoners or politically motivated prosecutions. This may be more difficult in rural areas or smaller cities, but a lawyer's politics might shine through in places you do not always immediately think to look. Is there an attorney in town who has done work for undocumented people or for prison rebels? Is there one who has volunteered time on human rights campaigns in other countries?

This is almost too obvious to say, but be sure that the attorney you choose practices criminal law. The law is very specialized, and an attorney practicing civil law can probably help you in a federal conspiracy case about as much as an eye doctor can help you with a heart attack.

Pro Se

In some rare instances, political defendants decide that their cases and/or movements will be best served if they represent themselves. This is called *pro se* (which means "on one's own behalf"). Some defendants decide that their political goals are the most important, so they are willing to run the risk of whatever legal consequences result from not using an attorney. Others simply become fed up with their lawyers and proceed on their own out of frustration. And, of course, some make bad decisions and are worse off as a result.

The Supreme Court has ruled that defendants have the right to represent themselves, but they must do so knowing the "danger and disadvantages of self-representation."[62] If you want to go this route, you have to file a motion with the court asking the judge for permission. The judge will question you closely to be sure you know what you are getting yourself into. In some instances, the judge may appoint a lawyer to give you guidance and advice in court. This lawyer might come in handy with procedural steps and other technicalities that you cannot reasonably learn before going to trial, so using a lawyer in this limited fashion may be beneficial even if you decide to represent yourself.

Political defendants most often go *pro se* when charged with misdemeanors, not felonies. They sometimes speak of the experience as incredibly empowering. Bear in mind, though, that charges such as trespass, disorderly conduct, and resisting arrest require less preparation and understanding of case law than do felony charges based on infiltration, surveillance, and/or entrapment. The consequences of getting it wrong in court are simply much graver in a felony case. Missing a minor detail may contribute to a guilty verdict at trial or destroy any chance for appeals or redress later on. Having a lawyer drastically reduces the chances of that happening, which is why most lawyers would never encourage anyone to go *pro se* on a felony charge. Even Lynne Stewart, who practiced criminal defense law for more than thirty years, hired an attorney to represent her when she was accused of providing material support for terrorism.[63] In contrast, Joshua "Skelly" Stafford of the Cleveland 4 went to trial *pro se* on federal conspiracy charges and was demolished in court; he was found guilty and sentenced to a decade in prison (which was a similar sentence to those of his codefendants, who all pleaded guilty). We would be remiss not to stress that several of the prisoners or former prisoners we talked with while writing this guide strongly advised against going *pro se*.

A Word on the Risks and Advantages of Going Pro Se

In 1984, Helen Woodson and three others took a jackhammer to the lid of a nuclear-armed missile silo in Missouri. Many Plowshares actions, such as this one, have taken place since 1980 and are characterized by property destruction aimed at calling attention to nuclear proliferation and US militarism. One court document from Woodson's case states: "Proceeding *pro se*, the defendants introduced testimony at trial on the destructive power of nuclear weapons, the 'offensive nature' of nuclear missiles, the escalation of risks from the availability of such weapons, the nuclear buildup, the role in history of civil disobedience, international law, and their theological beliefs. The district court instructed the jury that neither good motive nor moral, religious, or political belief was a defense to crime and that United States' nuclear policy was not on trial."[64] The defendants went *pro se*, which has been a common approach for Plowshares activists since they value making political and moral arguments over presenting legal defenses. Woodson and one of her codefendants received sentences of eighteen years in federal prison. Since she had eleven children at home, this placed a considerable burden on her supporters, who had not planned to care for them for nearly that long.[65]

In that same year, Ray Luc Levasseur and six comrades from the United Freedom Front (UFF)[66] were arrested on charges of bombing various military facilities, corporate buildings, and courthouses over the decade prior. Unlike the Plowshares activists, the UFF operated clandestinely and did not wait to be arrested at the scenes of their sabotage. The Ohio 7, as the defendants came to be known, were convicted on charges of conspiracy to commit property destruction and sentenced to fifteen to fifty-three years in federal prisons. In 1987, the federal government brought additional charges against them, this time for sedition and racketeering.

Ray Luc, already in prison, decided to defend himself on these new felony charges. When his trial opened in 1989, he explained his decision to go *pro se* in his opening statement to the jury: "What I'm simply trying to do is to add my voice to that of millions of others

who cry 'freedom!' from South Africa to
Central America to the south Bronx in New
York. They don't have much choice about it,
and I don't have much choice. I'd rather not
be here. But since I am, I want to defend
myself and I want to defend the issues that I
think are important. And the important issue
here is the issue of human rights."[67] After
several months, the jury acquitted Ray Luc
and his two codefendants on the sedition
charges and deadlocked over the racketeering charges. He walked free in 2004, seven
years before Woodson did.

In spite of these cautions—and the fact that personally we
cannot imagine representing ourselves against serious felony
charges—we offer some general advice for going *pro se*, from
people who have done it:

- Study the rules of the court and the rules of evidence
  closely in advance. You will need to know these rules
  to prepare your defense exhibits and to figure out court
  procedures (e.g., deadlines for filing motions, when
  you should object, etc.). Failure to follow what might
  seem like an immaterial or unimportant detail may result in the document you are filing being thrown out
  by the court. Important case law that could help you
  with this is *Ferreta v. California*, 422 U.S. 806 (1975).
- When you come across something you might not
  know or understand, do some thorough legal research.

Make sure you have a firm grasp on concepts and legal-ese that you might run across in the courtroom.

- If there is a law library nearby and you are not in custody, be sure to get help from the people who work there. Often law librarians can be extremely knowledgeable and helpful when navigating the legal research you will need to do for your case.

- If you plan to examine witnesses, either on direct testimony or on cross-examination, prepare an extensive and thorough list of questions. There is no time limit on the examination of witnesses (although the judge can apply limits on the lines of questioning you pursue and specific questions you can ask), so keep asking questions until you feel that you have covered the information you want. (If you are cross-examining witnesses, the questions you have prepared for them will most likely change after hearing how the prosecutor questions them.)

- Rehearse the entire trial in the way you think it will play out. Ask people from your defense committee to help you, and think of how they might see the trial play out so you can prepare for other possibilities.

- Do not assume that the prosecutor will cut you slack in the courtroom because you are not a lawyer. They will not. In fact, expect them to attack even more viciously because they know they can get away with doing so when up against a novice.

- Remind the jury frequently that your case is a serious matter and that your life is on the line, especially in opening and closing arguments. The prosecutor may try to make jokes to lighten the mood and win over the jury. Continually reiterate that this is a serious matter so the jury might be more likely to take what you have to say in the same vein.

▪ Always make eye contact with the jury and direct the witnesses to give their answers to the jury.

If you decide you want to represent yourself, have your defense committee help you find resources to assist you in building the best defense possible for yourself. In general, though, having even an inadequate attorney leaves you more room for appeals down the line, which might shorten the length of time you spend in prison overall. Again, your decisions about how to handle the legal defense in your case should depend on your overall goals for your case: personal, political, and legal.

Building a Healthy Relationship with Your Attorney

Lawyers can be amazing advocates, powerful insiders, articulate spokespeople, and even the core of a campaign to win your freedom. Additionally, as the legal process is illogical, unjust, and shrouded in jargon, your lawyer can make this process more understandable and less baffling. Unfortunately, they cannot make your charges go away, always get you out of jail right away, or get your belongings back instantly (or sometimes, at all). Blaming your lawyer for everything that goes wrong with your case can be easy, but it can also lead to feelings of resentment and anger, which are not particularly helpful when you have to work closely with someone in an inherently stressful situation. What follows are some basic suggestions for how to build a healthy relationship with your lawyer that will make working together easier, more efficient, and more productive. Basically, this advice falls into the categories of good communication and clear expectations.

Attorneys and Defendants: Comrades in Shared Struggle

If you are able to secure representation from a political or radical lawyer, your relationship can be one of comrades playing different roles in a shared struggle, in addition to the attorney-client relationship the court imposes on you. Your legal interests require you to maintain the attorney-client relationship well—and it is important that the attorney observes this, too, so they maintain their bar certification and continue representing radicals in the future. Yet we do not want the state to completely dictate the ways in which comrades relate to and associate with each other. As a radical defendant, treat your lawyer as your comrade in the ways that make sense given your situation, and insist that they do the same.

First of all, tell your lawyer that you want to be involved in your case and follow through on any promises you make or tasks you take on. If you expect your lawyer to stick to deadlines, the same should be expected of you. Demonstrating that you want to work on your case as a team will help your lawyer understand that you are serious about fighting your charges. Additionally, your attorney may be more likely to engage with you as an equal, rather than as a client paying for services.

Your relationship with your lawyer should involve open and honest lines of communication. Your lawyer needs to know everything that might be relevant to you and your case that could help at trial (which is not to say that your lawyer needs to know *everything about everything*, as there may be valid reasons for withholding information from your lawyer as you would withhold from other people who do not need to know it). Do not lie to your lawyer, including lies of omission. If they do not know something about you that the prosecution does, this could be extremely detrimental to your case. And, of course, your lawyer should be honest with you in return. Make sure your attorney knows that you need the truth about everything from attorney fees and timelines to possible defenses, plea agreements, and your chances at trial. In a best-case scenario, building good communication patterns between you and your attorney can lay a foundation of trust that can be crucial when dealing with the stress of state repression.

Further, make sure you tell your lawyer about any other legal problems you have (e.g., warrants, probation violations, child support or custody issues), but do not assume that they can help with them. Some of these issues can come up in court, including in bail hearings, and could affect whether or not you are released pre-trial. It is important for your lawyer to know about them upfront so they can figure out the best way to defend you.

Also make sure you both have a clear understanding of and are on the same page about other aspects of your defense, such as political support. The considerations could range from overall strategy and goals to tactical decisions about engaging with the media to deadlines for raising money for private investigators. For example, if together you decide that you will not speak to the media without first consulting your attorney, stick to that promise. Likewise, if you do not like the way your lawyer is pursuing a particular strategy, or feel it is not what you agreed on, tell them. If your attorney has a clear understanding of what you want and how you want to get it, they will be better able to respond to these changes with fewer mishaps and problems.

Needless to say, maintaining open, trusting communication with your lawyer means that you need to make sure you stay in contact with them. Return their phone calls and emails right away, as sometimes they are working on time-sensitive issues. Alternatively, they may be working on your case right at the moment they contact you, and will not return to your case for a few days (or more). Catch them while they are in "go mode"! If you are not in custody and are allowed to travel, let them know if you are going out of town and make sure they have a way to contact you.

If you are in custody, a defense committee can facilitate communication between you and your lawyer. Your lawyer probably cannot visit you as often as you would like, and defense committee members might be able to take up some of the slack. Use them as a channel to get the information you need about your case and to keep your attorney informed about what is happening with you. Always keep in mind, though, that jail visits with your defense committee are not covered by attorney-client privilege as your visits with your lawyer should be.

Perhaps most importantly, having reasonable and realistic expectations about what your lawyer can and cannot do will smooth the way for working with them. Even the greatest of lawyers cannot fix all—or even most—of the problems you will face as a defendant. They are still subject to the same whims and vagaries of prosecutors and judges as you, and are still working within a bureaucracy and system that does not care at all for people or justice. Try to discern between things that can and cannot be changed. Do not sell yourself short and be sure to hold your lawyer accountable when the situation calls for it. But remember that there are some things that are simply beyond their reach.

Common Problems and Pitfalls

No matter how hard you work at building a good relationship with your lawyer, things will inevitably happen that might be difficult to work through. And, unfortunately, lawyers can collaborate with injustice and oppression without even recognizing it. Treachery, dishonesty, and total incompetence are distributed throughout the legal profession, and are not confined to prosecutors alone. Lawyers can be unavailable, unsympathetic, inconsiderate, and inexperienced. They can erode your ability to proceed strategically and with integrity. These professional and personal shortcomings can be a major detriment to you and your case. Often, these challenges are unforeseeable and there is not always a right or wrong way to deal with them. But there are several pieces of advice we can offer for some potential problems and pitfalls.

Even when you are good at staying in touch, lawyers may not be. Often that is because they are legitimately busy people. Other times, it is not. Trying to communicate with someone who has so much influence over your life and does not return your calls can be incredibly frustrating—especially if you are calling from jail. At times like this, remember that they may be working on your case even though they do not return your calls right away. Be persistent, but not pestering: you do not want "client management" to get in the way of your lawyer's preparation.

If, however, you detect a pattern of leaving you out of the loop, or slippage on promises to "get back to you," document these instances. Lawyers should *not* be let off the hook for failing to communicate with you about how your case is unfolding.

Lawyers also often have an irritating habit of preparing at the last minute. Or they might work on your case constantly for a couple of weeks, then not at all for a few more. Usually they have so many cases going at the same time that they let things go until they are right up against a deadline. Since you are the defendant, you have only your own case(s) to worry about. You might be alarmed at the way they seem to have forgotten important aspects of your case, but try to be patient and understanding of their realities, too.

Most lawyers are never lacking in advice about how you should manage your case or make decisions. Often, that advice can be incredibly helpful. And, of course, their advice is not infallible, from either a legal or a political perspective. Sometimes, for political reasons, you might want something that your lawyer is legally bound *not* to do. It is not their fault if they cannot help you with that—and maybe you can do it without them anyway.

If you have issues, concerns, or frustrations with your lawyer, address them immediately. Left untended, they will only get worse. It can feel really awkward or even scary to confront your lawyer. Especially if you are in custody, you can feel like the lawyer is the only person on your side who has any power in the eyes of the law. But the farther you get into a case, the harder it becomes to address any issues or to fire your lawyer, if need be. And sometimes firing the lawyer is the best option.

Balancing what is best for both you and the movement you are a part of should be at the forefront of your thoughts and decisions. If that means firing your lawyer and hiring a new one, then you may have to do it, even if there are negative consequences as well. Hiring new counsel in the midst of pre-trial proceedings can be a huge set-back in a process that already feels long and drawn out. But the stakes are high and securing the best possible representation is critical. If you need to bounce your options off someone else, your defense committee might be a good place to start. Ultimately, the decision is yours, because your life is so centrally affected. Just remember that you will have to live with the decisions you make.

Similarly, you need to remember that your lawyer works for you. They likely learned in law school that the client is in the lead and the lawyer supports the client, follows their wishes, and encourages them to set the goals. However, because your lawyer knows the criminal legal system better than you do, it is easy to let them control the defense strategy—a role they may be all too willing to play. Look for a balance between your wishes and goals and the attorney's knowledge and experience in legal and courtroom strategy. The experience and perspective they bring, even if it is sometimes hard to hear, could prove invaluable to your defense.

Chapter 5
WORKING WITH YOUR CODEFENDANTS

IF YOU HAVE CODEFENDANTS, BUILDING A SENSE OF SOLIDARity and camaraderie with them can be powerful for both you and the movement that supports you. Having other people struggle alongside you can help you feel less alone and alienated, stronger, and more able to take on the daunting task of fighting the criminal legal system. Working with your codefendants can also be stressful and frustrating. Even when you are not the best of friends, you will likely need to work closely with your codefendants to coordinate your legal and political strategies.

People become codefendants in a variety of situations. Sometimes, people are charged for their organizing (e.g., the SHAC 7 and the AETA 4). At other times, people in friend circles get charged with conspiracy and other offenses (e.g., the Cleveland 4 and the NATO 3). There are also times when people are scooped up together and charged, even though they do not all know each other (e.g., the Asheville 11[68]).

These dynamics can be difficult to navigate, particularly if people do not know and trust each other, have never shared political analyses and goals, or do not even like each other. The case of the Chicago 8[69] is a good example of defendants facing adverse conditions for handling their charges together. The defendants all took an irreverent, non-cooperative approach to the court proceedings, ridiculing the judge and disrupting the proceedings frequently. Ultimately, they created and endured a highly publicized 4.5-month courtroom spectacle together.

Codefendants often have varying degrees of support (from family, friends, and the movement as a whole), different financial resources, outside circumstances that affect their abilities to focus fully on their charges, and uneven amounts of commitment to revolutionary struggle. All of these dynamics and considerations will come up as you deal with your charges. Below we offer some suggestions on working with your codefendants in ways that will strengthen you, your case, and your struggle.

General Considerations for Working with Your Codefendants

Creating a sense of cohesion and solidarity within your group is an important part of working together well. Solidarity does not spring out of nowhere, especially when you are under a lot of pressure from the legal system, the media, and/or your un-indicted comrades. Solidarity has to be built intentionally.

If you were part of a tight-knit affinity group before getting arrested, you are likely to have a good foundation to start from. Even so, it takes intentional effort to maintain your ties with the weight of your charges bearing down on you. If you were not part of a cohesive group before getting arrested, you may be forced to build affinity with each other while building your defense. Keep in mind that the state will be actively working to tear apart any sense of solidarity and affinity. Even though you might not always get along, you will likely be stronger if you stick together.

Start a clear, honest discussion about your personal and political goals as soon as possible after you are charged. Not everyone needs to have the same goals, but you should come to consensus about what you want to do with your cases, if at all possible. If you cannot reach consensus, then at least make sure no one person's individual decisions produce negative consequences for someone else. Having a clear sense of one another's goals and strategies from the beginning will help everyone stay the course for the duration of your case. Continue to check in about everyone's goals as the case progresses to ensure your initial agreements still hold.

Different experiences or factors may influence your codefendants' goals and how they want to proceed with the case. For example, a prior legal record could have real implications for a codefendant at trial or during sentencing. Some people may have situations that could make them particularly vulnerable to pressure from the state (e.g., chemical dependency, child custody or other dependent issues, learning disabilities, emotional health concerns). What support do they need from their codefendants, comrades, friends, family, and loved ones to stay in solidarity with everyone else? Try to be sensitive to and open about these issues while discussing your goals and strategies.

Managing group dynamics and interpersonal relationships while under extreme pressure can be difficult. Yet there are some simple techniques that may help. For example, try making up stories about how this prosecution will end. What is the best possible outcome? What is acceptable as a win, even if it is not the best result? What would be unacceptable? Another important technique is listening to each other without interrupting or changing the subject. In your meetings, you could observe time limits so no one person speaks all the time or more than others. If you tend to interrupt people because you are afraid you might forget what you have to say, write it down and come back to it when it is your turn to speak. Sometimes people will opt not to speak rather than compete to have their voices heard. We can often lose valuable insights as a result. Since the stakes are so high, make sure every opinion, insight, and possible piece of evidence is heard.

Inevitably, conflicts will arise. You are all under an amazing amount of stress, and the decisions you are forced to make have serious, long-term impacts on your lives. When conflicts arise, ask yourself, "What kind of person do I really want to be? What reaction will help us achieve our goals? How do revolutionaries need to act in situations like this to advance the struggle?" As you figure out your answers to these questions, strive to embody them in your words and actions, especially when doing so is hard in the moment. Remember that while no one is perfect and we cannot expect impossible things of each other, we *can* expect that each of us maintains a principled stance and conducts ourselves with integrity.

Be clear and transparent about your choices, priorities, and opinions—as well as about why these are so—particularly when faced with conflict. And ask your codefendants to do the same.

The Nuances of Solidarity and Conflicts

In *Love and Struggle*, David Gilbert[70] recounts his experiences after being arrested while working as an ally to Black Liberation Army revolutionaries in an expropriation of $1.5 million from a Brink's armored truck. During the expropriation, a security guard and two cops were killed in a shootout; three days later, a Black revolutionary named Mtayari Sundiata was shot and killed while fleeing the cops who had tracked down him and Sekou Odinga.

One of the BLA members, Sam Brown, was beaten so badly after his arrest that two vertebrae in his neck were fractured. His condition was untreated for eleven weeks until he eventually snitched on other revolutionaries in order to get medical care. Even though David suspected this cooperation, he and other captured revolutionaries urged supporters to make Brown their priority. David and another comrade also went on a hunger strike to demand surgery for Brown, which happened four days after they started their strike. While David and his codefendants could no longer trust Brown, they did not snitch on him or abandon him completely at trial.

Not many revolutionaries would take care of someone who was helping put them in prison for life. And certainly this decision flies in the face of a revolutionary ethic that calls for snitches to lose all support. While we do not advocate for snitches to receive support, clearly there are exceptional circumstances that could lead revolutionaries to figure out how to work together according to their own principles.

▬ ▬ ▬ ▬ ▬ ▬ ▬

At all times, ensure you do not let drama, interpersonal issues, or other needless sources of tension be the things you focus your time and energy on. Becoming distracted by making mountains out of mole hills can be all too tempting when the pressure is on and anything can seem more appealing than dealing with the real problems at hand. But getting caught up in drama only benefits the state since the more you are worn down by your situation as a whole, the more effective their pressure can be. At times, you may need to ask your defense committee or other trusted friends to step in and mediate situations so you can move past the drama and focus on what really matters. At other times, you may need to ask them to step out of the situation to stop stirring up drama. Whatever the case may be, keeping your focus on your goals and the broader political relevance of your case can help you avoid becoming stuck in the emotional drain of needless drama.

Another important aspect of working together as codefendants is checking in with one another regularly about how things are going in your personal lives. Becoming caught up in the urgency of your shared circumstances and allowing your case to be the only thing you talk about when you are together are all too easy. Thus, find time to talk about something other than your case once in a while. Having your case become your only point of affinity can become a weak foundation when put to the test as trial approaches. What are family and friends saying about your charges? Is anyone pressuring you to take a plea agreement? How is everyone getting along with their lawyer? Who is having financial problems? How are you feeling about your defense committee? Who is feeling discouraged? One codefendant might have more resources available to them than others. If that codefendant is you, consider sharing those resources. Your case and your emotional fortitude will benefit from everyone else feeling strong and healthy.

Occasionally, there might be a conflict or irreparable situation between one of you and a person outside of your group, your community as a whole, or your movement as a whole. Some of the worst situations that could fall into this category include one codefendant snitching (see below for more on this situation), assaulting someone sexually, stealing money from defense funds, or engaging in oppressive behaviors that cannot be tolerated. There are some measures that are often taken in cases such as these, including accountability processes, conflict resolution or transformation, and restorative justice circles. Unfortunately, none of these resources are guaranteed to work in every difficult situation. You, your co-defendants, and your defense committee will need to figure out what to do as best you can. There is also a temptation to downplay such serious conflicts in comparison to the high stakes of the legal charges. As radicals and revolutionaries, we cannot ignore behavior that harms comrades, even when the harm is caused by someone facing politically motivated charges. This can mean that codefendants may have to hold one another accountable for causing damage to their relationships or communities. If you are faced with one of these situations, do not be afraid to reach out to your defense committee and loved ones for help in handling it as best you can.

If All of You are in Custody

Being in custody and facing years of your life in prison is a terrible prospect. The stress can manifest in feelings of blame or anger toward your codefendants. Only the state benefits from this pointless blame, and your captivity is designed to create this dynamic (i.e., divide-and-conquer). Remember who put you in prison in the first place. Do not get caught up in thoughts about what might have happened if someone (yourself included) had done something or said something differently. No one can change the past and now you must all work together for your collective freedom in the future.

If you are in custody and are able to see your codefendants, try to balance your time together between working on your case and supporting each other emotionally. Play games, share books, tell stories. If you are not able to see each other, find creative ways of connecting through your lawyers and defense committee members. Your lawyers might be able to set up meetings where everyone is present so you can all work on your case together. While it is important to use this time strategically, use it to catch up with one another and reconnect as well. Just remember that while your communications inside of the room with your lawyer are theoretically protected, any conversation with your codefendants *outside* of that room is not protected, including in the hallways or elevators as you go to or from that meeting. Even if you first discuss something in a conversation protected by attorney-client privilege, that information is stripped of its confidential status once it is discussed outside of an attorney-client privileged setting.

The government is always monitoring your communications with your codefendants while you are in custody. Even when you are alone together, assume that other people are listening. While you can talk about your case or how you are feeling, bear in mind that anything you say could be played back to you in a courtroom. Do not discuss sensitive case strategy and facts unless you are in a private room with your lawyers.

If Some of You are in Custody and Others are Not

Sometimes, one or more codefendants are stuck in jail while the others are released pending trial. This situation makes it much more difficult to feel that you are in this together and to build solidarity within your group. Do not let the state divide you in these situations! Be especially cautious of rumors that one or more of your codefendants is cooperating with the prosecution. The state can lie with impunity, so do not believe anything they tell you until you have solid proof. Your lawyer and/or defense committee can help you find this proof, especially if you are in custody.

Similarly, do not speculate that one codefendant is cooperating because they got released from jail and no one else did, or because charges against them are dropped, or because the prosecution offers them a sweeter plea deal. The state's ultimate goal is to divide you and your codefendants so you will betray each other. Do not help the state out by jumping to conclusions or gossiping about your codefendants.

Beyond this primary firewall for solidarity, you will need to figure out ways of building or maintaining strong relationships and communication with your codefendants. Almost certainly, a codefendant who is out on bail will not be able to visit their codefendants in jail. Thus, your lawyer and defense committee may have to act as go-betweens. Creativity and persistence will be necessary to facilitate communication and a sense of camaraderie. Your defense committee may have more ability to help you in this situation since your lawyer needs to act in ways that do not compromise their own legal standing.[71]

Fighting a case from inside a jail cell feels much different than doing it from outside. The sense of urgency, while still present, can be a lot less dramatic if you are able to do ordinary things while you prepare your case. Be sensitive and responsive to the differences in your situations. Always remember that you are in this together and you have a responsibility to act in ways that help each other legally and personally.

If None of You are in Custody

If you are all lucky enough to be granted release pending trial, you will probably be way more capable of working on your case and assisting your lawyers. This can make a huge difference in how well and quickly your trial preparations unfold. With this relatively fortunate situation, you can all go through the discovery material (i.e., evidence) systematically. The discovery is usually too much for any one person to tackle alone. Figure out a method to get a collective understanding of it, which will be necessary for you in building a strong case. The evidence in your case can be confusing—like a million scattered pieces of a puzzle. And sometimes there are pieces that do not really fit anywhere at all. Your job is to create a picture out of the puzzle while figuring out what to do with the pieces that do not fit as you build your legal defense. You can also use this time together to catch up with one another or to answer questions you may have about each other's perspective on particular aspects of the case or the defense strategy.

When you take on an individual task, prioritize it so you finish on time. Flaking out undermines everyone's morale and can have serious implications for your case. Remember that this is not just *your* life—your codefendants' lives and well-being are on the line too. Your case most likely has implications for your movement as well. If you are feeling overwhelmed by the amount of work you have to do, say so! Take on only as much as you can finish. Being realistic about how much time you have and letting your preparations move forward at a slower pace is better than taking on too much and letting important tasks slip through the cracks.

Additionally, avoid letting the stress of your charges spill out in unintentional ways. Double- and triple-check your emails and text messages for sarcasm and nastiness. It is easy to read a tone of voice into an email or text. Ask yourself, "What tone of voice might the recipient of this message hear?" Avoid sending electronic communications to your codefendants, lawyers, or supporters when you are tired or cranky or sick. Be sure you are always saying what you mean and that you will not regret what you have written later.

If you are able to travel freely (or are able to get permission from the court to do so), go out of town together for a weekend. For example, go camping or hiking. Bring your partners and children, if you have them, but make sure you have some time together alone, too. A change of scenery can do wonders when you are under so much stress. Being out in the world can help you remember why you organize and resist in the first place, as well as why doing is important.

Similarly, seek ways to lighten the mood around your case from time to time. Find things to laugh about together. What is the funniest thing you could say to your judge? To the prosecutor? If any of you have artistic inclinations, draw cartoons of the *agents provocateur* who betrayed you (if applicable), or anyone else who irritates you. Alternatively, cook a meal for yourselves, your family, and your supporters. Have a dance as a fundraiser or sponsor a game night. Not all fundraisers have to be dour legal updates. There are excellent ways to have fun together while simultaneously reaching out to supporters and staying involved in your community. The more you remain present within your community, the stronger you will feel and be.

Non-Association Conditions

Although somewhat rare, radical defendants can be released pending trial under condition that they do not associate with each other. More commonly, defendants will be prevented from associating with people who are potential witnesses, although this is not always the case either. If your conditions of release include non-association clauses, talk with your lawyer to make sure you fully understand all the conditions, their implications, and the consequences if you were to violate them, whether accidentally or otherwise.

Dealing with Non-Association Conditions

If you are stuck with a non-association condition, the only way you can meet with your codefendants may be with all of your lawyers present. In the aftermath of the G20 protests in Toronto, Canada in 2010, dozens of people faced serious charges. In one case, seventeen codefendants had non-association conditions for their release pending trial.[72] Every time they met to talk about their case, there were seventeen codefendants and seventeen lawyers present in the room. Not only were these meetings hard to schedule, they were also incredibly long.

If you and your codefendants have non-association conditions, legal meetings may be the only time you can speak to one another. Such

> meetings have to include time to address in-
> terpersonal dynamics. After all, you and your
> codefendants benefit from catching up with
> one another and sharing laughter and tears.
> Nevertheless, you and your lawyer should be
> prepared for this situation and set realistic
> goals for how much trial preparation you can
> get done at these meetings.

— — — — — — — — — — — — — — —

Judges impose non-association conditions on defendants so they will become isolated from their defense committees, friends, and communities. You and your supporters will have to be creative to ensure you have the political and personal support you need to fight your charges. Often, the people who are best equipped to prepare you for dealing with things like jail and court appearances are the very people with whom you are denied contact. This restriction puts an extra responsibility on you, your lawyer, and your supporters to keep you informed about the legal process, help you make your decisions about your case, and ensure your decisions do not adversely affect others. Thus, you should strive to voice your needs clearly and work to find creative ways of getting them met despite draconian court restrictions.

When Codefendants Flip

Unfortunately, it is fairly common for one or more codefendants in a case to "flip" (start cooperating with the state), also known as snitching. This can feel devastating on several levels. Most obviously, the emotional fallout from this betrayal can be completely debilitating. When someone you considered a friend and comrade starts working with the state, the pain and anger can be overwhelming. Sometimes people claim they cooperate because they will be able to help their codefendants by presenting a story in court. This logic is, of course, completely absurd and plays right into the government's hands. The state would not work so hard to coerce people into cooperating if it did not work in the state's favor. Once someone decides to cooperate, they are completely at the mercy of the state. If they do not perform the way the state wants them to while on the stand, they may pay for it when it is time for them to be sentenced.

- - - - - - - - - - - - - - - - - -
A Fleeting Moment of Being the Cleveland 5

The case of the Cleveland 4 started out as the Cleveland 5. Shortly after the defendants were arrested, one snitched on the others in exchange for a lighter sentence. He was the least connected to the group and has a daughter, which was easy leverage for the state to use against him to force cooperation. The state seized on this opportunity and brought him to the stand when three of the remaining defendants (Brandon Baxter, Connor Stevens, Doug Wright) pleaded guilty to the conspiracy and other charges they were facing. His testimony made the situation for the non-cooperating defendants much worse

and was ammunition for the prosecution
to argue that the terrorism enhancements
should be applied at sentencing and that they
should all be given life sentences. These defendants were ultimately sentenced to eight
to eleven and a half years in prison, plus life-
time supervised release. The final defendant,
Joshua "Skelly" Stafford, took his case to
trial, representing himself, and was convicted
on all counts. He was sentenced to ten years
in prison plus life-time supervised release.

Had the state not been successful in breaking
solidarity between the defendants, they may
have been able to hold together to take their
cases to trial or negotiate more favorable plea
agreements. We can never know, of course,
but one codefendant flipping undeniably
benefited the state more than the remaining
defendants.

▬ ▬ ▬ ▬ ▬ ▬ ▬ ▬

When a codefendant flips, it can also seem devastating in
a legal sense. A cooperating codefendant presents significant
legal challenges, but it does not have to spell the end of all
hope for your chances at trial. You and your lawyer can mitigate the potential damage through revising your legal strategy and plans for what might happen in the courtroom. The
most obvious complication is what a cooperating defendant
will tell the prosecution, both before trial in a "debrief" and
while on the stand. You should have access to the statements

made by cooperating defendants before trial, which will help you prepare to defend yourself in front of the jury. The questions asked by the prosecution in these statements might give you insight into the arguments and angles of their trial strategy. As there is no real way to plan for everything a person might say while on the stand, be prepared for new and interesting interpretations of the "facts" a person has already admitted to during their debriefs. Again, since a cooperating defendant's performance at trial will directly affect how the government recommends they be sentenced, the prosecutor will hold this over their head to assure continued cooperation. Therefore, the cooperating codefendant will be loath to say anything that contradicts the government's version of events. Nevertheless, your attorney can attempt to question them in a way that challenges their credibility (i.e., impeaches them) or shines light on something more closely resembling the truth. If successful, this cross-examination can be a powerful moment in the eyes of the jury and can cast doubt on the government's entire story.

Another impact of cooperation is that someone who has been in on your strategy discussions has now gone over to the enemy. If you and your codefendants have discussed the discovery with your lawyers and begun developing your legal strategy, the snitch may tell the prosecution how you are using and interpreting the discovery materials. You should talk with your attorney about ways to mitigate any potential legal risks that could develop from those prior conversations.

A cooperating defendant can also affect your support, defense committee, and community as a whole. Snitching can be incredibly divisive. Your defense committee will have to navigate carefully as they inform the wider community that one of the people they have been defending has decided to co-operate with the government. They may be directly handling a lot of the fallout in the community when this happens, which can be an incredibly stressful experience. Hopefully, they can keep reminding everyone of the importance of supporting the folks who are still standing strong against the state, and cause a redoubling of commitment to you.

In the final analysis, when a codefendant becomes a snitch, you have lost a friend and comrade. This loss can make an already emotionally taxing situation feel unbearable. Remember, though, that you are not alone and there are good people fighting for you and your freedom.

Chapter 6
WORKING WITH YOUR DEFENSE COMMITTEE

DEFENSE COMMITTEES HAVE LONG BEEN A CRUCIAL PART OF radical movements. The state will inevitably repress political activity, and criminal charges are one of its most powerful tools. Because of this, supporting defendants and prisoners will remain an important part of radical organizing. Yet people who find themselves facing charges because of their politics will not always know how to draw on the support that is being offered to them. This chapter aims to help you figure out how to work with your defense committee regardless of your legal situation.

These committees typically do some or all of the following:

- Send money to your commissary account in jail or prison.
- Visit, write you letters, talk with you on the phone.

- Interview possible lawyers and act as a liaison between lawyers, family, and supporters.
- Do research for your defense.
- Stage noise demonstrations, rallies, and other solidarity actions as part of a political campaign in your defense.
- Fundraise to cover legal expenses, commissary funds, and other support expenses (e.g., photocopies, postage, gas money for people to visit you, etc.).
- Build a broader base of support for you and help you achieve your political goals for your case in the public, in the media, and within the movement.
- Conduct media campaigns to help you achieve your goals.
- Water your plants, feed your companion animals, help you with childcare, reassure family members that you are not doomed, move your stuff out of your apartment or house, and other tasks you might worry about because you cannot do them yourself (particularly if you are being held in custody).

This is an incomplete list because a defense committee's work depends greatly on the circumstances at hand. Since every case and defendant is different, new functions are created each time. The obstacles each committee will face also depend on the situation. Sometimes, the committee comes together easily from among your close friends. Other times, completely unknown activists step up to the work; hopefully, that happens quickly, though sometimes it takes months.

A strong defense committee will likely help you handle your case in the most effective way possible. Some cautions are in order, though: a defense committee is necessarily limited by your circumstances, and by the potential impact of their support on your legal case. For example, if you are in custody pending trial, you may never be able to speak freely with them about your feelings about your charges because you are constantly under surveillance. In the worst cases, you may find yourself far from your friends and family with no means of posting bail, in which case you may be relying on strangers or near strangers for political support. A defense committee is not the same as a strong affinity group, collective, or circle of friends, and you and your defense committee members all have to work at making your team successful.

Common Roles a Defense Committee Plays

The activities of defense committees vary based on the stage of the criminal legal case, the political context in which it is happening, and numerous other factors. There are several roles that defense committees commonly play, namely fundraising, defense preparation, direct support, and political support.

Fundraising

Your defense committee may be your primary fundraising crew. Some radical defendants can draw on their own financial resources, while others cannot. Likewise, some activists have family and friends with money, while others do not. Even if you have access to financial resources, it is highly unlikely that you will be able to fight serious felony charges without raising a lot of extra money. Your defense committee can help you do a tremendous amount of fundraising, often in a short time.

There are many ways to raise money, ranging from bake sales to house parties to art auctions to direct mail campaigns to selling t-shirts, posters, stickers, and patches to online appeals for funds to anything else you and your supporters can imagine. Set up online donation options as well as a mailing address where people can send checks and money orders.

Running donations through an organization with a 501(c)3 tax-exempt status is perhaps the best idea for raising tens of thousands of dollars. This arrangement, called "fiscal agency," typically involves the non-profit fiscal sponsor charging a small fee (usually 5–10% of each gift) for the service. Donors can then write their donations off on their own individual tax returns, and are more likely to give larger amounts. The fiscal sponsor will also take care of filing a tax return on behalf of the defense committee.

At the very least, your defense committee will benefit from a treasurer who keeps careful records and a business checking account. You probably do not want thousands of dollars going through personal bank accounts. Opening a business checking account will require you to have a business, which could be an easy operation or a hard one, depending on where you live. Whatever the laws are in your state, figuring them out and taking the steps needed to have a business checking account is well worth the effort, both because of the implications for individuals of large sums of money going through their accounts and for the ease of transparency regarding support funds. Distrust and fights over money regularly tear groups apart. There are also times when sharing financial reports of some sorts with supporters could be necessary or advantageous.

Of course, if you are in custody, you may not be able to get involved in these efforts much at all. In fact, restrictions imposed by the jail or the prosecution might make it necessary for you to remain uninvolved in fundraising and handling money. Do not be shy about asking your supporters to take the lead, and thank them warmly and often for their efforts. Be clear with them about how much input you want in to how the money is used. For example, discuss with them how much you are willing to pay for a lawyer, or whether your family needs travel money in order to visit you in jail or attend your court appearances.

Preparation of Your Legal Defense

Your defense committee can often help you with your legal defense. You can sign a waiver or otherwise come to an agreement that allows your attorney to discuss the case with them. They can then assist your attorney by doing research, taking notes in court, and providing information about how similar cases were prosecuted. Your supporters may know people or information that would help your lawyer prepare your defense. Additionally, if there is an informant, defense committee members might be able to dig up valuable information about the informant.

Sometimes, attorneys, defendants, and defense committee members partner on tasks such as reviewing discovery materials and transcribing audio and video recordings. If you and your lawyer are comfortable with it, defense committee members may be able to handle some of the work that is usually done by paralegals. For example, they could take on tasks ranging from interviewing witnesses to cataloguing evidence to writing *habeas corpus* petitions. This arrangement can speed up preparations and reduce costs, though it does require confidentiality agreements with committee members and supervision by your attorney.

But remember: your defense committee may contain potential witnesses for your defense. Always be careful in your dealings with potential witnesses. For instance, it might be best for them not to review discovery documents, and you might want to avoid talking with them about what is in the discovery. That does not mean you have to be unfriendly to your potential witnesses, just that you should explain that you must keep them in the dark about anything that might come up on the witness stand. You and your supporters should always work closely with your lawyer to ensure all the necessary precautions are taken as you prepare your defense.

That being said, having defense committee members working with your lawyer can be an invaluable part of your legal defense, so this possibility should not be precluded hastily. Additionally, there are often sound political reasons for sharing some information about your case with your supporters or the public, even if there are potential legal consequences of doing so. Your defense committee should be able to help you sort through the questions of what, when, how much, and what sort of information to talk about publicly. Only the state benefits from your case being shrouded in secrecy!

Direct Support

Defense committees frequently help defendants with their life needs, such as housing, travel, childcare, and weathering the emotional ups and downs of legal proceedings. If you are in custody pretrial, your defense committee can write letters, send in books, put money on your commissary, and visit. All of these efforts go a long way towards keeping you strong—both physically and mentally—and more able to fight your charges.

Your defense committee can also function as a sounding board as you define and refine your political strategies and weigh your legal options. While you should generally not discuss the details of your case with them unless you have specific agreement from your lawyer, you will benefit from talking about the political and personal implications of your case and decisions. For example, you might not want to talk about the cell phone records the prosecutor will likely introduce at trial, but you might want to talk about the importance of understanding how technology can be used against radicals in court. Your defense committee might also have access to information that you do not, particularly if you are in custody. These discussions can inform the decisions you are making about your personal, political, and legal goals. Additionally, since your defense committee should talk to you honestly about your case and options, they might sometimes challenge your thinking or positions.

Sometimes, defense committees end up providing invaluable support to a defendant's family (chosen or biological) or loved ones. The legal system is incredibly confusing, daunting, and scary to people who know nothing about it. Your defense committee may help your family or loved ones through this difficult time by helping them make sense of what is happening to you, navigate the court system, find and work with a lawyer, prepare for jail visits, and so on. Your family may also want to actively support you as you fight your charges. If your family is supportive, suggest that they join (or at least work closely with) your defense committee. This approach can give them a structure to plug into while helping them understand the politics of the case, if that is something they need. Having one member of your defense committee act as the liaison between your family and your lawyer can make things easier for your lawyer and reduce the chances that they will be bombarded by multiple emails and phone calls whenever there is a new development in your case.

Political Support

Defense committees can conduct political campaigns that neither you nor your attorney can undertake. Your attorney may have to face your prosecutor and judge over many other cases during a year, while a defense committee usually does not. That leaves a defense committee freer to, for example, work against the prosecutor's re-election, or to discredit the prosecution's handling of similar cases, or to take actions that will enhance your image in the general public or within your movement. The defense committee also has the advantage of being able to use humor in campaign, including ridiculing the entire system if they want.

For example, the RNC 8 Defense Committee once staged a small circus outside the court building after the prosecutors accused the defendants of trying to turn their trial into a circus. Clowns representing the sheriff and the county attorney played with some of the most dubious pieces of evidence against the defendants: a household deadbolt lock that the county attorney maintained was intended for a lockbox and a bicycle inner tube that was supposed to be a slingshot. This fun and creative protest was part of a broader pressure campaign against the county prosecutor. You and your lawyer are not likely to see positive legal results from using humor in public or in the courtroom, as the government will take everything you say and do both literally and in the worst light possible. Your defense committee, however, often has more freedom in this respect.

Whenever you go to court, even for a simple hearing on a motion, ask your defense committee to pack the courtroom full of your supporters. The number of people in the courtroom sends a clear message to the judge and the prosecution that you are not going to be easily bullied, the community cares about you and your case, and the court process is being watched. Seeing the room full of friendly faces can also be invaluable emotional support for you, as the court system is designed to make you feel isolated, overwhelmed, and outnumbered. That can be especially important if you are in custody.

Your defense committee can also keep political allies updated on your case. Having a website, announcement listserv, and social media presence are generally the most effective ways to get the word about your case out to the greatest number of people as quickly as possible. If there are popular websites, publications, pod casts, and radio shows among your potential support base, ask your defense committee to connect with them and spread the word.

The Dangers of Social Media

Using any form of social media carries potential liabilities and dangers. Social media posts are regularly used against defendants to justify indictments, pre-trial incarceration, high bonds (or denying bond entirely), and

> stiff sentences. Thus, the use of platforms such as Facebook should be undertaken as responsibly as possible and with extreme caution, if at all. On the one hand, we believe that there is no truly responsible and safe way to use social media platforms. For example, the prosecutor will likely try to introduce postings on your defense committee website, Facebook page, Twitter account, and so on into the pre-trial proceedings or the trial itself to smear you. On the other hand, it is almost impossible to build a political defense without using some media that you do not like much and without saying things that a judge or prosecutor can use against you. So an important thing to remember when making your tactical and strategic decisions about using social media is that your enemies follow the news, check the internet (including your website), and monitor social media as a matter of course. (See Chapter 7, "Working with the Media," for much more on this topic.)

- - - - - - - - - - - - - - - - - - -

As is likely clear by now, your defense committee may also use a media strategy. This can be tricky or dangerous for your legal case, as well as necessary for movement strategy and broader public support. You will likely find it most beneficial for your defense committee to check with your attorney before releasing statements to the press or granting interviews, even to friendly media outlets. As this setup is not always possible or ideal, your defense committee should feel empowered to speak for itself while remembering its responsibility not to damage your legal case, put your freedom in jeopardy needlessly, or go against the goals you have set for your case. (See Chapter 7, "Working with the Media," for more on navigating the dangers and opportunities of setting a media strategy.)

The Committee to Defend the Panther 21

On April 1, 1969, the New York City cops arrested a group of Black Panthers and charged them with "conspiring to murder New York City policemen and to dynamite five mid-town department stores, a police precinct, six railroad rights-of-way and the New York Botanical Gardens....No actual act at all was charged."[73] Twenty-one people were charged and most were held on $100,000 bail for months or for the entire two-year pre-trial process. Dhoruba Bin Wahad, one of the defendants, wrote, "On May 13, 1971, the Panther 21...were acquitted of all charges in the less than one hour of jury deliberations, following what was at that time the longest trial in New York City history."[74] This case was a clear example of the state using criminal charges to destroy the organizing capacity of a revolutionary group in a particular location as part of a broader attack against the Black liberation movement nationally.

The Committee to Defend the Panther 21 formed to raise money for bail and legal fees, put out propaganda about the case and the Black Panther Party, and publish trial bulletins.[75] In a fundraising letter, the committee described its purpose and fundraising goals:

> The Committee to Defend the Panther 21 has been formed to raise funds for the defense effort, to focus local and national attention on the case, and to inform people about the full scope of what is happening to the Black Panther Party....The total defense costs are now projected at well over $100,000, even though the lawyers are volunteering their services.[76]

Many parallels exist between the organizing of this defense committee during a tumultuous era in the Black liberation movement and more recent support efforts for prisoners from other movements (e.g., earth liberation, animal liberation). There are also significant differences, such as the defense committee publishing an open letter from many of the defendants to the judge during the trial. In this letter, the defendants wrote:

> You have implied contempt charges. We cannot conceive of how this could be possible. How can we be in contempt of a

court that is in contempt of its own laws? How can you be responsible for 'maintaining respect and dispensing justice,' when you have dispensed with justice, and you do not maintain respect for your own Constitution? How can you expect us to respect your laws, when you do not respect them yourself? Then you have the audacity to demand respect, when you, your whole Great System of Justice is out of order and does not respect us, or our rights.[77]

We do not know of many similar statements that defendants have made directly to judges while the trial was in progress—particularly when the legal outcome of the trial was acquittal for all defendants! The lesson to draw from this historical example is not that writing open letters to the judge will guarantee victory in court, but that various tactics can be used by defense committees and defendants that may at first glance seem ill-advised or too dangerous. The political context and defendants' goals will be key in determining which tactics to use.[78]

- -

Some Considerations for Working with Your Defense Committee

Working with a defense committee gives you particular responsibilities that you may not have had before. In broad terms, many of these responsibilities can be thought of as ensuring a group of people come together to help you with a specific project despite differences in politics, interests, goals, personalities, and experience levels. You, as the defendant, are not solely responsible for ensuring the defense committee's success, but you do have a role to play since you are the one most affected by the committee's actions and inactions. Likewise, the committee members all have the responsibility of ensuring they work with you well and deliver on what they promise. Having clear and direct communication with your defense committee members and the group as a whole will undoubtedly help you work successfully with your committee.

Radical defendants have said that working with a defense committee can be a frustrating experience as well as their most valuable lifeline while facing charges. If you have the luxury of choosing who will be on your defense committee, look for people who are closely aligned with you politically. While not everyone has to share your politics on everything, you will likely find your support will run smoother if there are not significantly different approaches to the tasks at hand. For example, if you were injured while you were arrested, you may have no interest in trying to address the situation using the legal system, while some of your supporters may want to launch a campaign to get the cops charged with assault or file complaints against them with Internal Affairs. Arguments such as this can distract the committee from doing what you need them to do.

You may find that having people on your committee who have experience with the criminal legal system, either from having been on defense committees in the past or having faced serious charges of their own, is especially valuable. These supporters can be particularly well equipped to provide you with "critical support," i.e., understanding the complexity of your decisions about your case and challenging you to live up to your principles as a radical. Similarly, talking with them can help you feel some sense of agency over your life and help you make informed decisions.

Being in custody obviously makes it harder to handpick your defense committee members. Jail is designed to make you feel disempowered about everything, and your defense committee may be the only people you can always expect to listen to you. Ask them to seek individuals with the skills to ensure you receive the support you want and need, if the committee does not already have them. You should always voice your needs to your defense committee, whether you are in custody or not.

At times, you may need to ask people to step back from your support organizing if they are not aligned with the direction you want to go, or if they are a drain on the committee. If you participate actively in the committee, people may turn to you to resolve disputes within it or to take sides in a debate. You may find it necessary to draw boundaries for how much of the internal dynamics you will engage in. Your highest priority must be your trial preparations, and you do not need another drain on your emotional resources. The degree of your involvement in your committee can be a delicate balance to strike since you may also need to take an active role in ensuring the success of your defense committee at times.

All this being said, an important thing to remember when working with your defense committee is that accountability flows both ways. You are accountable to your defense committee (and more broadly, to the movement that is supporting you). Be clear with them about your goals for your case, and be honest about your situation (even though there will be many aspects of your case that you cannot discuss with anyone but your lawyer). In order to offer you the best and strongest support, they will need you to communicate with them about developments or changes in your situation—including if you are considering taking a plea, or if you are having seemingly unresolvable issues with your codefendants. You must earn the solidarity that is being extended to you, as well as show respect and appreciation for your supporters. They are investing themselves in both you and your case, so they have a legitimate stake in the outcome as well, even though it is drastically different than your stake. Remember to thank them often and well for helping you in your time of need.

Defense committee members are accountable to you, too. They must take seriously their responsibilities not to damage your legal situation or work against the goals you have set for your case. Just like you, they must be honest in their communications about your case and approach your support work with integrity. They need to be transparent with you about how the funds they have raised for your support are being used. They should also work as effectively as possible with your legal team to ensure coordination between your legal and political defense as much as is possible and makes sense. Since all of you may be in this for the long haul, your defense committee has to discuss with you the boundaries on the support they can offer you, honor your wishes as best they can, and tell you directly when they cannot honor them. If you are in custody, talk with them about how often they can visit, how much money per week/month they can put into your commissary account, and how much they can do in other areas of your life, such as helping with childcare and covering your rent.

Potential Liabilities of Having a Defense Committee

While we clearly believe that radical defendants benefit from defense committees, we would be remiss not to talk about the potential downsides. The state is aware of the power of defense committees, especially for incarcerated defendants. Since the criminal legal system intentionally alienates people from their communities, and since defense committees intentionally get in the way of that, the government increasingly demonizes these committees. You, your defense committee members, and your lawyer should be prepared for attacks against the defense committee both in the media and in the courtroom—mostly directed at you as the defendant. In Marius Mason's case, for example, the prosecution argued that his defense committee constituted a network to help him go underground if he was not remanded into custody prior to sentencing.

In the case of Scott DeMuth[79], a few members of the RNC 8 (who had been charged with terrorism and conspiracy in an unrelated case), attended Scott's court hearing. The prosecutor commented on their presence as a part of his strategy of labeling the defendant a domestic terrorist because of his alleged politics (i.e., anarchism), which he did repeatedly in court and in his written motions.[80] The prosecutor's statement singling out the RNC 8 defendants was clearly meant to make the defendant and his supporters nervous or afraid because they were known to the state and being watched.

Having a defense committee, particularly one that is open to people with only loose affiliations with each other or with you, can create opportunities for informants to become involved. The case of Leonard Peltier offers a clear and disturbing example. As Leonard wrote in 2007, at least one informant became involved in AIM and had access to discussions and information that should have been protected by attorney-client privilege. Leonard explained that:

> In the Wounded Knee Trials, Douglas Durham [the informant] was similarly advised by the FBI not to engage in any activity that would violate confidences of the defense, nor to engage in any activities or relate to the FBI any information that had to do with defense tactics, or any legal aspect of the operations of AIM or the defense at that point. In spite of the advice he allegedly received from the FBI, Mr. Durham testified in the United States Senate about the 1974 trial of AIM leader Dennis Banks: "If Dennis and I were sitting in a room and an attorney would walk in and start talking, I couldn't jump up and say, 'I can't be here, the FBI won't allow it.'"[81]

While an informant being present at attorney-client meetings might be an unusual situation, the risk of this happening is inherent to having a defense committee. Similarly, particularly in loosely organized defense committees, there is the risk of members or the committee as a whole making statements (e.g., in the media, over social media) or taking actions that could damage your situation.

These risks may motivate some attorneys to advise their clients not to associate with other radicals, and not to accept support from defense committees. While we think the benefits of having a strong political defense overwhelmingly outweigh the possible dangers (again, the government counterattacks only because that political defense is so clearly effective), these risks can be real and can have serious consequences for you. Accepting support—and being prepared for the government's underhanded tactics—is most likely the strongest position a defendant can take.

Chapter 7
WORKING WITH THE MEDIA

MEDIA WILL INEVITABLY PLAY A PART IN CASES AGAINST RADI-
cals and revolutionaries. Yet this does not mean that engaging
with the media needs to be inevitable. The use of media in
your defense is a strategic decision that should be focused
on helping you meet your personal, political, and legal goals
while advancing your struggle (or at least not doing damage).
Sometimes, this means actively engaging in a sophisticated
and robust media strategy. Other times, it means avoiding
media coverage as much as possible. The approach that you,
your supporters, and your lawyer take to media will necessarily change at different stages of your case. In this chapter, we
explore the role of media and social media in handling serious cases from a movement perspective. We also offer some
advice on ways of using (or not using) various forms of media
effectively. (Throughout this chapter, we generally say "you"

even though it is not always advisable for defendants to be actively involved in the media for their cases since anything they say will be used against them in court.)

Some Basic Truths about the Media

The capitalist media (aka the mainstream media, or MSM) is not your friend. Reporters from capitalist media outlets will likely view you and your comrades as enemies of the public, the state, and the status quo. You should expect them to vilify you and your comrades as a matter of course, even when they are not being intentionally and blatantly malicious in their coverage. Likewise, you can expect them to be more interested in staying on good terms with the cops and prosecutors who will feed them breaking stories and leak them documents than in helping you speak your truth.

The Duplicity of the Mainstream Media

While the NATO 3 were incarcerated pending trial, there was coverage of a solidarity rally on a local TV news affiliate that, on the surface, appeared to be favorable. In a voice-over, the reporter explained the supporters' analysis of the political motivations of the charges while footage of hooded and masked protesters standing outside of the criminal courthouse was aired. The segment also aired snippets of speeches that supporters gave at the rally. Then the reporter moved on to explain that three of the Cleveland 4 were to be sentenced the next day. The story implied that, in both cases, the defendants were guilty of terrorism—while in fact the NATO 3's trial had not yet begun. The segment as a whole was not the most terrible news coverage in the NATO 3 case; however, making this connection between those cases was not beneficial to any of the defendants or to protesters in general.

▬ ▬ ▬ ▬ ▬ ▬ ▬ ▬

Independent media is not necessarily your friend either. Having leftist media can be an indispensable part of building support and solidarity for defendants while bringing attention to their movements. Yet a journalist's sympathy does not always mean that they will help you advance your cause. The reality of journalism is that journalists need to break news, produce original content that cannot be found elsewhere, make names for themselves, or become prominent in the public eye. Thus, all journalists have interests that, at the best, co-exist with your interests and, at the worst, conflict with your interests. Yet independent journalists are often our best shot at getting our issues and analyses out to the public, so it is often worthwhile to invest time and energy in cultivating strong relationships with them. Even so, be wary of mistaking them for comrades in the struggle too easily, as the role they have chosen requires them to remain at least somewhat removed from those struggles in order to "objectively" report on them.

▬ ▬ ▬ ▬ ▬ ▬ ▬ ▬ ▬ ▬ ▬ ▬ ▬ ▬ ▬ ▬ ▬ ▬ ▬

When "Political" Journalists Do the State's Work

Independent journalists writing for Truth-Out.org prior to the NATO 3 trial wrote a damaging article about the defendants. Their so-called investigative journalism included obtaining footage from a gas station camera showing one of the defendants purchasing gasoline that was used to create four Molotov cocktails. One of the undercover cops who entrapped the activists accompanied the defendant, and was also caught on the tape. Rather than writing an article critical of police entrapment, the journalists presented narratives from the prosecution's legal filings as if they were verified facts in the case, referencing documents they had received from the court file without posting them publicly for their readers to evaluate for themselves (although they later posted some after pushback from the defendants' defense committee). They also posted pictures of a couple of the defendants from their Facebook profiles and speculated that they were drifters and ne'er-do-wells before they were arrested.

This article did much more to promote the state's narrative of the case than it did to help the defendants. Indeed, the journalists went beyond even what the prosecutors had claimed about the defendants in their original press conferences, which celebrated the arrests and the valor of the cops in catching terrorists prior to the NATO summit.[82]

-- -- -- -- -- -- -- -- -- --

In contrast, movement media is media that activists create for themselves. As such, they have full control over what is given public airtime. This media can be something that defendants, defense committees, or supporters make on their own. It can also be trusted media makers who do their own programs, run their own websites, or otherwise produce their own journalism (e.g., Submedia.tv, The Final Straw radio show, Crimethinc's podcast, Unicorn Riot, and It's Going Down, to name just a few). Producing content in this way can provide defendants and defense committees with the opportunity to present the narrative of the case that they want to advance without having to deal with all the liabilities of engaging with capitalist or independent media. This approach can be an invaluable part of raising support and solidarity for defendants. One drawback can often be that this media only reaches people who are inclined to be sympathetic and supportive anyway, without having the potential to contribute substantively to political pressure campaigns against prosecutors or elected officials who hold sway over the cases or to affect the views of the "general public." Another drawback can be that these media outlets might have goals and agendas that come into conflict with the defendant's, such as describing the defendant as a die-hard animal liberation warrior when they plan on using an entrapment defense to plead not guilty.

These considerations indicate that it is best to conceive of the media as a tactic to use when doing so is strategically beneficial to defendants and their movements. Particularly when working with the capitalist and independent media, the benefits of engaging with the media should be carefully weighed against the liabilities of doing so. Likewise, the benefits of *not* engaging with the media should be carefully weighed against the liabilities of *not* doing so. For example, jumping into a full-fledged media campaign for the sake of winning the "hearts and minds" of the public when that win does not affect the outcome of the case does not have any more strategic value than does passing up an opportunity to wage a successful pressure campaign to drop the charges because of a steadfast refusal to engage with the media under any circumstances.

Decisions about whether, when, and how to engage with capitalist, independent, or movement media are best made with the ultimate goals for the case in mind (see Chapter 2, "Setting and Balancing Personal, Political, and Legal Goals"). If you decide to engage with the capitalist or independent media, though, you should be prepared to play their game and to play it well. You will likely not have much (if any) success in trying to reform the media, educate or enlighten reporters, convey sophisticated and nuanced political analyses instead of mere soundbites, and so forth. But you can have success in using the media to further your cause and weaken your enemies' positions.

Engaging the Media as
Radicals and Revolutionaries

Before we move into advice on engaging with the media, we want to talk about what it means for us as radicals and revolutionaries to do so. One of the most important things to do when engaging with the media is to be scrupulously honest in your presentation of your case and the issues involved in it. This is *not* the same as talking about the facts of your case! There are many ways to talk about a criminal case with honesty and integrity that do not compromise your legal situation—that is, that do not amount to a confession or to snitching on others. Even if you decide that you do not care about the legal repercussions of talking about the actions you took, you still have the responsibility to talk about your case honestly and in a way that will not implicate others. For example, when the government targeted you because of your political activities or associations, saying that your academic research, your identity, or some other factor got you in trouble misconstrues the reality of the case against you. It also sets you up to lose support later, on if your supporters feel tricked. Deception, spin, and rhetoric all have their roles in radical struggles, but have no place in the way you present your case to your supporters and the movement as a whole.

Playing the media's game well does not mean believing that their rules are fair, and that they will even observe their own rules. We can be ready to be subversive of the capitalist and independent media, and their rules. Even the most sympathetic journalists are not really on our team, though we may be able to make them work for us just as much as they make us work for them. When capitalist and independent journalists are hostile, our responses to them can be irreverent and caustic—as long as that helps us to achieve our overall goals for the case.

Asserting and defending our principles maintains our dignity and supports the validity of our struggles. In doing so, we undercut the efforts of our enemies to demonize us, paint us as terrorists, and convince people to discount or hate us. For example, if our enemies are calling us unreasonable because we engage in militant tactics to stop the exploitation of animals, the destruction of the Earth, racism, transphobia, or anything else, we can easily fall into the trap of proving their point for them by engaging in the debate on their terms, according to their values. If instead, we counter their perspectives with our unwavering dedication to a world free of exploitation, domination, and oppression, we can show the sense in our perspectives and the unethical, (self-)destructive nature of theirs. We will always wield more power by setting the terms of the debate ourselves, rather than allowing our enemies to do it. We will not necessarily win any particular battle, of course, but we will be fighting in ways that have the potential to advance our struggles.

Strategic Media

Whenever you decide to engage with the media, the next question you should be asking yourself is, "How can engaging with the media be strategic?" Any engagement, whether a one-off interview or a concerted campaign, should be designed to help achieve your personal, political, and legal goals. Not all of these goals can or should be met through media, of course—favorable media coverage is not a goal, but a tactic. There are several ways media can be used strategically in political cases that are worth examining here: combating the state's narrative of the case while creating your own, political pressure campaigns, building support and solidarity, and fundraising.

Combating the State's Narrative

We are engaged in a battle for the story—the way in which the public understands the issues that led to your prosecution, the state's actions that brought the charges against you, and the implications for the future depending on how your case is resolved. You will likely have quite the fight when waging this battle. The state presents their charges according to the narrative that benefits them, and has full cooperation from the mainstream media in doing so. Thus, cases are generally talked about in terms of defendants being "guilty" or "not guilty." That is, the state often sets (and narrows) the terms of the discourse surrounding the case. In some cases, that may be important. For example, the defense campaign for Mumia Abu-Jamal worked hard for decades to prove that he was unjustly convicted of murdering a police officer and ultimately resulted in his sentence being commuted from death to life in prison.[83] While this is a limited win at best, as a life sentence is basically a slow-death sentence and the prison has repeatedly tried to kill him through medical neglect, he is now in a less precarious legal position from which to continue contributing to social justice movements.

When radicals work to set the terms of the discourse, they often find that they are not simply trying to win the debate set by the state. For example, when the government charges people with terrorism, they generally assert that the defendants are terrorists and the public is fortunate that the police saved the day. Any debate on this issue is restricted to the terms set by the criminal legal system, in which the question of "guilty or not guilty?" is supposed to be put to a jury. When the targets of these cases are activists, a typical response is for the activists and their supporters to claim that activism is not terrorism and therefore the government is wrong. This line of reasoning can easily be morally superior to the state repression at hand and thus gain support from a range of people, and even help radicals stay out of prison. Even so, the government excels at writing laws that define various types of activism as terrorism (see, for example, the Animal Enterprise Terrorism Act). Thus, sticking to the terms of the debate set by the state can validate the state's narrative by the mere act of engaging with it.

In contrast, there can be a lot of power in combating the state's narrative of the case entirely. For example, there are significant differences between debating the guilt or innocence of the defendants, decrying the inappropriate application of the laws the defendants are being charged under, and challenging the legitimacy of the authority the state is claiming in the first place. The first allows the state to fully control the narrative, the second challenges the functioning of the state without addressing the root of the situation, and the third calls into question the existence of the state itself. Indigenous activists and Puerto Rican *independentistas* have attempted to do this many times, and some major shifts have resulted, particularly in the area of treaty rights. Any approach you take will necessarily depend both on your own politics and on your personal, political, and legal goals.

Working to set the terms of the debate according to the issues you care about and want to be primary in the case can create an effective attack on the state's narrative. Some questions to consider are: "How can my movement benefit from a successful campaign to focus the narrative of my case on the validity of my struggle rather than on guilt or innocence? How can the workings of state repression and/or systemic oppression be further revealed by shifting the focus of the narrative to these realities? How can focusing the narrative of my case on promoting my revolutionary principles inspire more resistance in the future?"

Engaging with the media can be one way of successfully waging the battle of the story. When working with the capitalist media, of course, you should never assume that they will be receptive to your narrative or will want to adopt it over the state's narrative. You will therefore need to find ways to push your narrative through your interviews, press releases, press conferences, and so forth (we explore some of these ways in the next section). The same can be true of working with independent media, although in the best-case scenarios these journalists will be receptive to your narrative and the politics informing it, even if they do not share those politics. As mentioned previously, when creating your own media or working with movement media, you will have much more control over the way your narrative is presented. None of these efforts will guarantee that you will win the battle of the story, but they all can be routes to take when doing so is strategically beneficial.

Finding Strategic Leverage with the Media

A concerted media campaign was used in CeCe McDonald's case to shift the focus from the state's narrative of the case. The county prosecutor said that they needed to uphold law and order by both charging CeCe with murder after the death of the white supremacist who attacked her and her friends, as well as by charging one of the white people who had attacked her with assault. CeCe's defense committee worked to shift the narrative to the realities of racism and transphobia, particularly the trend of trans women of color being attacked and murdered because of their gender identities. As part of a broader pressure campaign against the county prosecutor, the defense committee took a variety of approaches to push their narrative in the media and force him to engage with them on those terms. This media campaign gained some success when a mainstream media program produced a show about trans people and used her as an example. This break into the mainstream media just a month before trial helped bolster the pressure campaign against the county prosecutor and undoubtedly played a role in her receiving a more favorable plea agreement. Most mainstream media coverage of the plea agreement and sentencing favored the state's narrative of the case despite this victory, but the defense committee was highly successful in bringing international attention both to CeCe's case and to attacks on trans women of color in general. More importantly, their efforts helped her get released after about three years in custody rather than the two decades she had been facing.

In contrast, there was not a concerted effort to wage a battle for the story in the AETA 4 case. The strategy taken in this case was mostly a legal one, culminating in the indictments being thrown out for being unconstitutionally vague. While the strategy taken was ultimately successful, at least one of the defendants was frustrated by the way the narrative of the case became about allegations of terrorism versus the right to free speech rather than focusing on vivisection and the animal rights issues that the activists were fighting for in their campaigns.

Political Pressure Campaigns

Media can be an effective part of political pressure campaigns against elected or other state officials who have the power to drop the charges (e.g., head prosecutors, district attorneys) or influence the course of the case (e.g., governors, the president). Pressure campaigns generally include other tactics as well, such as demonstrations outside of the offices of these officials or at events or fundraisers in their honor, call-in campaigns to their offices, petitions gathering hundreds or thousands of signatures in support of dropping the charges, and so on. A media strategy can bring attention to these efforts in ways that make it politically desirable for the targeted officials to capitulate to the supporters' demands (or at least make concessions).

For these campaigns to be successful, they generally need clear goals (e.g., to get the charges dropped), clear demands (e.g., "Drop the charges!"), and effective ways to get leverage over those with decision-making power. This leverage could be changing the political climate so the officials could suffer negative consequences of continuing the prosecution, shaming the officials, tarnishing their reputations in the minds of the general public, and exposing illegalities or unethical behavior on the part of those officials or others involved in the case (such as the cops). Getting attention in the media outlets that these officials care about can be a crucial part of applying pressure on them.

These campaigns also need to be sustained to be effective. Political leverage is cumulative and generally has a tipping point that needs to be reached for those in power to make concessions. Dabbling in pressure campaign activities such as demonstrations or call-ins without having a sustained strategy can simply annoy or anger those with power over the defendants (which can sometimes have extremely negative consequences for our comrades in jail or prison). Media can help with maintaining this pressure by causing the officials embarrassment or by simply making it difficult for them to go about business as usual because they have to deal with the political implications of the media coverage of your pressure campaign activities.

The Potential Power of Pressure Campaigns

The RNC 8 were eight anarchists who organized against the Republican National

Convention in St. Paul, Minnesota in 2008. They were initially charged with felony conspiracy with terrorism enhancements under the Minnesota state version of the USA Patriot Act. Due to a successful pressure campaign against the county prosecutor, who was in the local Democratic party, the charges with the terrorism enhancements were dropped, thereby leaving the defendants with two remaining felony charges each. This pressure campaign included demonstrations outside of the county prosecutor's fundraising events for her bid for governor, rallies outside of the court building at each hearing, and a media campaign to decry the state's targeting of the defendants for their politics. The media campaign targeted mainstream media, independent media, and movement media to shift the narrative of the case away from the allegations of terrorism to the issues of state repression.

Building Support and Solidarity

The media can also be engaged effectively to build support and solidarity for defendants. Independent and movement media are often the best for achieving these goals, of course, as they are well positioned to connect you with potential supporters. When engaging media for these purposes, it can often be helpful to think of the mindsets of the people you could possibly connect with through each journalist or venue. Some people will be active supporters who are rearing to jump into organizing fundraisers and solidarity actions, some will be passive supporters who are sympathetic but not inclined to take the initiative to support you, and some will be undecided or indifferent but could be moved to become passive or active supporters. Understanding your audience and tailoring your messages to them can help you build support and solidarity.

At times, the mainstream media can be engaged successfully to build support and solidarity. Getting a respected community leader or public official to speak on your behalf to a mainstream outlet is influential, for example. While these venues will generally connect you to people who are passively or actively hostile to you and your cause in addition to potential supporters, you may be surprised by the potential supporters who follow these venues. Even getting outraged comments from these people on news websites can contribute to winning the battle of the story or applying pressure on elected officials. All the aforementioned cautions about engaging with the capitalist press apply in these situations, of course.

Fundraising

All the different types of media can be engaged for fundraising purposes, too. As with building support and solidarity, independent media and movement media are usually best for this purpose. Movement media venues are often the best for directly requesting funds and fundraisers from supporters. Not all independent media will want to include direct appeals for funds on their websites or in their publications, but some will. And almost invariably they will link to your support website.

The capitalist media will rarely (if ever) include fund-raising appeals in their coverage of your case, but there are ways to bring attention to your fundraising efforts none-theless. Even something as simple as having signs with your support website address at rallies that potential supporters can see in photos and videos can direct them to your web-site when they otherwise would never have known about it. You can also reach out to mainstream news venues for coverage of certain fundraisers or other events. For exam-ple, if there is an art auction fundraiser for your legal ex-penses, the local news weekly might be willing to put it on their calendar or send a reporter out to cover it from the angle of the eclectic art mix, with the politics of the case being an interesting side note. There are drawbacks to having your case approached from anything aside from the politics of the case, but there are also limitations to repeatedly asking your closer circles of friends to donate to your mounting legal expense bills.

Media Strategy

There are many in-depth resources for conducting media campaigns from a range of groups, so this section will not attempt to re-create that wheel or condense all the possible advice into a few hundred words. Some resources worth checking out include *Media Training Manual* by The Ruckus Society[84], *SPIN Works!* by the SPIN Project[85], *Communicate Justice 101* by Youth Media Council[86], *Re:Imagining Change* by Patrick Reinsborough and Doyle Canning[87], and the handouts produced by Seeds for Change[88]. Defendants and supporters may also be able to find local organizations or media-savvy individuals who would be willing to conduct a training for the defense committee.

Some general advice, however, is to be prepared with your narrative and analysis of the case and to focus all your statements (including answers to questions) on the story you want to tell. Whether you are engaging with the capitalist media or the most sympathetic movement media, it will be important to convey your story as clearly and concisely as possible. This story will serve you best by being both offensive and defensive. That is, it should assert your analysis of the charges, the political context surrounding the charges, and the real issues at stake in the situation while also countering your enemies' assertions, analysis, claims, and attacks on you and your perspectives. Remembering that there is always a battle for the story to be waged will likely help you consider the points you should convey as well as your enemies' points to address and disarm.

After crafting your basic narrative and analysis, it can be helpful to create clear talking points that you can have at the ready for interviews, press releases, and articles you produce. Talking points are most effective when they are written as sound bites—statements you can make in just a few seconds to convey your main messages and assert your narrative and analysis. For example, if you are asked, "So what is this case really about?", your answer will be much more likely to be broadcast if it is short and to the point: "This case is about the government criminalizing social justice movements and saying that activists are terrorists." Going into a complex, nuanced examination of state repression in general and the history of repression against your particular movement will typically not be successful communication with the media—and will almost certainly not be included in their story. While sound bites necessarily strip down what you are able to convey and therefore require you to make concessions about what you want to impress on people in that moment, engaging with the media means you need to speak their language and play their game.

Learning to speak in sound bites without watering down or selling out our politics is quite an art. Work to make your political analyses and revolutionary principles understandable to other people in ways that are easy to grasp intuitively. A good metaphor, an ironic question, or a clever pun can go a long way towards identifying and attacking our enemies' premises, assumptions, and worldviews. Sometimes, these short gems pop out in casual conversations. Watch for language and images that may shape the terms of the debate when put out through media outlets without requiring that the general public have a sophisticated understanding of the political context or history of our radical struggles. Instead, try to force our opponents to try to explain themselves and their unjust, corrupt system.

Speaking in sound bites is a good rule to follow whenever engaging with the media, and particularly in hostile interviews. Having these statements memorized can help you keep your cool in a heated, high-stress situation and maintain your focus on getting what you want out of the interview. You can always default to your talking points when you are not sure what else to say. Defaulting to your talking points can feel awkward at times, especially when they interrupt the flow of the conversation. The important thing to remember, though, is that an interview is not a conversation—it is an exchange of thoughts and ideas between people who all want to achieve different goals. The interviewer and anyone else speaking to you in a media engagement (e.g., a debate with an opponent) may want to get a juicy story, tear you apart, make you appear foolish, or simply talk about issues that you do not find relevant or important. Whatever their goals and interests, these may have nothing to do with your own. Your goals for that engagement will likely be to convey your messages in a way that helps you achieve your personal, political, and legal goals for your case. Defaulting to your talking points has a greater chance of helping you achieve these goals than does improvising your responses or going down the rabbit holes that the other people in the interview can create (maliciously or otherwise).

Since interviews are exchanges of communications for particular purposes rather than conversations, you never need to answer the questions posed to you. You should always answer the questions you want to answer, even if you are not asked them (maybe especially if you are not asked them). If you do not like a question, you can deflect by saying something such as, "The real issue here is..." or "A better question to ask is..." or "What's more important than that is..." and then launching into a talking point. Likewise, if a question or statement from someone else in the interview challenges one of your positions, you can choose to address it on their terms, address it on your terms, or ignore it. Responding with one of your talking points can be an effective approach when you are being challenged. Doing so may make for an awkward conversation but for a strong interview. (Remember that interviews are often prerecorded. They will not be played in their entirety, but will be cut into little pieces with the best sound bites spliced in with the interviewer's commentary.)

Another good piece of general advice is to make the media's job as easy as possible. The more you speak their language and present them with sound bites they can plop into their pieces, the more likely you will be able to convey your messages through them (and the more likely they might be to seek interviews with you in the future). In addition to speaking in sound bites, this can entail writing your press releases as if they are articles (including succinct quotes that can make their way directly into articles). For example, one activist press release after the 2008 Republican National Convention in St. Paul, Minnesota was picked up by the Associated Press (AP) newswire and sent out to newspapers across the country word-for-word as an AP article. Some editor at AP likely figured that it was good enough to use, so it was sent out without any additional research or writing at all.

Making the media's job easier can also entail presenting them with the spectacles they need to engage their audiences and working on their schedules. If you are engaging TV news, for example, having a vibrant, colorful protest will be much more newsworthy in their eyes than a group of somber people marching wearily while mumbling uninspiring chants. Photographers for print media will likewise value interesting spectacles over drab ones. Further, you will benefit from working on journalists' schedules, which often means sending press releases at five or six in the morning (right when they are getting to their desks), scheduling press releases for late morning or lunchtime so they have time to work your statements into their pieces due in the early afternoon for the five o'clock news, and having statements prepared or talking points at the ready for spontaneous interviews at the courthouse, at protests, or at other newsworthy occasions.

You will also likely benefit from cultivating relationships with friendly journalists (while remembering, of course, that they have their own interests, not yours, at heart). Calling them after sending out press releases or announcing press conferences will both bring those to their attention as well as show them that you value their attention to the matter. You might be able to do an impromptu interview with them on those calls, which would make both of your jobs easier since you want to get your messages across and they want to produce content on deadline. Once they get to know you, they will also have someone they can call for quick quotes and sound bites as they are putting their pieces together. These relationships can also be useful if you need to set up in-depth coverage of breaking news when there is an important development in your case.

Often it makes sense to designate one or two media contacts within your support group (or legal team) who can field questions, respond to requests, and interact with the media at public events, court hearings, and so forth. This approach will help ensure that your message and narrative are cohesive and on point with every media interaction. While it might be difficult for others who care about you and your case to "keep quiet" with the media, it can be extremely important for them to do so in your pursuit of your goals.

Finally, tracking and analyzing media coverage can help you ensure your approach remains strategic. You can monitor news coverage to see what the media got right, where they are confused, what gets traction with different outlets, what the state is using for talking points. Such an analysis can help you learn from your mistakes and anticipate changes in the state's media strategy. Conducting these analyses shows how media engagement is a dynamic process that often includes mistakes, missteps, and fruitless attempts. Thus, ensure you are forgiving of yourself and other spokespeople when you are not successful.

Social Media

Websites such as Facebook, Twitter, Instagram, and many more have become integral parts of people's lives and consciousness, so much so that many people cannot imagine what it would be like to not have them. Some of these people work for the FBI and National Security Agency (NSA), which is one reason that social media is so dangerous. (PRISM, a top-secret data-mining project run by the NSA, was exposed in 2013 through Edward Snowden's leaks. This disclosure proved that the government taps directly into the servers of many social media websites to collect data without users' knowledge and, perhaps, without the knowledge of the companies either.[89]) We cannot in good conscience recommend that anyone use social media, either personally or for political organizing. Yet we realize that people do use social media and will continue to do so despite the increasing use of it against us and our comrades in the criminal courts. We want to address social media as a dangerous tool that has just as many liabilities as it has benefits, if not more liabilities.

An undeniable truth is that Facebook, for example, has become one of the easiest ways to get the word out to tons of people about breaking news, events, actions, fundraisers, and so on. Yet getting the word out over social media does not always result in increased attendance at events, more money being donated to defense funds, or more solidarity for people when it is needed most. Too many activists are too willing to sit at home or on their phones looking at an endless stream of social media rather than taking concrete action. And too many organizers are too willing to create social media announcements and call that an end to their organizing for the day (which inevitably leaves out folks who have made a conscious, responsible decision to *not* use social media as well as those who do not have access to this technology). This reliance on social media can have clear pacifying and limiting effects on our organizing and movements, despite their ultimately limited usefulness in bringing people out to events, raising funds, and so on. At a certain point, people in movements will have to decide how much they want to value and prioritize the perceived conveniences of organizing approaches based on social media and how much they want to value and prioritize more security-conscious and relationship-based organizing approaches.

Social media provides our enemies with important data about us, our organizations, our networks, and our movements regardless of how effective or ineffective our uses of social media are at any given time. Many critics of social media have pointed out how much information we willingly hand over to the state to help them map out our relationships—information that the state previously had to dedicate a lot of investigative resources to discovering before being able to use it against us. This information provides the state with guidance on how to conduct their investigations into our movements, targets for their efforts to neutralize and disrupt our organizing, and ammunition to use against us in legal proceedings (including all stages of criminal cases, from bail hearings to sentencing and beyond). On a tactical level, providing our enemies with ammunition against us, our friends, and our communities is counterproductive to our goals, to say the least.

If you decide to use social media in your political defense efforts, ask yourself every time you post whether you would want to see this in the evidence being used against you or your comrades at trial. Your supporters should ask themselves the same question whenever they are creating posts about your case. This consideration obviously cautions against making any incriminating statements either of yourself or others. And this consideration applies whether you are using accounts linked to your legal name, a pseudonym, or an organization's name. You probably already know that you cannot always control the comments section of social media and website posts. What you may not realize is that the state can use these posts against you as well (including any that the cops might post themselves).

Statements made over social media can provide the state with information that can be used against other people in the criminal legal system—even if they are not defendants. For example, social media posts that identify who was at particular events or meetings could provide the FBI and prosecutors with a list of people to subpoena to a grand jury, subpoena as witnesses against you at trial, interview in the lead-up to trial, and otherwise harass to undermine your support. We can never know how the data we provide to the state will be used against us, so the point is to provide them with as little of it as possible. Some risks are clearly necessary to achieve our goals, so the question is once again about whether or not using social media is an acceptable risk.

This caution does not just apply after people are charged. The state routinely pulls data from social media sites into trials to use against defendants, and much of this data was generated before people ever became targets of investigations. Social media sites and email providers such as Gmail routinely provide cops and prosecutors with individuals' account data—including pictures, videos, text messages, private messages, and chat histories. Even when companies are considered "good" about protecting user data, they provide some or all of the data requested of them nearly all the time.[90] When people become involved in radical politics and revolutionary movements, they should always be considering the risks of using social media and always making smart decisions accordingly.

Social Media Accounts Equal Damning Evidence

When Eric McDavid was arrested along with Zachary Jenson and Lauren Weiner in 2006, their support team took down Jenson and Weiner's social media sites almost immediately (Eric did not have one, due to security concerns). Unfortunately, the government had already been monitoring them for months, and dozens of pages from Jenson's MySpace ended up in the discovery against the defendants and was used as evidence against both him and Eric repeatedly, especially during their bail hearings. Even though Eric never had a MySpace page, his codefendants' use of one ended up working against him throughout his case.

One final note of caution about social media: defendants and their supporters should always be careful not to present defendants (or grand jury resisters) in ways that create cults of personality around them. When people need support and solidarity, they will necessarily need to be put in the public eye to a certain extent. Yet there is a difference between portraying a defendant as a radical or revolutionary in need of support and making them look like a hero who should be celebrated, adored, followed, looked up to, and so on. The difference largely lies in the focus being on the politics of the situation rather than the personality or identity categories of the person involved.

Social media lends itself to highlighting the most appealing aspects of a defendant to the public at large. These aspects are often physical attractiveness, age, gender, race, body type, and so on. Of course, such a picture of a defendant reinforces and perpetuates many systemic oppressions that we should be fighting against in all our thoughts and actions. The principled stands taken by targets of state repression are far more important than their physical attractiveness, public-speaking abilities, prowess as writers, and so on. It does not matter if they are cute in black clothing or are people of color or know how to use the jargon of theory to talk about their cases and politics—our solidarity should be based on respect for people fighting for their principles.

Additionally, seeking celebrity status can lead those who have been targeted to tokenize themselves for the sake of gaining attention. They may give in to the temptation to highlight a part of their identity that is oppressed to claim that as the reason they are being targeted, or to speak on behalf of all people who share that identity. Likewise, seeking celebrity status can cause people to gain an inflated sense of their own importance and of the value of their contributions to their movement.

We must be careful not to confuse attention with solidarity, or celebrity with integrity and commitment to revolutionary principles. Revolutionary movements need revolutionaries who are willing to stand strong on what they believe in when faced with consequences for doing so. These movements do not need shooting stars who shine bright and fade quickly. When people are targeted and seek support, they have the responsibility to be honest in their presentation of their cases and to act with integrity when receiving support and solidarity. This responsibility entails both not snitching and not selling out their expressed principles. Another part of this responsibility is distinguishing between gaining solidarity for a principled stance and rising to celebrity status.

Celebrity Culture Does Not Equal Solidarity

In June and July 2012, the FBI raided houses and issued subpoenas in Portland, Olympia, and Seattle as part of the investigation into property damage at a courthouse in Seattle on May Day in 2012. The FBI broke down doors, seized anarchist literature and black clothing from the houses, and subpoenaed several known anarchists. Additional subpoenas were later served.

The grand jury resisters[91] and their supporters quickly issued statements decrying the political witch hunt targeting anarchists in the Pacific Northwest. Most of the resisters and their supporters did a brilliant job of presenting photographs and statements of the resisters that showed them to be principled, dedicated people who were willing to suffer the consequences of their revolutionary commitment and actions. Their strongly worded condemnations of the grand jury were often accompanied by pictures of them dressed nicely with smiles on their faces, usually with furry animals in their arms. These photographs were effective in countering the state's depictions of them as violent criminals. They also provided the media with images aside from mug shots, which helped humanize the resisters in the public eye. Further, they gave the resisters' supporters around the world glimpses into who they were as people and helped inspire solidarity actions ranging from banner drops to attacks against ATMs and other symbols of capitalism.

This media and social media work brought a lot of attention to the resisters and helped their supporters raise much-needed legal funds. Those who appeared before the grand jury refused to testify, some publicly sharing the questions they were asked and their refusals to answer. Others successfully avoided appearing before the grand jury at all. Those who appeared and refused to testify were held in civil contempt of court. Three of them ended up serving several months but one, Leah-Lynne Plante, was only held for about a week before she was released. She subsequently dropped communication with most of her friends and supporters, refusing to explain publicly what had happened that led up to her release while the others were still being held hostage. This refusal was quickly taken by many anarchists as an indication of her cooperation with the grand jury and her defense committee withdrew their support of her.

While the social media presence the resisters gained helped them individually and collectively in many ways, this attention was not by itself sufficient support for their resistance. This fact is seen most clearly in Leah's case. She received a lot of attention, such as a website focused solely on her support. She also issued a video statement saying she was ready to go to prison to uphold her beliefs, which was shared widely on social media. Her unexpected release and refusal to explain what had happened suggest that she was not actually prepared for or equipped to handle the consequences of resistance.

Gaining celebrity status in the lead up to going to prison was clearly not the support she needed to endure the harm inflicted by the state and to remain true to her expressed principles. Yet there are undoubtedly things that could have helped her resist the way she said she wanted to; part of our responsibilities as participants in revolutionary movements is to provide each other with the support, resources, and options we need to resist and withstand state repression, rather than simply making our comrades into celebrities.

- -

Special Considerations for Criminal Charges

If you decide to engage with any form of media around your case, there are different considerations to keep in mind at different stages of the case, from the initial arrest or grand jury subpoena through to the conclusion of any supervised release after incarceration. In general, creating clear talking points for each stage of the case can help you engage with the media strategically, and you may find that these points vary greatly over time. Many of the considerations presented in this section will be moot points if you decide to reject the authority of the courts or take a strategy that involves admitting guilt while demanding trial so you can argue your political points in court. Yet many of them will apply regardless of the approach you take since media engagements can be used for garnering support and for political pressure campaigns. We offer this look into the various stages of criminal cases to help you make the most strategic media decisions all throughout your ordeal.

Pending Trial

Most legal strategies benefit from defendants not admitting guilt.[92] This fact combines with the criminal legal system's precepts that (1) defendants are innocent until proven guilty and (2) that anything defendants say will be used against them in court to mean that anything said publicly that could be construed as admitting guilt will be used against the defendant in court. A truism among both cops and prosecutors is that defendants lose cases the moment they open their mouths. This is true both in the interrogation room and in front of cameras, on computers and smartphones, in visitation booths in the jail, in jail cells, and on phone calls from jail. Thus, it is prudent to avoid saying anything in any form—including "private" messages through social media—that could amount to a confession or an incriminating statement made against other people. This is especially true since the "presumption of innocence" is actually an illusion; most jurors presume that defendants are criminals and are therefore guilty, which can cause them to see all the evidence presented as indicative of guilt, even the most innocuous statements.

Most lawyers will instruct their clients to never make any statements to the media for fear that they will make an incriminating statement or one that could damage prospects for a civil suit after the criminal trial concludes. The lawyers are clearly prioritizing the defendant's legal goals in these instances, often with the assumption that concluding the case with the lightest possible consequences is the goal. Many times, it is also in the defendant's best interests personally and politically not to make statements to the media before trial, but this is not always true. There are certainly times when the political value of defendants making statements outweighs the potential negative consequences in legal terms. Whatever the situation may be, there is also a difference between the defendants making statements, the lawyers making statements, and defense committee members making statements. Any of these on their own or in combination could be a useful approach to take overall, so the important thing is to make smart decisions that are aligned with your personal, political, and legal goals for your case.

This stage of the criminal legal process is typically the most restrictive on defendants in terms of their abilities to speak their minds. Many choose not to speak publicly about their cases, their analyses of the politics involved, or their feelings about what has happened to them and what they are experiencing in the courts until after trial, which can often mean going years without openly addressing some of the most significant events in their lives. Having our speech stifled is clearly a terrible experience that most if not all of us would balk at under any circumstances, but it is important to keep your overall goals and strategies in mind as you make your way through this stage and decide when to speak or not speak.

During Trial

Once the trial has begun, defendants sometimes have more of an ability to speak about their cases, although not necessarily through the media. Within the criminal legal system, these opportunities are tightly controlled and extremely limited. Mostly, this means testifying on your own behalf if that becomes part of your legal strategy (defendants cannot be compelled to testify if they do not want to). Some defendants who are working closely with their lawyers insist on making their own opening and closing statements during trial, but typically defendants only do this if they are representing themselves. Since nearly all trials are open to the public, the media can report what you say in court. Even so, the media coverage of the trial is different than talking directly to the media (capitalist or independent) or making your own media. (If you are in custody, you may not have the opportunity to talk to any media directly anyhow.) If you do have this opportunity, your lawyer is likely to instruct you not to make any statements, since trials are such sensitive and unpredictable events with so much hanging on the line.

Lawyers and defense committee members have much more of an ability to talk to the media during trial. If the trial has received a lot of attention, the media will most likely try to get statements from lawyers and supporters at every opportunity, especially after big developments in court. Anyone speaking to the media would do well to have clear talking points in advance so they can be sure to make greatest use of the chance to achieve the defendants' overall goals for the case. If media spokespeople anticipate that facts or assertions could come up in testimony that would significantly change the narrative of the case during trial, they would do well to develop alternative talking points for various scenarios. It would be hard for them to speak strategically when their heads might be spinning. For example, many times the prosecution puts witnesses on its list who may or may not actually be called to testify. If there are possible witnesses whose testimony could damage the defense's case badly, talking points can be created in advance to deal with these developments. (Spokespeople can be ready to attack the credibility of the witnesses' testimony, and/or point out how this weak testimony shows that the state is grasping for straws to prove its case.)

Between the Verdict and Sentencing

After the trial concludes and the jury issues its verdict, or after a plea agreement is entered, the legal situation fundamentally shifts. Statements made at this point will not be brought into court through testimony or prosecutors' arguments to prove guilt, although they will certainly come to the judge's attention when considering the sentence. There is also a chance that the verdict can be overturned through appeals and the case can be sent back to the original court to be tried again. In these situations, which are somewhat rare, any statements made or evidence discovered after the original trial might be admitted the second time around.

In general, do not underestimate a judge's ability to be petty and vindictive when issuing the sentence. Defendants who refuse to accept responsibility for their alleged crimes after being convicted almost invariably receive harsher sentences than those who stand meekly before the judge and beg for leniency. The same applies to those who decry the injustices or illegitimacy of the criminal legal system. Any statements made to the media or to the judge in court are likely to influence the judge's sentencing decision. Yet even saying everything that the judge wants to hear will not necessarily lead to leniency during sentencing.

The message here is not that you should sacrifice your dignity, forsake your principles, or otherwise throw yourself at the mercy of the court. Rather, consider any statements in court and media engagements—including social media—during this stage carefully, and focus sharply on achieving your overall goals for your case. The same goes for your lawyer and members of your defense committee.

During Incarceration

If you serve time after your trial, you will likely find that you have more freedom to talk about your case in certain ways, but not in all ways. If you are appealing your case, speaking publicly about your ordeal will likely not be in your best legal interests. Also, many politicized prisoners, political prisoners, and prisoners of war have been targeted by prison officials and guards because of their political speech. These prisoners have been beaten, thrown in solitary confinement, moved to super restrictive units within the prison, transferred to prisons far from their families and communities, and otherwise punished. The realities of being in prison often prevent people from speaking out about their cases, further stretching out the length of time that they are prevented from speaking their minds.

However, now the defendants' lawyers and defense committee members usually have greater freedom to speak out about the politics of the case and against the criminal legal system and prison-industrial complex. Media engagements can be part of pressure campaigns to change the conditions the prisoners are experiencing or the conditions within the prison as a whole. Defense committee members can also create a lot of movement media to tell the story of the case and keep up solidarity with more freedom than when the trial was looming. At times, lawyers and prisoners can arrange media interviews in prison that are acceptable risks for any pending appeals or other legal procedures (the same applies to interviews through the mail or prison email systems).

Seeking Parole, Pardon, Compassionate Release, Habeas Corpus Petitions, Etc.

For prisoners serving long terms, there are various legal maneuvers to get out of prison before the expiration of their sentences (or after serving a significant period of time on a life sentence). The available remedies vary depending on each person's situation and the jurisdiction they are in, as states differ from each other and from the federal system as well. Media engagements during these times must of necessity be extremely strategic, as they are often the prisoner's last shot at freedom or could mean the difference between dying in prison and recovering from a life-threatening illness on the outside. At times, the prisoners speaking for themselves will have the most powerful impact and be the most strategic move, whereas at other times the best course of action could be to pursue these legal measures as quietly as possible so as not to attract media attention.

On Parole, Probation, or Supervised Release

When people are released from prison, they usually have to spend some amount of time under state supervision. There are generally a number of restrictions they have to abide by and requirements they have to meet so they can stay out and not be sent back to prison to finish their sentences. These restrictions can directly or indirectly affect their ability to speak publicly about their cases. While it is theoretically unconstitutional for these restrictions to prevent freedom of speech, prisoners can easily be punished for their speech while under the thumb of the state.

‒ ‒ ‒ ‒ ‒ ‒ ‒ ‒ ‒ ‒ ‒ ‒ ‒ ‒ ‒ ‒

Speaking Out from the Inside

In April of 2013, Daniel McGowan was arrested while on probation after serving almost seven years in federal prison for his role in Earth Liberation Front (ELF) actions. The majority of his time in prison was spent in highly restrictive Communications Management Units (CMUs). While he was on supervised release in 2013, he wrote an article about the CMUs and their politically motivated uses within the Bureau of Prisons (BOP). He was arrested three days later at the halfway house and told that he had violated his terms of release by publishing the article. After Daniel's lawyers pointed out that the regulation used to send him back to jail had been found unconstitutional in 2007, the BOP released him back to the halfway house. Nevertheless, he was still required to sign a document upon his return to the halfway house that included this clause: "writing articles, appearing in any type of television or media outlets, news reports and or documentaries without prior BOP approval is strictly prohibited." However, the BOP quickly backtracked and claimed that he would not be punished for publishing articles.[93]

‒ ‒ ‒ ‒ ‒ ‒ ‒ ‒ ‒ ‒ ‒ ‒ ‒ ‒ ‒

Free and Clear!

Once people have been released from prison and have completed their supervised release, they generally can engage with the media and speak publicly about their cases. This point may not come for many years or decades, unfortunately. Even when it does, former prisoners should be careful not to say anything that could incriminate other people or bring additional charges.

This is not to recommend that former prisoners keep quiet and forgo participation in revolutionary movements, of course! Our movements need our prisoners to return to them after they have been returned to us. Since our enemies do not forget about us once we have finished all their legal processes and will continue to target and repress us, our communities, and our movements, we must never forget that every media engagement or public statement should be part of our strategy for achieving the goals of our revolutionary movements.

Chapter 8
RESOLVING YOUR CASE

THROUGHOUT THE EXHAUSTING MONTHS OR YEARS THAT you spend fighting with the criminal legal system, there will be many opportunities to resolve your case. There are two basic options if the state does not drop all your charges: hang tight and go to trial, or negotiate a plea agreement. This chapter will examine both of these end-game scenarios. Of course, your personal circumstances may change, the importance of your legal battle to your movement may change, the political climate in the country may change, the relationships between you and your codefendants and supporters may change, and your legal team may change. All these factors influence what you do and when you do it. Once again, we urge you to make decisions in the context of your movement and with the help of your comrades, rather than thinking only of your personal situation.

A Conspiracy against Defendants

Only around 5% of criminal cases make it to trial; the vast majority result in plea agreements instead.[94] The criminal legal system depends on people pleading guilty and receiving punishments of various sorts (e.g., fines, imprisonment, probation). The system is rigged this way for a variety of reasons. Perhaps most importantly, the criminal legal system is the direct pipeline into the prison-industrial complex, which is not only a crucial part of state-sanctioned slavery (see, for example, the Thirteenth Amendment to the United States Constitution[95]) but a major industry.[96] Defendants are generally forced into plea agreements in part due to the tremendous workloads of the prosecution, defense, and judges—all of who have a vested interest in defendants resolving their cases as quickly as possible. The overwhelming expense of fighting charges, the time required to do so, the threat of more severe punishments, and the fear of the unknown all conspire to force plea agreements as well. Coercing people to take plea deals drastically increases the number of convictions (i.e., wins) the state can claim, which helps them justify the existence of their courts and cages. Overall, the criminal legal system is a well-oiled machine that is designed to control the population by keeping people locked up and otherwise under the thumb of the state.

Prosecutors are highly skilled in coercing plea agreements. After charging defendants with as many crimes as they can think up (the scarier the better for their purposes), they typically start offering to reduce the charges in exchange for an admission of guilt to one or more of the charges (although not necessarily to the original charges) as the trial date approaches. Usually, the first offer is terrible. Sometimes, the longer you hold out, the better the offers become. The logic is that no one wants to go to trial, so the state has an incentive to offer you an acceptable plea agreement so that you will waive your constitutional right to a trial.

We must stress that there are no certainties in plea agreement negotiations. Only the prosecutors know whether they will ever offer you anything better than their first offer, so the negotiations and the decisions you make about whether or not to go to trial are always a gamble. So while plea offers may get better the longer you hold out, they are by no means guaranteed to get better. The danger of waiting too long for a better plea agreement is that the prosecution could take their plea offer off the table.

The judge can also retaliate against you for insisting on your constitutional right to a trial and pressure your lawyer and the prosecution to coerce you into accepting a plea agreement. The judge can also give you a worse sentence out of spite. Judges will never admit to having any preference for a quick resolution to the trial, of course, just as they will never admit to making sentences harsher out of spite. Rather, they will be careful to ensure the court record shows that they did everything possible to protect your rights. Likewise, they will ensure the record reflects that you were fully informed of your rights and made your own decision to plead guilty without any coercion from anyone. The idea that any guilty plea is free of coercion is ludicrous, of course—no system built on coercion can produce a result free of coercion! Even so, their system is designed to support itself by ensuring it can lock up defendants as effectively as possible.

-- -- -- -- -- -- -- -- -- -- -- -- -- -- -- --

The Deck is Stacked Against You

Brandon Baxter of the Cleveland 4 filed a *habeas corpus* petition (known as a 2255) that argued in part that he had not been properly advised by his lawyer and thus was unable to make a fully informed decision to plead guilty. The appellate judge summarized one of Baxter's arguments as:

> petitioner claims that counsel was ineffective because counsel advised petitioner to plead guilty to avoid retribution from the Court for exercising his right to trial. According to petitioner, counsel told him that if all of the other defendants pled guilty and petitioner was the only one to proceed to trial, "this would 'not be taken well' by the court." Further, counsel allegedly told petitioner that the Court "wanted to get this case done and over with as soon as possible" and that if petitioner went to trial and was found guilty, the Court would sentence him harshly as a punishment.[97]

The appellate judge then ruled, in part:

> the record shows that petitioner's plea was, in fact, voluntary and intelligent. A guilty plea entered by a defendant who is fully aware of the direct consequences of

the plea is voluntary in a constitutional sense "unless induced by threats ..., misrepresentation ..., or perhaps by promises that are by their nature improper as having no proper relationship to the prosecutor's business....A plea is intelligent when the district court verifies that the defendant understands the "applicable constitutional rights, the nature of the crime charged, the consequences of the guilty plea, and the factual basis for concluding that the defendant committed the crime charged."[98]

In other words, the court's ruling seems to assert that plea agreements are valid as long as there is no proof that the plea was coerced and the judge asks the defendant a series of questions to show on the record that the plea was not coerced. Obviously, the prosecutors and judges are extremely adept at ensuring the legal record meets these criteria and that defendants pleading guilty provide the answers that allow the prosecutors and judges to ensure the conviction while covering their asses.

Your own attorney may not want to go to trial either, especially if the trial is likely to last for several weeks or even months. Trials are expensive, hard, and uncertain—they could be a lot of work just to lose at the end. While some lawyers will be willing to go to trial (even eager), some may not be and may unintentionally or intentionally pressure you into taking a plea agreement. Many defendants who receive court-appointed attorneys have struggled with this pressure, perhaps in part because these attorneys are generally so overworked. Defendants have struggled with this pressure from radical lawyers as well. And sometimes lawyers just do not have your best interests in mind and do not want to fulfill their professional obligations of giving you a rigorous defense at trial. Your lawyer's wishes about going to trial are not the most important factor, though. This is your life—and you will have to deal with consequences of the choices you make.

Preparing to Resolve Your Case

As soon as you have been arraigned, the process of figuring out what to do about your charges begins. Sometimes this process can take years. Other times, defendants finish with it in a matter of minutes by pleading guilty right away and suffering whatever punishment the state hands out. We obviously think that it is best for radical defendants to wait out their charges long enough to make a decision that will benefit or at least not harm their movements. As we said in Chapter 2, "Setting and Balancing Personal, Political, and Legal Goals," we believe that radical and revolutionary movements need members who will approach their legal cases as part of the struggle with the dedication to turning a terrible situation into a part of winning that struggle.

As your trial date approaches, the pressure on you will increase significantly, perhaps exponentially. Review your goals for your case frequently to keep clear on what you want. Ask yourself some of the same questions you asked yourself when you were setting your goals at the beginning of your case. For example, "How important is it for me to get my day in court? How will a trial bring my politics and the issues I care about to a wider audience? How important is it to me to stay out of jail? How have the needs of the movement and my codefendants changed since all this started? How have my loved ones' needs changed since this all began? What do I need from my loved ones and supporters as I make my decisions?"

You will also likely have new questions to ask yourself as you figure out more about your situation. If you are preparing a legal defense, you might ask yourself questions intended to take a critical look at your legal situation. For example, "What will the judge allow or not allow me to bring up at trial? How might the current political climate affect the jurors or potential jurors in my case? Will I be able to bring in the witnesses I want to support my defense? How prepared and reliable are my witnesses? Who is the prosecution likely to call to testify against me? What is my relationship to those people? If they are friends or comrades, how will being subpoenaed by the prosecution affect them?"

This list is not exhaustive and these questions are solely offered as examples. You will be in the best position to figure out the most important questions to ask yourself. Try writing the questions and your answers out. You can also ask your trusted friends, comrades, and loved ones to help you answer these questions. Even if you are incarcerated and cannot speak freely because all your communications are being monitored, you can talk about these issues in general without going into specifics about your case. Members of your defense committee will try to be helpful as you sort through the personal and political considerations at play. While you may not be able to describe all the factors weighing into your decisions, you can get informed reactions from them.

Your comrades will be aware that you personally have more riding on the outcome of your case than anyone else. As such, they may be reluctant to tell you what to do or to offer advice if they have never been in a similar situation. If, for example, you want or need them to think more about the political implications of any given resolution to your case than about your personal welfare, tell them so. Ask them to help you weigh the political pluses and minuses of going to trial, taking a plea agreement, receiving probation, serving time in prison, and anything else that is on your mind.

If you have a strong working relationship with your lawyer or another member of your legal team, you can discuss some of these questions and concerns with them as well. In general, you will likely benefit from finding a balance between looking inside yourself to answer these questions and reaching out for support in ways that do not endanger you or anyone else. Make sure you have a good discussion with your lawyer to get their candid opinion about your chances at trial. Going to trial is always a risky business—if convicted, you may get more time in prison and/or on parole or probation than you would if you strike a bargain with the prosecution. A good attorney will be able to give you a reading on how likely you are to be acquitted on some or all of your charges based on the evidence against you, your viable defenses in the face of that evidence, and the judge's decisions about the way you can present your defense to the jury. An honest estimation of how trial will likely go can be crucial to your decisions, though it is important to remember that an estimate is not a guarantee. And sometimes, despite steep odds, it may be necessary to risk a trial in order to protect or strengthen revolutionary struggles.

Whatever your process and your final decision, we cannot stress enough how important it is that you never do or say anything that could harm anyone else—either directly through snitching or indirectly through giving the state further leverage over them.

Going to Trial

Going to trial is often the right choice for a variety of reasons and we urge all radical defendants to consider doing so as part of their resistance to state repression. For example, if you do not consider yourself guilty of the charges against you, pleading guilty could be not only distasteful but against your principles. Or perhaps you were entrapped and want the government's behavior to be put in the spotlight by your trial. Or maybe you were never offered a plea that you could live with and going to trial seems like the only option. No matter your reasons for going to trial, once you make the decision, remember that the legal arena is one of the many battlegrounds where we must fight. Also remember that significant victories have been won in that arena—even if some of those victories took a long time to achieve.

Additionally, remember that you are not destined to be found guilty and spend years or decades in prison. Anything can happen at trial—acquittals and hung juries happen, the jury could acquit on more serious charges but find you guilty of a lesser charge with a lighter sentence, or you could get convicted but then have your conviction overturned on appeal. Of course, you can also be found guilty of all charges and sentenced to the worst possible punishment. We do not intend to sugarcoat the risks involved in going to trial.

Yet there have been unlikely successes in the courts when everything about the case would suggest that a reasonable person should cut their losses and accept a plea agreement. Consider, for example, the trial of Russell Means and Dennis Banks on charges stemming from their occupation and defense of the town of Wounded Knee, South Dakota, in 1971. The 1868 Treaty of Fort Laramie was at the heart of their struggle, for the United States government had originally guaranteed hunting rights in large portions of Wyoming, South Dakota, and Montana to the Lakota Nation. Furthermore, white settlers were excluded from the basin of the Powder River (which runs through Wyoming and Montana), and the Lakota had sole access to the sacred Black Hills of South Dakota. Obviously, in the following century, the government violated the treaty repeatedly and whittled the treaty lands down to five reservations in South and North Dakota. Meanwhile, the Black Hills had been extensively mined (by white people) for gold.

Means and Banks, while charged with seventy-three counts of criminal behavior in relationship to the occupation of Wounded Knee, wanted to get the 1868 Treaty of Fort Laramie into their trial. They argued that the treaty was still in force and that the United States government had no legal jurisdiction over the land on which the crimes allegedly happened. While the judge never ruled on the admissibility of the treaty, their defense team referred to it continually and eventually brought a physical copy of the treaty into the courtroom. The dismissal of the charges against Means and Banks, while welcome, proved less important than the way in which their insistence upon the validity of the treaty supported the struggle for indigenous sovereignty. Through aggressive use of the media, relentless questioning of the FBI's collection of evidence, and eloquent opening and closing statements by the defendants, the autonomy of First Nations within the United States became the take-away message of the trial.[99]

If you decide to go to trial, there will be particular considerations and decisions for you to grapple with as you figure out exactly what you will do to defend yourself. If you are taking a legal approach to your case, you will benefit from discussing these thoroughly with your lawyer. We will explore some of these considerations in general terms since many of them are not obvious. These areas are much too important to neglect in your conversations with your attorney, though, so we urge you to explore them thoroughly as you prepare your legal defense. If you have decided to go to trial but are not worrying about your legal defense (e.g., you are using the trial to mount a strictly political defense), then these considerations may be less important. Their importance depends on the goals you have set for your case.

The considerations to ponder include preparing yourself to withstand the pressure of trial, aligning your court support with your goals, dealing with the judge's totalitarian hold over the courtroom, preparing for witnesses testifying against you, calling your own witnesses to testify on your behalf, and deciding whether you want to testify yourself.

Preparing Yourself to Withstand the Pressure of Trial

Trial will be an incredibly stressful time for everyone: you, your defense committee, your loved ones, your supporters.

Many defendants and supporters get so caught up in trial preparations that they forget how daunting of an ordeal a trial can be. Do your best to prepare for trial emotionally, physically, and mentally. Communicate with your defense committee about any extra needs you might have at this time. You will likely need to get creative to figure out how to meet these needs, especially if you are locked up and/or have other beings who depend on you for support and care (e.g., children, companion animals).

Your defense committee members can help you with many tasks during your trial that people in your life might assume that you will do personally. For example, they can help keep your family and friends informed about what is happening in court each day so you do not have to update them over email after a long day in court. Ask your defense committee to take notes during trial and to spread the word about what is happening. These notes can also be helpful for your lawyer, who might not always be able to keep track of everything that happens in the courtroom.

Your defense committee can also recruit supporters to come to trial every day. Having a room full of supporters raises your spirits and affects all the courtroom actors. Having supporters filling the seats shows the prosecutors and judge that people care about your case and are watching the proceedings. Jurors may also be impressed with the number of people who care about your case. If the media is covering your case, having a show of community support may affect their perceptions of the case and provide your defense committee with an angle for getting your messages out through the capitalist media (if you decide to engage this tactic).

An important consideration that is often overlooked is giving yourself some outlets for stress, fatigue, and burnout. As best you can, set time aside for having fun, joking around, and thinking about anything aside from your trial. If you are in custody and can receive visits while your trial is in process, consider talking about anything except your trial or limiting the time you talk about your trial in your visits so you can also talk about other things. You can also ask your supporters to send you in novels or other books that you want to read for pleasure to take your mind off your trial each night after court. Likewise, if you have been released pending trial, try to set some time aside for yourself each night to unwind before you have to go back to court in the morning.

Aligning Court Support with Your Goals

Another area that is often neglected is considering how the court support you ask for is aligned with your goals. Are you taking a legal approach to your case? If so, you might want to ask your supporters to follow all the court protocols and obey all the judge's orders, regardless of how you or they may feel about those orders. This approach may include standing when the bailiff or court clerk says "All rise!" before the judge enters the courtroom. While following these rules can irritate radicals, abiding by them can be to your strategic advantage during trial and later during appeals if you are convicted. Additionally, this approach may include asking people to dress nicely so as to appear respectable to the jury.

Even if you have decided that you are not going to engage a legal defense and will run risks (e.g., contempt of court) in order to achieve your political goals for your case, you may not want your supporters to run the risk of contempt or of the judge closing the courtroom to the public (or making supporters view the trial through monitors rather than being in the courtroom itself). Then again, if you want to throw wrenches into the system at every opportunity, you may want to ask your supporters to take the risks they are comfortable with as they stand in solidarity with you (even if that means that some do not come to court out of fear of arrest). There are no right answers, just better and worse ways to align your court support with your goals.

Dealing with the Judge's Totalitarian Hold Over the Courtroom

As you will undoubtedly have seen well before trial, the judge will have a totalitarian grip on their domain—the courtroom. Judges can do even the most unconstitutional of actions in the trial courtroom with virtual impunity. Most of the time, your only legal recourse is to appeal based on their violations of your rights or of the criminal legal procedure. Any relief that comes from these measures will arrive well after the fact, though, so you would be subjected to their whims and outbursts in the moment. Judges have been known to yell at attorneys and defendants during trials (although usually not in front of the juries) and put harsh restrictions on defendants and their supporters. In one of the most appalling examples from a political trial, Bobby Seale of the Black Panthers was bound and gagged in the middle of the courtroom during the Chicago 8 trial after getting in a heated argument with the judge (who was white). While the judge cited legal precedent to justify his draconian response, it had a profound effect on the jury. The power the judges can wield in their courtrooms can be incredibly hard to suffer through and often catches people off guard. Be prepared to evaluate each challenging instance and your responses in terms of what will best serve your goals.

Many important rulings happen before the trial starts or outside of the jury's presence during trial. Throughout the trial, the judge will likely send the jurors to the jury room so the lawyers can argue points of law that determine how the trial will proceed. These hidden courtroom battles may involve the kind of evidence that will be admitted, the questions both sides can and cannot ask witnesses, instructions to the jury for their deliberations (the process of determining a verdict at the end of the trial), and the responses given to jurors when they ask questions during their deliberations. The judge is always the one who decides these critical issues, which can greatly affect the jury's verdict. If the judge rules unfairly, your only legal recourse is to appeal these procedural issues in the future. Of course, the judge's decisions could also cause you to re-evaluate your goals and priorities as you go through your trial. If this happens, prepare to shift your strategies and tactics to achieve the new goals you set for yourself based on how the situation has changed from when you were simply anticipating how all this would go down.

Preparing for Witnesses Testifying against You

You could be faced with one or more types of prosecution witnesses: hostile witnesses (e.g., cops and snitches), expert witnesses (who may or may not bother to appear neutral in their stance), willing witnesses (e.g., people unconnected to you who have some information about the alleged offense; these people could be hostile or neutral, but not likely on your side if the prosecution subpoenas them), and unwilling witnesses (e.g., your comrades who have been subpoenaed against their wills). Each type of witness will add different perspectives and information to the state's theory of your case (i.e., the story they are trying to convince the jury to believe), and thus each will require you to respond in different ways. These differences are true regardless of your goals for your case, although your responses to them will clearly be dependent on your goals. An important part of trial testimony is that the testimony can be impeached (i.e., challenged). So just because, for example, a cop gets on the stand and tells a well-rehearsed story about how you are a terrorist who masterminded the whole plot does not mean that this story will appear credible after your attorney punches holes in it through cross-examination. The prosecution is also supposed to provide you with a list of their potential witnesses (at times even a list of the ones they will call for sure) before your trial begins so you can have the opportunity to interview them yourself (they do not have to talk with you, though).

Preparing for hostile witnesses can be relatively easy in some ways since you may be able to anticipate their testimony. For example, you can probably expect all the cops to have the same basic narrative and to support each other's testimony. Likewise, you can probably expect any snitches in your case to say exactly what the state wants them to say (the truth be damned). Willing witnesses who favor the prosecution's narrative of the case may be harder to predict, however, as you may not be able to determine what they know or what they might say on the stand. Nevertheless, your lawyer can still tear apart their stories and call into question their reliability during cross-examination. A successful impeachment of such a witness or their testimony might even turn them into a liability for the state rather than a benefit. The same could be said for expert witnesses, as some might be clearly biased towards the prosecution, have questionable expertise, or contradict themselves upon cross-examination.

Another note must be made about testimony from snitches: you should prepare yourself for the emotional impact of watching the government's witnesses testify. Listening to snitches on the stand can be gut-wrenching. While this may be some of the most emotionally taxing testimony during your trial, it could also be helpful for you and your case. A good defense lawyer may be able to get more of the truth out of the snitches than the state would like. When the government's own witnesses tell the jury facts that contradict the prosecution's version of the story, it can affect the jury powerfully. Likewise, your lawyer can work to destroy the snitch's credibility in the eyes of the jury during cross-examination and even subpoena them as a defense witness later on.

Similarly, if there was an informant in your case, the prospect of testimony from them can be scary. However, this testimony is not guaranteed to damage your case as much as you may fear. For example, Eric McDavid went to trial in 2007 on charges stemming from the activities of an informant known as "Anna." She worked for a year and a half to build a case against Eric and two of his comrades. The culmination of her entrapment efforts took place at a remote cabin that was completely wired with audio and video surveillance that captured the groups' every move the entire time they were there. Towards the end of Anna's testimony, the prosecutor prompted her to tell a story in which McDavid supposedly woke her up by waving a knife over her head. Defense attorneys jumped on this allegation during cross-examination because they knew the government would be unable to produce any surveillance footage to substantiate this claim. They also knew that there was no mention of this alleged incident in the mountains of reports that were part of the evidence in the case. Jurors who heard this testimony later stated that this story was quite unconvincing. Informants are on the stand because they are skilled in lying, so if your attorney can highlight their basic dishonesty and tendencies to exaggerate, their testimony may not be enough to sway a jury.

The type of prosecution witness that might be the least anticipated is a comrade who is subpoenaed to testify against you. Being served with one of these subpoenas puts them in a tough predicament. If they refuse to testify, they will likely be held on contempt of court and be sent to jail for the duration of your trial. At times, they may be simply released after your trial is over and there is no more reason for them to testify. But they could also be charged with criminal contempt of court and face legal problems of their own. These witnesses will need to decide how they want to respond to the subpoena and what risks they are willing to run. For example, they could refuse to show up, show up and refuse to testify, testify but refuse to provide information that they think could damage you or others, testify but invoke their Fifth Amendment protection against self-incrimination, and so on. Each of these approaches carries different risks for them, you, and others. These witnesses would benefit from talking with a lawyer about their options, but they may be prohibited from talking with you or with your lawyer (unless your lawyer is interviewing them as a potential witness).

Unwilling witnesses for the prosecution, like radical defendants who are targeted for their politics, should keep the best interests of their movements in mind. There will be times when being involved in revolutionary struggle requires people to run the risk of criminal contempt charges or other punishments for refusing to take part in the proceedings. Ultimately, these witnesses will have to make that decision for themselves and we hope that they will draw on the perspectives offered in this guide as they do so.

- - - - - - - - - - - - - - - -
To Testify or Not to Testify?

We hope that this title made you do a double take! When people are called to testify before a grand jury, the best policy is to refuse, even if it results in civil and/or criminal contempt charges and jail time. However, being subpoenaed to testify at a jury trial is different for a couple of reasons. First, grand jury testimony often results in charges being filed against someone and always provides our enemies with more information to use against us. If someone is testifying at trial, we generally know who is at risk and what the stakes are. With a grand jury subpoena, there may not be any indication (even in the grand jury room) of what the case may be about or who may be the target of the investigation.

Another difference is that both the witness and the defendant theoretically have more legal protections in place during trial testimony.

In a trial, the defendant has a lawyer present, who can object to the direction of the prosecution's questions and can ask questions of their own (cross-examination). The judge can also block inappropriate lines of questioning, although they might not. Further, witnesses may be able to invoke their Fifth Amendment protection against self-incrimination (this protection is limited, however, so consulting with a lawyer is advised if you are ever subpoenaed to be a witness).

Even so, testifying at a trial always entails risks for the defendants, the witness themselves, and other people involved in their political communities. Deciding what to do in response to being subpoenaed should also include thorough considerations of what is in the best interests of the witness, the defendant(s), and the movement as a whole. The perspectives in this guide for defendants can also be useful for those who have been subpoenaed by the state.

━ ━ ━ ━ ━ ━ ━ ━ ━ ━ ━ ━

Calling Your Own Witnesses

Whether you are using a legal or political defense (or some combination), you may decide to call people to testify on your behalf. You also may want to call hostile witnesses so you can ask them questions that your lawyer was not able to ask on cross-examination (typically, cross-examination can only go into areas brought up by the first side's original questions). Thoroughly think through who you will and will not call as a witness. For your friendly witnesses, you probably know the version of the story they can and cannot tell better than your lawyer. When deciding on witnesses to call, remember that taking the stand is incredibly nerve-wracking and stressful; it is not for everyone or for every situation. These witnesses will need to understand the role they play at your trial and may need to talk with their own lawyer about their questions or concerns.

Also ensure that your witnesses understand that they will likely need to answer questions from both your lawyer and the prosecutors. While answering questions from your lawyer might be relatively easy, they should be prepared to answer the questions that are posed to them carefully and clearly in addition to honestly. Your lawyer might ask them strangely worded questions to get to some information while not touching on other information; they should be sure they answer only what is being asked of them. Additionally, they will likely need to answer questions from the prosecution that are just as carefully crafted—except these questions will be designed to make them look bad and to hurt you. Prosecutors are well practiced in making people uncomfortable, upset, and angry, as well as in getting them to say what they need them to say to ensure a conviction. For example, the prosecutor might make a statement and ask for a simple "yes" or "no" answer. Tactics like this are extremely limiting for a witness and can force them to tell a version of the story that is less than complete or accurate. A good defense lawyer should be able to help your witnesses and prevent the prosecutor from bullying them by objecting to certain questions or challenging the prosecutor's behavior, but the judge does not have to rule in your lawyer's favor or prevent the prosecutor from tearing into your witness. Thus, the damage done by the prosecution's questioning can be hard to prevent or undo.

Another consideration when deciding who to call as a witness is that witnesses generally cannot be present in the courtroom until they have completed their testimony. Consider the full range of your needs during trial and weigh your options carefully if you must decide between having someone present with you during trial and available to take the stand as your witness. Since the prosecution will present its case first, your witness might miss the bulk of your trial. Having this friend or loved one in the courtroom for support throughout your trial might make more of a difference to you than the quality of the testimony they are able to give.

Testifying on Your Own Behalf

Many times, defendants assume that they will need to testify to get their story across (whether this is for a legal, political, or combination approach). Testifying is not always necessary or even advisable, though. You do not even need to present a defense at all if you do not want to since the state theoretically bears the burden of proving your guilt (i.e., as opposed to you having to prove your innocence). You should carefully assess the potential benefits and dangers of testifying before you decide to take the stand in your own defense. Often lawyers will advise their clients to *not* take the stand. There can be many reasons for this, including evidence that the prosecutors could introduce into the trial during cross-examination that they would not otherwise be able to put in front of the jury. Defense attorneys know how skilled prosecutors are at twisting a witness's words and stories to get the jury to believe their version of events. If you decide to take the stand, make sure you are constantly on guard and think through everything you will say before you say it. Perhaps most importantly, make sure your words do not implicate others in any way.

When testifying on your own behalf, listen carefully to each question your attorney asks you and answer only that question. Be careful not to jump ahead in your narration of events, answer questions that your lawyer's question brought to your mind, or answer the question that you think your lawyer should have asked (your lawyer should have the opportunity to ask you additional questions in the redirect examination, which should occur after the prosecutor cross-examines you). When you are being cross-examined, pay particular attention to what you are being asked and answer only what you are being asked—unless, of course, the answer would implicate you or others. In either of these cases, you will need to make a spur-of-the-moment decision on how best to protect yourself, your comrades, and your movement.

Finally, remember that the jury always watches for your reactions while you are in the courtroom. Work to present yourself the way you want to be seen and ensure this way is aligned with your goals for your case. Since they are human beings, your jury members will invariably use many subjective factors to come to their verdict. Thus, it is best to assume that they will be constantly measuring your words and your attorney's arguments against your appearance, facial expressions, and casual behavior. As long as you are anywhere near the courthouse, consider yourself to be on stage and in character in this judicial theater piece.

Negotiating a Plea Agreement

Since the vast majority of cases end through plea agreements, we would be remiss not to explore them fully even though we believe that going to trial usually presents radicals and revolutionaries with more options for fighting back against the state in the long term. In political cases, plea agreements can be tricky because of the implications they can have for you, your codefendants (if you have any), other people facing similar charges even if your cases are not joined, and the broader movement of which you are a part. *If you decide to take a plea, we strongly urge you to hold out for terms that are acceptable to you and do not damage your movement.* Do not agree to testify against any codefendants or political comrades who may be charged with crimes in the future in exchange for reduced charges, less prison time, shorter probation, and/or smaller fines for yourself. Do not implicate others in your statement of facts when you admit guilt or in your sentencing statement. The government wants you to sell out your comrades so they can divide and conquer your movement. Do not do it!

The plea agreement document will likely not use the term "non-cooperating," but you should ensure that the government is clear that you will never share information about other people. Pushing for a clause in the agreement that says that you will never be called to testify against others will likely not hurt, even if the government refuses to include it explicitly. More likely, the agreement simply will not contain any language requiring cooperation with the state. However, if a person *is* cooperating, often their plea agreement will contain a "5K1" motion (this is for federal cases). The prosecutor will use this motion to ask the judge for a downward departure at sentencing in exchange for cooperation. This is one thing to watch out for in looking over anyone's plea agreement.

Although prosecutors extol the ways you will benefit from turning snitch, cooperation does not necessarily result in lighter sentences. The Crimethinc Ex-Worker's Collective analyzed sentences received by defendants in the FBI's Operation Backfire.[100] Eight defendants cooperated with the government and four did not. The four who did not cooperate did not necessarily receive harsher sentences than the eight who did. While the case against each defendant was different, this chart shows that there is no clear benefit to cooperating. Some cooperating defendants received longer sentences than the non-cooperating defendants and had a terrorism enhancement applied at sentencing. The non-cooperating defendants who were facing the most charges received significantly less time than the cooperating defendants who were facing the most charges. And the non-cooperating defendant who was facing the least number of charges received only a marginally higher sentence or an equivalent sentence to the cooperating defendants who were only facing a few charges. The overall lesson to be learned from this chart is that cooperation does not necessarily mean a lighter sentence. This lesson supports the principle of non-cooperation by showing yet another way that the state lies to coerce cooperation and plea agreements.[101]

The term "non-cooperating" is broad, and the devil is in the details. These details will necessarily vary according to the peculiarities of your case. When negotiating a non-cooperating plea agreement, there are some points worth considering:

- *On-going investigations*: You may not be the only person the government would like to charge coming out of the event(s) which led to your arrest. It may take years for them to build up enough evidence against someone else, and they may be in the process right now. Assume that a grand jury is already looking into people you might have been working with or who simply know you. Examine everything in a proposed plea agreement through that lens. Could anything in your document be used to indict someone else?

- *Specify the crimes you are pleading guilty to*: One or more of the charges brought against you may be dropped in exchange for a guilty plea to the one(s) the government cares about the most. Alternatively, your charges may have "lesser included offenses" that you can plead down to (e.g., from a felony down to a misdemeanor or from a felony with a stiff penalty to one with a lighter penalty). Before you accept the prosecutor's offer, consider the implications for your life of a conviction on those crimes as opposed to other options that may be (or become) available to you. Your attorney can probably advise you about what may become available, based on their knowledge of the prosecutor's office, courthouse politics, and cases similar to yours.

- *Specify the facts you stipulate to*: As you decide which crimes you will plead guilty to, you should work out with your lawyer what you will say in your statement of facts. (Sometimes the procedure is that your lawyer will ask you questions in front of the judge to establish the facts. Work out both parts of your script, in that case.) Be careful that the facts you stipulate to do not incriminate anyone else, whether they have been charged or not—especially if you are charged with conspiracy. Do not provide information about other people, groups, or organizations that would aid the state to gather intelligence about radical movements and communities. Additionally, be careful not to set yourself up for a perjury charge later.

- *Negotiate jail/prison sentences, probation/parole, fines, and restitution*: Your plea agreement should clearly specify the terms of the punishment the government has agreed to recommend. Often, prosecutors will try to leave elements of your punishment vague so they can hit you with something at sentencing. Would you rather serve a prison sentence than be restricted by probation for years? Let your lawyer know what you want, because many times defense lawyers think of jail or prison as being the worst punishment and try to avoid it through probation.[102] The prosecutor, in contrast, will likely push to make you serve the most time possible *and* have probation afterwards. Have you already spent time behind bars on these charges? If so, you should receive credit for time served and have that taken off the remaining time you spend in prison. While this process is often fairly automatic, it is likely better to have it explicit than to trust the state to play by their usual rules. Do you have ethical issues about paying fines or restitution? If so, make sure your plea agreement does not leave room for the judge to impose these at sentencing.

- *Terms for codefendants*: Solidarity pays off in negotiating a plea agreement, and the pressure of the negotiations also strains solidarity. Not all of you may be equally willing (or able) to push through to trial. Not all of you may be willing to accept the same terms for your punishment. In other words, you may be negotiating not only with the prosecution, but also with one another. If you have a team of lawyers, they may not be particularly helpful if they still think about you as individual clients rather than as a collective. In these situations, you may find yourself bucking everything about the typical plea negotiation process to approach it on your terms and with both your individual and collective needs, values, and priorities at the forefront of your minds. Be prepared for this and work with each other to stand strong and united. Also be careful that such strains among you are not communicated to the prosecution because they will take advantage of any splits they see developing.

- *Specifically state that you will not testify at related trials*: In conspiracy cases, it may be necessary for one codefendant to settle more quickly than the others, for any number of good reasons. If so, insist on a clause that excuses you from being called as a witness at the trial of the remaining defendants. If you believe a grand jury may still be working on further indictments, push for language that specifies that you will not cooperate against anyone in the future either. The government might not agree to this, but stand firm on your non-cooperation stance even if you are not able to get specific language in your plea agreement.

- *Factor in other consequences*: Consider the impacts of your conviction on other areas of your life. Could a long prison term put your children in a precarious position or cause you to lose custody of them permanently?

Some health conditions mean that a long prison sentence would be a death sentence; what arrangements can you make in your plea agreement that speak to this issue? If you are trans / intersex / gender-nonconforming and going to serve time, will you be placed in a unit that will be as safe as possible? If you are on hormones, would you be able to continue receiving them? If not, what health consequences could this have for you? Convictions also have implications for certain jobs. Ask your lawyer about the possibilities of getting the conviction expunged from your record later on and figure this into your agreement with the prosecution.

▪ *Other minutiae*: The government is quite adept at sneaking in details that seem unimportant now but might matter to you a lot later. For example, do not agree to terms which would bar you (or anyone else) from filing Freedom of Information Act (FOIA) requests. Filing FOIA requests can be a powerful tool for a defendant during any post-conviction proceedings (such as appeals or *habeas corpus* petitions), and you do not want to deny yourself any tools or resources you might need in the future.

Gaining Leverage in the Negotiation Process

Knowing what you want out of a plea agreement is much different than knowing how to get what you want. Approaching your negotiations from a position of strength can be valuable even when you feel like you are being totally defeated. The government desperately wants convictions to justify their repressive tactics and apparatus, win the battle of the story in the public's eye, seal the deal on new legislation that criminalizes dissent, and destroy the movements that threaten their hold on power. The court system is also short on time and money for lengthy trials, so the prosecution always has that incentive to work out a plea agreement with you.

Apart from these more obvious factors, you can be creative and strategic in your efforts to find leverage over the state as you negotiate a non-cooperating plea agreement. For example, you may be able to take advantage of government missteps and malfeasance. Daniel McGowan was one of the Operation Backfire defendants who moved to uncover evidence of National Security Agency (NSA) domestic spying on him and the other non-cooperating defendants. Unconstitutional spying could potentially have led to his case and other Operation Backfire cases being thrown out. The judge ordered the government to reveal whether the NSA had been involved in any surveillance in the case. Shortly thereafter, McGowan's attorney withdrew the motion and McGowan and his codefendants accepted plea agreements that explicitly stated that they would not have to provide information on any other activists. The threat of having to admit to illegal spying seems to have led the government to offer one of the most favorable plea agreements to date in political trials. While this was a lucky break in some ways, it is not unusual for law enforcement to overreach in its investigations of activists. As another example, most members of the Weather Underground Organization and Prairie Fire emerged from hiding and negotiated minimal sentences for bombings they committed in the 1960s and 1970s in part because the government collected evidence against them through illegal means.[103] Looking for the things the state really does not want people to know about can be both valuable political work and beneficial to you in your plea negotiations.

Sealing the Deal

When you sign a plea agreement, you are generally making a final decision and should treat it as such. Agreeing to plead guilty means that you waive a laundry list of "rights" that you would normally have at trial, including the right to confront your accusers, the right not to incriminate yourself, and the right to most appeals. The last of these is perhaps the most important. Getting redress through the courts for things such as improper sentencing and mistakes made during trial is notoriously difficult and becomes infinitely more so when defendants take plea agreements. Make sure your lawyer fully explains to you both what your plea means for you now and how it could affect you and your case in the future.

Judges are *not* bound to abide by the plea agreement, although they often do. The plea agreement is worked out between you and the prosecution, but the judge ultimately decides your punishment. If the judge's sentence varies considerably from the agreement, you may be able to withdraw your plea. That is not always possible and is never easy, so this is yet another gamble you will be taking in your case.

While it should go without saying by now, if the prosecution will not agree to a non-cooperating plea agreement, scratch a plea agreement off your list of options. Let the prosecutor know that you will be going to trial. Let the prosecutor know that they will get nothing but headaches out of your trial if this is aligned with your goals. For example, you can assure them that you will not provide any information on other people if you testify on your own behalf, even at the risk of contempt of court for this refusal; you will not testify against anyone if the prosecution calls you to testify in *their* trials either, even at the risk of contempt of court for this refusal, too; you will bring out evidence that they wish you would not, even if the judge tells you that you cannot; your defense committee will make a big scene outside the courtroom, in the media, and in every possible way—even if that means more arrests. Being willing to suffer the consequences of our resistance can help us disarm the criminal legal system.

Sentencing

If you are found guilty by a jury or if you plead guilty to reduced charges, you will be sentenced to some sort of punishment. Generally, several months pass between the time you plead guilty and the time you are sentenced. The probation office usually spends this time doing a pre-sentence investigation to make a recommendation to the judge about what your sentencing should be (this is true at the federal level and in many states). Both the prosecution and the defense generally object to some or all of the Pre-Sentence Report (PSR) submitted to the judge. The prosecution often objects because they feel the report is too lenient, whereas the defense often objects because the report is too damning and will make the defendant's prison sentence that much worse. (For more information on federal PSRs, see Appendix A, "The Criminal Legal Process.")

You and your defense committee can also use this time to prepare for whatever happens. Fundraising for your long-term support in prison and/or your needs once you are released is incredibly important and most defendants will receive more donations more easily early on in their ordeals rather than years down the road. Depending on your goals and politics, you might want to ask your defense committee and/or lawyer to gather letters asking for leniency from the judge. These letters can come from family members, community members, teachers, co-workers, and supporters. You and your defense committee can also spend this time researching the facilities to which you could possibly be sent. If you find one that you prefer over others, your lawyer can ask the judge to make a recommendation to the prison administration (e.g., the Bureau of Prisons for federal sentences) that you be sent there. Even if your judge complies with this request, though, the bureaucrats in the prison administration who decide your placement do not have to honor the judge's recommendation. And do not forget to spend some of this time taking care of yourself and spending time with those you love (even if that time has to be through visitation where you are being held).

At your sentencing hearing, you will be able to make a statement to the court if you so choose. This statement can be as brief as you want, although perhaps not as long as you want because the judge can cut you off whenever they want (again, with the threat of contempt or incurring their wrath and receiving a harsher sentence, or both). You will likely benefit from deciding on what you want to say as if you will be able to say it all. Choose your words wisely and think about the messages you want to convey to the judge, the state, your supporters in the courtroom, and the broader movement. Your defense committee can later publish this statement for you.

One political prisoner who gave us feedback on this guide told us that, when he was figuring out how to handle his case, he received much inspiration from reading and re-reading the trial statements of Kuwasi Balagoon, a member of the Black Liberation Army convicted of an expropriation of a Brink's armored car. Balagoon's sentencing statement concludes with:

> Legal rituals have no effect on the historic process of armed struggle by oppressed nations. The war will continue and intensify, and as for me, i'd [*sic*] rather be in jail or in the grave than do anything other than fight the oppressor of my people. The New Afrikan Nation as well as the Native American Nations are colonized within the present confines of the United States, as the Puerto Rican and Mexicano Nations are colonized within as well as outside the present confines of the United States. We have a right to resist, to expropriate money and arms, to kill the enemy of our people, to bomb and do whatever else aids us in winning, and we will win. The foundation of the revolution must rest upon the bones of the oppressors.[104]

Balagoon identified as a prisoner of war and decided not to participate in much of the trial proceedings. As such, his opening, closing, and sentencing statements are all brilliantly aligned with his politics, priorities, and goals for his case. You can craft an equally well-designed sentencing statement by considering your goals along with the messages you want to convey. And you do not have to make a statement at all, which could be in your best interest at times. For example, if you plan to appeal your case or your sentencing, what you say at this time could be used against you in those appeals. Thus, deciding on whether or not to make a sentencing statement and deciding what to say are both strategic decisions that are best made within the context of your goals and with the long road in view.

When considering your options for this part of your ordeal, remember that you may be able to have a few people speak on your behalf at sentencing. If that is an option and you decide to use it, coordinate with them as best as possible to figure out what they will say. If you have codefendants, consider how one defendant's use of an influential or notable speaker may positively or negatively affect those without the same connections or status. Even at this late date in your case, continue to work out a collective strategy.

- - - - - - - - - - - - - - - - - -
Staying True to Your Revolutionary Principles at Sentencing

Jeremy Hammond is a hacktivist serving a decade-long federal prison sentence after pleading guilty to participating in a hack of Stratfor (Strategic Forecasting), a private intelligence firm. Jeremy was working with Anonymous and was betrayed by another hacker known as Sabu (legal name Hector Xavier Monsegur). Sabu turned informant and set up Jeremy and other hacktivists after being arrested and threatened with more than 100 years in prison.[105] Below is an excerpt of Jeremy's sentencing statement[106]:

> The acts of civil disobedience and direct action that I am being sentenced for today are in line with the principles of community and equality that have guided my life. I hacked into dozens of high profile corporations and government institutions, understanding very clearly that what I was doing was against the law, and that my actions could land me back in federal prison.[107] But I felt that I had an obligation to use my skills to expose and confront injustice—and to bring the truth to light.
>
> Could I have achieved the same goals through legal means? I have tried everything from voting petitions to peaceful protest and have found that those in power do not want the truth to be exposed. When we speak truth to power we are ignored at best and brutally suppressed at worst. We are confronting a power structure that does not respect its own system of checks and balances, never mind the rights of its own citizens or the international community.
>
> While in prison I have seen for myself the ugly reality of how the criminal justice system destroys the lives of the millions of people held captive behind bars. The

experience solidified my opposition to repressive forms of power and the importance of standing up for what you believe.

When I was released, I was eager to continue my involvement in struggles for social change. I didn't want to go back to prison, so I focused on above-ground community organizing. But over time, I became frustrated with the limitations of peaceful protest, seeing it as reformist and ineffective. The Obama administration continued the wars in Iraq and Afghanistan, escalated the use of drones, and failed to close Guantanamo Bay.

Around this time, I was following the work of groups like Wikileaks and Anonymous. It was very inspiring to see the ideas of hactivism coming to fruition. I was particularly moved by the heroic actions of Chelsea Manning[108], who had exposed the atrocities committed by U.S. forces in Iraq and Afghanistan. She took an enormous personal risk to leak this information—believing that the public had a right to know and hoping that her disclosures would be a positive step to end these abuses. It is heart-wrenching to hear about her cruel treatment in military lockup.

I thought long and hard about choosing this path again. I had to ask myself, if Chelsea Manning fell into the abysmal nightmare of prison fighting for the truth, could I in good conscience do any less, if I was able? I thought the best way to demonstrate solidarity was to continue the work of exposing and confronting corruption.

I targeted law enforcement systems because of the racism and inequality with which the criminal law is enforced. I targeted the manufacturers and distributors of military and police equipment who profit from weaponry used to advance U.S. political and economic interests abroad and to repress people at home. I targeted information security firms because they work in secret to protect government and corporate interests at the expense of individual rights, undermining and discrediting activists, journalists and other truth seekers, and spreading disinformation.

The government celebrates my conviction and imprisonment, hoping that it will close the door on the full story. I took responsibility for my actions, by pleading guilty, but when will the government be made to answer for its crimes?

The U.S. hypes the threat of hackers in order to justify the multi-billion dollar cyber security industrial complex, but it is also responsible for the same conduct it aggressively prosecutes and claims to work to prevent. The hypocrisy of 'law and order' and the injustices caused by capitalism cannot be cured by institutional reform but through civil disobedience and direct action. Yes I broke the law, but I believe that sometimes laws must be broken in order to make room for change."

Chapter 9
SURVIVING IN PRISON

While we would love to believe that no one reading this guide will ever need a chapter like this, the unfortunate reality is that some will. If you are convicted or take a plea, more than likely you will be spending at least a little time in prison. Every facility is different—with different rules and a different group of prisoners. The varieties of experience and opinions on how to handle those experiences will become even clearer to you as you read some of the responses below, which often contradict each other in both tone and content.

What follows is basic advice about how to survive in prison (much of this will also apply to you if you are in custody pre-trial). Each section begins with a few words from us, but the bulk of the chapter consists of feedback and advice from a handful of current and former political prisoners/prisoners of war about how to do time. We were not able to contact everyone we would have liked, so this chapter is necessarily an incomplete examination of these issues and topics. We hope it will be useful nonetheless.

General Advice

Probably the most oft-repeated piece of advice from folks who have spent time in prison is to keep your mind and body active. If you are healthy, both mentally and physically, you will be more capable of handling whatever comes your way, even if you cannot always be fully prepared for it. And in prison, you can never be quite sure what that might be. Additionally, although spirituality means many different things to many different people, almost everyone we talked with also advises you to nourish your spiritual growth.

Some other bits of advice that stood out are:

- If you are in a position to do so, learn as much as you can about where you are going before you get there.
- Talk to other people who have been to prison/jail, especially former political prisoners/POWs.
- Know your "rights," which are greatly diminished in prison. But there are still rules and regulations that prisons are supposed to follow (whether or not they do). Knowing what those are—and the bureaucratic processes for navigating them—might help you win small battles while in prison.
- Use the law library and talk to other prisoners who have experience navigating the legal ins and outs of prison. Just a word of caution, though: not all prisoners who claim to have legal skills do. If you seek help or

advice from other prisoners, make sure you can verify that their advice is sound and trusted by others.

JOSH HARPER[109]

One thing that I try to be really careful about, and sometimes I'm not as careful as I should be, is extrapolating my prison experience and saying it's *the* prison experience. Every prison sort of has its own culture. Even depending on the era that you're in one prison, it can change quite drastically. There's an old political prisoner by the name of Claude Marks and he did time out at Sheridan, where I did my time, and even though there were some similarities between the prison environment that he was in and the one I was in, over a space of ten years, there were also some very drastic changes. I talk a lot about the negative things that happened to me in prison because I want people to know when they're being asked to make sacrifices for a movement, that those sacrifices are real and severe. But what happened to me will not necessarily happen to others...

I think that there are a few basic things that people can hear, but there's really nothing that can prepare you. Prison, incarceration is an experience that's not quite like any other... I guess what I would say is that there are some things that people can do to keep themselves safer while they're in. One thing I always tell people is do not gamble, do not drink, do not smoke, and do not do drugs. I think some folks immediately assume I'm saying that because I might be straight-edge. I'm not... But in prison, the thing is that one of the quickest ways to get abused or exploited is to get in debt. And gambling is a quick way to get in debt. Cigarettes cost $7 each and they're addictive. And you're in a stressful environment where you're going to want access to these vices. And so you're going to start purchasing them on credit and I knew people that ended up having to prostitute themselves to be able to afford their cigarette habit. So don't smoke. The people that manufacture alcohol in prison have a commodity that everyone wants and what that means is that you've got to have it protected, which means that if you're manufacturing it, you're almost certainly part of a gang, almost certainly high up in the gang, because you're going to have revenue. Don't get involved with those people. Don't purchase alcohol, because, again, you're setting yourself up to be vulnerable, in a weakened state, mentally impaired, and then you're going to owe money to people who are quite dangerous, as well. There's also some very commonsense things: don't gossip. That was a hard one for me. Don't run your mouth. Listen more than you talk. Finally, I would say you've got to be very conscientious. There are people in there who are going to be there for the next thirty years, forty years. There are people who are never going to see the street again. And that means that that environment is their environment. It's their home. You can't fuck things up for them. If you get angry at your girlfriend on the phone and you slam that phone down, well that phone might be the only way that they have to communicate with their child, their mother, so you can't get away with that stuff. You've got to be clean. You've got to be tidy. It sounds like a weird point to make about staying safe. If you disrespect that space, you're disrespecting someone's last bit of comfort in a hellacious environment. And so, keep your voice down, don't whistle. Keep your cell mopped and make sure you're respecting that environment.

Jake Conroy[10]

I think a couple of the big things are that you should be prepared. If you're a political prisoner, and someone asks you, and everyone will ask you, what you're in for, you need to have a quick answer. You can't sit there and be like "Well, it's this law called the Animal Enterprise Protection Act. Let me tell you all about it." They want to know what you're in for in about five seconds, and if you can't give them a clear and concise answer that they're going to understand, you're suddenly different, and being different in prison is a terrible thing because that means you're going to be exploited, you're going to get beat up, be taken advantage of, and eventually you're just going to get rolled off the yard, beat up so you get moved out of that prison yard because they don't like you, they don't want you there. You kind of have to appear normal. And that's difficult for certain political prisoners that have certain politics who go into prison. … You just have to be aware that people are looking at you and they're sizing you up and they're judging you constantly, and you have to be prepared to put on a particular face, give them the impression that you're a normal person, you're not to be fucked with. The second big thing for me was that was told to me before I went in that I thought was great advice was that when you first get there, it's best to just sit back and watch. Just observe what's going on. I was told to spend two to three months doing that, until you see the inner workings of the institution and your unit, and your cells, and the politics, the gang politics and the racial politics, and how all that works, and learn it and understand it before engaging in it. I remember that after two or three weeks I thought "I've got all of this down," and I started spending more time in front of the TV and trying to get to know the people I was in with and I felt a little cocky about the situation and one of the few people that I became friends with, on a dime, he did something wrong, and in a heartbeat, this guy had his face rearranged by two skinheads, beaten up so badly that you wouldn't be able to even recognize him, and it really clicked in my head that I don't know what's going on. I never felt ready to enter this prison world, but after a couple weeks I thought "I can handle this," and it was just a real big reminder that you really need to take this process really slow and carefully and really thought-out, or you're going to get seriously hurt.

AUGUST SPIES[111]

Two big things to keep in mind: 1. Don't believe a word anyone tells you, ever, and 2. patience. There's a lot of ignorance and disrespect (contrary to popular beliefs) in prisons. Be patient.

Other advice: keep a journal, develop a healthy routine, use the time to learn, grow, build a solid foundation.

EMMA GOLDMAN[112]

I have several [coping mechanisms] for trying to keep my mind active, to keep learning and challenging myself. I've really tried to push my guitar skills by tackling just horrendously difficult pieces of classical music. It's satisfying to get a fussy run down, to mix harmonies with slides and fast picking... Mostly, though, the guitar playing helps to relate to other folks here. I learn songs people like and teach a class whenever the Rec folks will let me... Music is probably my most important stress release, my meditation and connection to my core beliefs and the vision of a changed world—but it's also an easy good time to share when people are also feeling lonely and disconnected. We sing together and it's better. We can mark holidays and learn something about each other, too. … I've tried to increase my strategies to distract and calm myself. I've increased the amount of exercise I do every day, lots more time on the treadmill and the yard. The exercise helps to de-stress, for sure. I read a ton, both fiction and non-fiction. I keep trying to challenge my memory and my mind. I also study and read in both French and Spanish… and want to take up the study of Japanese… And finally, but probably most challenging to me is my painting practice. I want so much to get better and know that I need to learn so much more. I read everything I can get my hands on to study and more to the point, get a lot of meditative value out of just practicing. When the California prisoners went on hunger strike—one of their demands was to be allowed to get art supplies. This is no small thing. When you spend so many hours locked in a small cell, it matters to your sanity that you can see colors so absent from your environment and that you can use art to connect to your culture, memories, family and vision of the world. Art can be very healing to your psyche, both as a way of communicating with your unconscious mind and as a way to work through trauma and pain. Art can give you a voice in the world, allow you to connect and be part of an ongoing civic debate in the world. I think prisoners need this more than anyone, sometimes.

Voltairine de Cleyre[113]

The best way to survive in prison is to refuse to engage in the prison culture, stay out of people's business and mind your own. Don't ask another prisoner for anything, and don't accept anything from them. Keep your personal business all to yourself.

Get involved in education pursuits, and stay in school learning something. Visit the library as often as you can.

Be polite and very courteous to everyone, including prison staff and especially to the screws. Leave female staff the hell alone.

JOHN TUCKER [114]

Learn local racial and/or gang structure before becoming active in an area and learn how to carve out a non-affiliated safe place for yourself once incarcerated. Gang and race relations vary from place to place and you must be wary of lingo, symbols and ingrained responses. For example, words like "folks," "people," "king" and "gent" have gang meanings within Cook County, Chicago, IL and use of the wrong word, possession of a peculiar tattoo (i.e., a five or six pointed star, numbers such as 7-4, 2-4, a crown, a skull, a pitchfork or even a heart) or simply being in the wrong place at the wrong time can make your life hell or cause you harm while incarcerated.

Be prepared to explain your case vaguely but effectively. Other inmates will look into your case over time and simply stating that you "don't want to talk about it" can be an invitation to violence in some situations as that can be misconstrued into another form of case and you could serve as a scapegoat for a host of issues that have been burning since before your arrival.

LUCY PARSONS [115]

Be yourself. Your presence is unimpressive, no one knows who you are or cares; you're just another body that comes and goes. Be observant of people around you and wary of those who approach you—while some people may have the best intentions toward you, others will usually want to know something about you: like whether you are street smart, stupid, have any vices, or are weak or strong. Guys in prison are good at finding these things out. Whether you realize it or not, their eyes and ears are on you at all times. Informants are likely to be among them, too. So be vigilant, not paranoid. Be yourself and you'll get by. Some people may test your will through physical force, intimidation, coercion, drugs, and the like; and should they succeed, you become their prey and they will shamelessly exploit you. So at the first sign of this, nip it decisively in the bud, otherwise nobody will respect you. And word gets around: fortunately, most people in prison are not predators and they will at times intervene on another's behalf if that person readily fights for his own self-respect and self-interest. But you cannot rely on that. You have to handle your own affairs! Mind your own business, choose your own company, make your own decisions.

JOHN BROWN[116]

Whether in custody or out, it is good to take on projects, speaking, writing, expanding solidarity with other causes, both for the benefits of the work *and* because it provides an opportunity to get your head out of your own situation. Facing charges is being under attack, and it can have the effect of forcing you into a "barricades" mentality, dwelling on your own situation and losing sight of the larger context. An hour at a Food Not Bombs is good therapy. Writing statements in support from the county jail is good therapy too. Be prepared for captivity before facing it. Speak to those who have survived the experience. It is less traumatic when you know what to expect. Also, if you read KUBARK[117] and other materials, you learn the "why" behind the "what"—as in, "Oh, this is why they do this, because they want it to affect me like this..." And when you have the benefit of that analysis, it lessens the trauma.

Some key points. Whatever you experience—isolation, harsh conditions, confrontations from hostile staff or other prisoners—remember: This is *temporary*. Not permanent. Not forever.

Also, a somewhat counter-intuitive approach from the standard prison movie: Be yourself. It's disarming. *Remember who you are*, despite all the State does to strip you of identity and force you to accept their definition of you. *Remember who you are*, despite all the efforts of other captives to pressure you to conform to established norms (racism, gang membership, shunning other captives based upon charged offenses, etc.). There is power in deciding that *you* will define *you*.

This is not to say that you will not be affected by your experience or that you can somehow transcend reality by clicking your heels together. You can't.

The politically conscious captive is a rare thing. You are in a small minority. It can be lonely. Frustrating. The vast majority of the prison population is opportunist at best (looking to get over at the expense of others) and predatory at worst.

You are getting an up-close-and-personal view of what this social disorder produces. Many are unalterably fashioned in the image of their cultural creator. You are largely going to live among assholes who think you're slightly crazy.

Key is to develop real and genuine relationships with the small minority of captives who are conscious. Such relationships are never easy because all captives are in constant flux—transfer from unit to unit or prison to prison, etc., and prison is a place where it is much safer to care about no one. But "safe" isn't necessarily healthy.

Everywhere I have been held captive, I made friends with good people whose character and integrity I respected and admired—real and trusting relationships. Those relationships can be a kind of "resistance" in that such relationships deny the State the power to decide what we mean to each other, deny the power to force us into dysfunctional social spaces.

Interaction with prison staff is always detrimental. Everyone working in prison is trained to perceive you as qualitatively and quantitatively different from them. Like the Jews in concentration camps for the Nazis, you are not fully human, not real to the captors.

Accept that reality. Expect it. If you ever encounter that rare prison staffer capable of being fully human, consider yourself lucky until that staffer is set up and fired because his or her co-workers cannot trust that staffer.

These are the things the prison complex can do to you:

- Smash, destroy, confiscate your property.
- Place you in isolation.
- Transfer you from one state of captivity to another.
- Assault you.
- Kill you.

These are the only five activities the prison complex knows how to do. The mundane activities of life—chow, programs, visits, etc.—are simply the busy work, the window dressing, between instances where the prison complex finds an excuse to do one of the five activities listed above.

Expect that. Anticipate it. Your captors are irrational, unreasonable, and incapable of anything other than 1–5. Generally, administrators are not hired for their expertise or acumen in reforming offenders, but for their specialty in cutting the costs of bread and potatoes—however it is done.

Staying True to You

Being in prison can be a real test of your principles and integrity. A lot of the social ills that exist on the outside are greatly magnified on the inside. And either ignoring them or responding to them might carry much heavier (and swifter) consequences than doing so on the outside would. Confronting racism, acting in solidarity with other prisoners, and exercising mutual aid are just a few examples of some ways you might be able to continue living your life in a way that feels personally and politically fulfilling from inside prison. Remembering some of the reasons you might be in prison in the first place could help guide you through your experience.

August Spies

Staying true to one's principles in prison is only possible in your own life, in your own walk. I imagine this is true of life in general. For instance, I confront my own racism and my own notions of race and racism in general. To attempt to confront racism beyond myself would not be unlike punching a brick wall. Mutual aid is only ever on an individual basis, and one must be wary.

Emma Goldman

My vegan diet is a daily reminder of how I want to try to make my personal consumption choices in line with my beliefs in the valuing of all life forms, all beings. It's been a little confusing for me, as I've had to make a decision to accept medicine that is not vegan, as my bones were thinning in some places, my teeth cracking and thinning, some other physical effects... This feels bad, as I'd have more options on the outside (or would have been fine, having access to a balanced and nutritionally superior vegan diet). But it matters to me to keep my dietary constraints, even if I can't claim to be totally "vegan" because of medicine and footwear anymore.

Lucy Parsons

In staying true to your principles, you can face racism in one of two ways—directly or indirectly, depending on the circumstance. Regardless of how you approach it, you will attract attention to yourself because the "race card" is often played in jail. It's a decisive tool the guards use to bolster their control and exercise their own racist sentiments. Some whites condone it in expectation of "white skin privilege"— fewer hassles, choice housing and program assignments. For a white to directly challenge such practices is to be scorned by the guards and fellow whites in subtle and not so subtle ways, and to be treated with contempt and regarded as a "race traitor." The other more direct approach is to voice one's criticism to fellow whites in private. Remember, people be checking all this out and your standing among them hangs in the balance.

Acting in solidarity with fellow prisoners is important and is expected. But a cautionary note is advised. Rely on your common sense. Avoid entanglements in dumb things. If you feel or think something should not be done, keep out of it and exercise discretion when your stand is questioned. People in here and on the streets may understand. (In blind anger and frustration, people may turn on you and—should you survive their attack—express contrition at a later time. Poor traumatized you. Malcolm X said: If people knew the meaning of revolution that they would "jump back into the alley.") Bear in mind that neither you nor your principles are running a popularity contest. The life you've chosen bears a terrible burden with grave responsibilities for others and for yourself.

Political Development in Prison

Many people have found that spending time in prison is one of the most radicalizing experiences a person can have. You will truly be in the belly of the beast and will experience firsthand what the state is capable of. You will probably also have more time on your hands for things like reading and writing—using that time to learn the history of struggle and figuring out your place in it can be an incredibly empowering thing to do from inside of a prison.

LUCY PARSONS

Out of sheer boredom or a desire to enhance your own political understanding, you read more while imprisoned. Your cell is both classroom and office. It's where you can improve your education, hone your communication and organizational skills, self-introspect, develop "do-able" projects that can be implemented on the streets. Hence, you find yourself organizing from afar; it becomes a school and a study in your own and others' capabilities, in human character. Not everyone is the same and thus you learn to relate to people accordingly. Most important is that you learn to become friends with yourself; you learn that you're more than a mere body that breathes and thinks; you discern (over time) that you're far more than that.

EMMA GOLDMAN

I have to depend on the great books that I get from AK Press and from friends to keep me informed of what is being learned and discussed on the outside. I read the *Earth First! Journal*, the *Industrial Worker*, *Fifth Estate* and *Monthly Review*, follow the mainstream news and engage in some discussion here with my fellow inmates. There's not that much interest in this community in specific groups, but rather in broader questions about how we all could live more responsibly (as in energy consumption, unionism, materialism, etc.).

JOHN BROWN

Political consciousness in prison is deviance. Reading and writing are deviance. A vegan diet is deviance. Different equals deviant. Deviant equals punishable.

There are now literally hundreds of free books to prisoner programs. In terms of reading, writing, and possibly small group discussions, prison is the place to be for political development. For anything beyond that—not so much.

Staying Connected

Staying connected to your friends, loved ones, support crew, and community will be vitally important to you while you are in prison. Letters, phone calls, and visits are the primary ways in which this will happen. Many federal facilities also now have email for prisoners (although, not internet access). If you need financial assistance to help cover some of these costs, there might be resources available to you. Ask your defense committee for help in tracking them down. If that is not possible, try contacting groups such as the Anarchist Black Cross (ABC). Maintaining strong, healthy relationships with people from inside a prison might seem like a daunting task and it certainly will not be easy. The state will do everything in its power to break down your connections with the outside world, which can sometimes make holding on to those connections seem even more important. Remember that all of your communications are monitored, but do not let that interfere with the emotional connections that need to happen for you to stay healthy and strong.

August Spies

Definitely crucial. I have been blessed with constant communication, visits, and so on. This has helped immensely. Really I cannot speak of what it is like to go without this connectedness.

This communication is vital for so many reasons. It helps in the more obvious ways of solidarity, love, warmth, etc. There are also the benefits of long-running dialogues, conversations through paper that allow us to focus our thoughts/experiences and trace our developments. And there is the additional vitality of synchronicity, and the immense value of sharing dreams, desires, experiences, and so on.

Voltairine de Cleyre

Stay connected to family and friends. If you really cared about them on the outside, don't let being in prison change that relationship.

Also, just because someone is close to you while on the outside, but out of touch during your imprisonment, don't necessarily mean they no longer care about you. Maybe they have a difficult time "seeing" you locked up. Never pressure anyone to visit you or write. The decision ought to be theirs only.

Should you decide to remain connected to and supportive of radical causes, remember you might pay a price for it. The prison administration might not take kindly to it, especially the parole board.

Lucy Parsons

You should be there for family, supporters, friends, and loved ones; and you should refrain from placing undue demands or requests on them. They did not put you where you are. They love and support you but, my dear friend, you yourself have to weather this adversity. Every tub has to stand on its own bottom.

Maintaining connection and continuing political work are expected of political prisoners, though at times the insurmountable charges, the sentence that has been imposed may dishearten some. Stay connected with those who support and love you, who are politically allied with you and are the lifeline of your tomorrows. It is hoped that your strength of spirit and character will eventually sort through all this, which makes you stronger and better prepared to confront the challenges ahead.

John Brown

In one fundamental way, prison is a matter of geography. You are on one side of a fence. Everyone you love is on the other side. You are not physically present. But you can be present in every other way. It just takes more work.

In dealing with others, it is very important to communicate well. You are dependent on others in a number of ways—missing a lot that you once took for granted. In my own experience, [my support website] is largely the work of others who transcribed my writings and designed the site and continue to post updates, etc.

A frustrating dynamic to avoid: Because people care about you and want your needs met and want you to be connected and engaged, supporters will have a tendency to take on too many projects or activities or support functions. Discourage this. Communicate that the worst possible scenario is for supporters to say "yes" but do "no." It is much better for supporters to only take on support they know they can do. Also, they have to know that if they take on support they cannot handle, they need to let you know as soon as possible: that there is no "penalty" for not accomplishing something; that it does not make them bad or wrong or uncaring, and that you benefit greatly from being informed so that you can find some alternate means for having that need met.

It can be a toxic dynamic if supporters take on too much and then leave the dependent captive with unmet needs as a consequence.

The importance in communicating needs. An example. A friend of mine from high school is fairly wealthy, wanted to "support" me. He bought me clothes boxes and food boxes and other luxuries designed to make me comfortable.

He considered that if he were in my position, his creature comfort would matter more than anything. But, for me, I wanted freedom. Legal struggle. An investment of resources into counsel and vindication, not into creature comforts. It is important that support knows the needs of the captive and responds to those needs. So, it is important that the captive expresses needs.

One constant struggle for any politically conscious captive is related to comforts. Do I want to be comfortable and therefore less motivated to struggle, or do I want to forego comforts and suffer hardships and stay hungry in the struggle? Do I want a television set or do I want the equivalent in books by revolutionary writers? Do I want a CD player and CDs? Do I want a food box with lots of bags of potato chips and feel like I'm "back on the block"?

Express your priorities.

Weathering Appeals

Post-conviction legal maneuvering can be an important part of a person's legal battles. But it is important to remember that the majority of appeals, *habeas corpus* petitions, and other forms of redress post-conviction are met with failure. This is not meant to discourage you from pursuing whatever options are available to you. It is meant instead as a word of caution about putting your hope in a legal system that has more than likely already failed you many times over.

Sometimes you will need to find a different lawyer to help you file appeals and *habeas corpus* petitions, as trial lawyers do not always specialize in this particular area. If you need help finding a lawyer to help with appeals, there might be resources available to you. Ask your defense committee, supporters, or loved ones to help you in your search. Remember that often appeals need to be filed within a certain time frame; once the time frame has passed, you lose your chance. The court will refuse to hear anything that is not filed in a timely manner—no matter how good you think your arguments might be. Even though the court wants *you* to act in a timely manner, they will take their time. There is often no set time frame for a court to respond to appeals, *habeas corpus* petitions, and other legal filings. Be prepared to wait a long time (often years). If you are granted oral arguments at the circuit level, you will probably not be present for them. Prisoners are not required to be present in court in most cases during the appeals process. For more information on the appeals process, see Appendix A.

LUCY PARSONS

You will find your court experiences trying, for they are like no other. By all means, submit your appeals and petitions to the court, but place your faith in none of them. That's just the way things are. In prison, it's generally understood that it's easy to put someone in prison and is hard for him or her to get out.

MONDO WE LANGA[118]

One thing that occurs to me is the matter of prisoners' expectations...what happens is that, often times, when a prisoner learns that a law or court ruling is favorable to him or her, he or she will come to believe that the state or court has to do something or other. This can be dangerous for a prisoner's state of mind. If and when his expectations get stepped on, the disappointment can be devastating…there is a world of difference between what a court should do or is empowered to do and what it will do. Realism, optimism, pessimism, etc. need to be talked about in the context of the criminal "justice" system. I would suspect that political prisoners are less vulnerable to victimization by unfounded faith in "the system."

JOHN BROWN

Courts are slow. Glacially slow. Also, courts rarely reverse. The fact that you're in prison proves that an upstanding and wise member of the bar selected for his or her outstanding acumen and judgment wants you in prison. Such an upstanding and wise judge cannot be second guessed. So, piece of advice, live in reality. Live in now. Do not escape from it in fantasies of vindication. Be effective in the now.

When facing a lot of time, it is a good coping mechanism to involve yourself in projects and activities that engage your mind and give you purpose. Also, you aren't doing 25 years. You're doing today. This week.

Nobody can eat a large pizza. But they can eat a slice, and then another one… Same with time. I've been locked up almost 23 years. I didn't do 23 years. I did a day—almost 8,000 times.

So, appeals and legal work and *habeas corpus* petitions are other-worldly events. Work, research, write, analyze, communicate, and wait…a lot. And while you wait, fill your life with other purposeful activity.

Another idea on supporting your needs. The best thing others can give you is purpose.

Ricardo Flores Magón[119]

Weather appeals, *habeas* petitions, etc…this is a psychological/mental challenge. My case has been challenged in every court it could be challenged within—multiple times in each court. I have filed every action I could think of and even seem to have created a few others—and each has been denied. For a person in my position—it is difficult to keep hearing a court tell me that I will die in prison. Sure, the court doesn't actually say that but the denial of the challenges simply reiterates the trial court decisions—life in prison. So, each denial was like being re-sentenced. But worse when I filed something the court agreed and would state in writing that I was correct—but still denied vacating the conviction… When that happens it can be difficult for the prisoner—really difficult. Even with outside support it can be a horrible thing to try to deal with.

Eric McDavid[120]

The way I've come to weather the time during the appeal/2255 process has been to let go of the way I've been molded to react with power dynamics—the system moves with bureaucratic mechanizations meant to be completely known by no one and regularly used by a specialized few; its ratcheting through time tends to cause confusion and disorientation to humyns caught within… Being in a space outside of trying to control it seems to have caused a shift in the pressurization intended by the process—letting go of the "knee-jerk" reactions creates room for something else, something that feels a lot healthier ~ feels like this may also speak to my experience at trial as well.

Dealing with Loss

Dealing with the loss of a loved one is never easy and from prison it can become infinitely more complicated and painful. And, of course, prison is set up to create a sense of loss in your day to day. Losing contact with friends, family, a beloved companion animal, your favorite place to watch the sunset…all of these can cause a real sense of loss. This is why it can be so important to maintain those ties as best you can. It may feel like you are dealing with loss all alone, but remember that lots of people are outside thinking of you, always—even if they cannot call you on the phone to send their love.

Lucy Parsons

Though your political activism might result in your arrest and imprisonment, you may never contemplate the possibility that a loved one might die or fall gravely ill during your imprisonment; prison officials seldom permit a "bedside visit" or allow one to attend a funeral. It happens! And your emotional support—a wife, girlfriend, an old friend—may grow weary of your circumstances. You may feel that they're moving on with their life without you. Sad but true; it happens! Yet there are also those who stay the course regardless of what you face. Suffice it to say that that's when friendships and commitment are put to the test; you may discover a surprising reality. It happens! And despite all this, you are expected to meet these challenges with equanimity and a brave heart. This is how we grow and earn the privilege to teach and lead, and learn.

Voltairine de Cleyre
We must be our own emotional supporters, because other inmates don't want to hear about your troubles: they have their own to worry about.

Emma Goldman
This has been the hardest. When my mother was dying of cancer two years ago, being away from her side was killing me. I used all of my phone minutes to call, and when she could no longer speak—my sister (who was her end of life caregiver) and I spoke almost daily so that I could encourage my sister and share her grief… It has been tremendously painful to have to be at a distance when I wish so much that I could be part of the family and friends holding [my children] up. I do what I can to let [them] know how precious [they] are to me, how much I love them and value them…but there are so many limitations, I'm so distant and blocked that it feels like a failure as a parent. That feels terrible. …

John Brown
Trauma is often magnified in prison. Dealing with loss, a prisoner often desires some privacy, some time and space apart from the daily madness in order to grieve, but prison is a place where there is no privacy, no solitude, no time or space away.

If you have developed real relationships with a select number of prisoners, then you have the luxury of expressing grief and receiving comfort on a local and immediate level. I have not lost anyone close to me while in prison, but I have known people who have. Grieving is experienced through sleeping a lot, or through talking through it, or through translating pain into anger and getting into a fight. Some coping is better than others.

Typically, those prisoners in a grieving captive's circle of friends will offer support, to include making food so the grieving captive doesn't have to go through the very public and social experience of going to the chow hall. That also helps the captive avoid confrontational scenarios while vulnerable and emotionally unsettled.

Concluding Thoughts

As these responses have undoubtedly shown, a common theme is that prison is a hard place that makes living difficult, especially living according to your revolutionary principles. Yet another theme is that staying connected to loved ones and radical movements is possible—doing so just takes a lot of sustained effort and internal fortitude. Many of the comments offered in this chapter are from people who have spent decades in prison. They have managed to survive while maintaining their revolutionary ideals and their connections to radical struggle. Their continued commitment to struggle makes them an integral part of our movements and communities, and an inspiration to those of us on the outside. You too can lead a life inside the reflects your ideals and commitments in a way that will make doing your time feel like your life is moving forward, instead of being put on pause by the state.

CONCLUSION

By now, you know that you have a long, hard road ahead. We hope that what you found in these pages has helped you achieve more clarity on what you are up against. Likewise, we hope this book has helped you figure out how to move forward in a way that allows you to maintain your integrity while moving closer to your personal, political, and legal goals for your case. We will not mince words—this sucks. It is a scary, frustrating, and overwhelming situation. There are a lot of unknowns, which can sometimes feel like the worst part about it. But remember that you *can* and *will* get through it. And you will not be alone.

Do not be afraid to ask for the help you need. There are people who have navigated this before you, both prisoners and their supporters. Their experiences and support will be invaluable to you as you move forward. Always remember that your responsible participation in your own defense is crucial. Act thoughtfully and carefully, with your movements and your comrades in mind. Remember that legal defense does not have to be a zero-sum game. Done well, legal defense work can leave our movements stronger while simultaneously discrediting the state (even if we do not achieve all of our legal goals). That does not mean that you will not make missteps along the way. You almost certainly will. Yet that does mean that you must always have your strategy in mind and your intentions must be clear. Be prepared for losses, but do not let them force you to lose sight of the bigger picture: handling your case in ways that strengthen radical and revolutionary movements.

Although it might seem that there is no end in sight, one day you will have gotten through this. Many people will have helped you reach that point, including people you have never met but whose experiences and wisdom have helped pave the way for radicals and revolutionaries such as yourself. The best way to show your love, respect, and gratitude to all of these people is to continue this work. For some, that can mean continuing the struggles you were engaged in before your arrest—either from outside the prison walls or inside. At the very least, that means supporting other people who find themselves facing the prospect of being locked up. Keep these future radicals in mind as you move through the laborious process of fighting your criminal charges. The lessons you learn today might help someone else stay free tomorrow.

Appendix A
THE CRIMINAL LEGAL PROCESS

The day of a person's arrest to the day they arrive in a federal or state prison can span a painfully long period of time. All the steps in between can be disorienting and confusing, and no person's experience is ever exactly the same as another's. But there is a basic process to the criminal legal system that remains fairly consistent for everyone. What follows is a brief description of the judicial process in the *federal* system (note that there will be differences in each state system).

1. Grand Jury/Preliminary Hearing

The prosecutor must show that there is "probable cause" that someone has committed a crime to hold them after an arrest. This usually happens in one of two ways—either through a grand jury indictment or through a preliminary hearing. All felony cases in the federal system require an indictment from a grand jury (these can be bypassed for misdemeanors). If the grand jury finds that there is probable cause, they will then issue a formal indictment that charges the person with a specific crime or crimes. Grand juries basically just rubber stamp indictments for prosecutors, so this process is a mere formality. For more information on grand juries, visit GRANDJURYRESISTANCE.ORG.

In some jurisdictions (not a federal case), probable cause will be established through a preliminary hearing. The preliminary hearing can happen before or after an arraignment. The preliminary hearing, which is held before a judge, is when the prosecutor must establish that there is reason to hold a person for a particular crime. Hearsay evidence is often admissible and the defendant's attorney is present.

2. Arraignment

The arraignment is often the first time a person will appear before a judge. During this time, the person will be told the charges against them and informed of their right to representation. They will also be asked to enter a plea (e.g., guilty or not guilty) and bail may be set. The court may also set a date for trial, but this is almost never when the trial will actually happen. The arraignment may be combined with the preliminary hearing.

3. Bail Hearing(s)

The bail hearing is often combined with the arraignment, but sometimes a separate hearing may be set, or there might be multiple bail hearings. Bail hearings determine whether or not a judge feels that someone meets the requirements to be released from jail pre-trial. These requirements include whether or not the person is a flight risk and whether or not they are a danger to their community. The judge can consider factors such as prior criminal history, the nature of the offense (e.g., was it "violent"? did it involve narcotics?), a person's financial resources, their physical/mental condition, and more. There is a lower standard of proof during a bail hearing. Social media pages have been used against defendants at bail hearings, and so has prisoner support. A person may be released on their own recognizance, or they may be forced to post bail or bond. At these hearings, defendants can benefit from providing the court with evidence that a person is not a flight risk and not a danger to the community. This evidence can take the form of letters from family and loved ones to prove that the person has a close-knit family and strong, long-term ties to their community. A person can also call witnesses during a bail hearing, such as parents, employers, teachers, supervisors from volunteer agencies, etc. This is also a good time to bring up any medical conditions someone might have that would necessitate their release pre-trial. Make sure you have a note on the doctor's stationary about these conditions

If bail is not granted the first time around, you can keep trying. Sometimes circumstances change that might make a judge more likely to grant bail at a later date. In some instances, a Pre-Trial Services report (PTS) might be prepared to help the court assess whether or not a person should be released pre-trial (it might also be referred to as an OR report ["Own Recognizance" report] if release without bail is an option). The office in charge of these reports will interview the prisoner and ask them for phone numbers of friends and family so they can confirm the information given to them by the prisoner. If someone is contacted by a person preparing one of these reports, it can be very helpful to provide them with information confirming what a wonderful person their friend is; however, people need to be extremely cautious with situations like this. They should absolutely NOT talk to law enforcement about their friend under any circumstances. People should confirm that they are, in fact, speaking with someone who is working on a PTS or OR report. They should only answer questions to confirm things such as addresses, job histories, volunteer histories, and so forth.

4. Pre-trial Motion Hearings

Pre-trial motions are filed by both the defense and the prosecution. The motions are submitted in writing (and often filed online); many are argued at a hearing before the judge. The motions address various issues that need to be hammered out before a case actually goes to trial. These can include issues like what kind of evidence can and cannot be introduced, who can and cannot testify, and on what grounds the case could possibly be dismissed altogether. For example, if a person was illegally wiretapped, or if there was no search warrant issued when the house was raided, there could be grounds to exclude that evidence from being used at trial. Motions addressing various discovery issues can also be heard during these hearings. Although they are usually tedious courtroom experiences, laden with lots of legal details and jargon, many important issues are decided at motion hearings.

5. Trial

Trials can last anywhere from a couple of days to a couple of months, depending on the amount of evidence to be presented and the number of witnesses to be called. Most trials will not go longer than a couple of weeks. The first day of a trial is usually comprised mostly of jury selection. Then opening arguments are presented. The prosecution will present its case first (along with all of its witnesses), and then the defense will present theirs (if they choose to do so—defendants are not required to present any defense against the state's allegations). The trial concludes with closing arguments, generally from the prosecution first and the defense second.

After all the evidence has been presented, the jury will file into the jury room and begin their deliberations. If they have any questions for the court about the trial proceedings, witness testimony, legal definitions, or the instructions the judge gave them for deciding on their verdict, those questions must be answered in open court to allow the attorneys an opportunity to object to the responses given. Juries must deliberate until they have a unanimous verdict (this is true in a federal case but can differ a bit from state to state). This decision can often take several days.

Once a verdict is reached, the jury will notify the court that they have reached a decision. Once this happens, there is generally not much time for supporters to get back to the courthouse. Thus, it might be necessary for folks to stay close by while the jury is in deliberations. The lawyer can call someone to tell them when a verdict has been reached. If the jury is unable to reach a verdict, they will inform the judge that they are deadlocked and a hung jury will be declared. At this point, the prosecution must decide whether or not they will demand a new trial.

Trial is, obviously, an incredibly emotional time for everyone. Listening to the government and their witnesses lie about you and your comrades to a jury who will decide your future is frustrating, maddening, and sad. But this may also be a time when you will really need to help your lawyer as they prepare each evening for the next day of trial.

6. Sentencing

If you are convicted, the next phase will be sentencing. This can be one of the hardest things to wait for. Knowing that you are going to prison—but not knowing for how long, or to what kind of facility, or to where—can be incredibly nerve-wracking.

There are a couple of things that must happen before someone is sentenced. A Pre-Sentencing Report (PSR) must be filed by the probation office. This report is the result of the pre-sentence investigation (PSI), an incredibly thorough interview of each prisoner by the probation office prior to their sentencing. The PSI/PSR contains general information about the defendant's history and characteristics, but also specifically includes: prior criminal records, the defendant's financial condition, any circumstances affecting the defendant's behavior that may be helpful in determining a sentence or "correctional" treatment, victim impact statements, and so on. The PSR must also calculate a defendant's recommended sentence based on the advisory United States Sentencing Guidelines.

The PSR is crucial. Not only does it guide the judge in deciding what kind of sentence they will dole out, it also follows a prisoner throughout their experience within the BOP. This report helps determine the prisoner's security designation, what geographic location they will be sent to, work assignments, transfers, etc. It can affect how they are treated by the guards and other prison staff. Because of this, it is important to get everything into the PSR that needs to be there. This can include things such as dietary needs (e.g., vegan), medical issues, work experience, education, etc. The PSR is written by an employee of the federal government, so do not expect it to be fair and balanced. The defense attorney can and should submit a formal objection to any inaccurate information in the PSR. Also, the defense attorney should accompany the defendant when the interview is being conducted.

Both the defense and the prosecution can submit sentencing memorandums. These are usually filed after the PSR is written and contain each side's arguments for or against the sentence recommended by probation. These arguments will be heard by the judge at the sentencing hearing. The judge is the ultimate decision maker when it comes to sentencing, and it is not uncommon for a judge to depart from what probation recommends (unfortunately, that departure is usually an upward departure). The judge can also make a recommendation that a person be sent to a specific facility, which is usually made in an effort to get someone as close to home and their friends/family as possible. By law, the BOP is supposed to consider the recommendation of the sentencing judge; in practice, they only do this when they want to for some reason. A judge's recommendation does not mean that a person will end up in that specific facility; it should never be expected that a person's request will be honored. For people interested in doing on-line research about this and other federal sentencing issues, a good place to start is Alan Ellis's website, WWW.ALANELLIS.COM (this law office specializes in sentencing and post-conviction actions for federal criminal defendants and has helpful tips, resources, and publications on their website).

Being transferred to a federal facility after sentencing can take several months. Again, this might be some of the hardest waiting that you will have to do. Once the transfer process begins, it can take several months for a person to reach their final destination as they bounce from county jail to federal facility to county jail. Communication can be sparse and difficult at this time.

7. Appeals

If you plan to file an appeal (e.g., of the conviction, for problems with the process at trial, of the sentencing), you must do so within a specified amount of time. For federal cases, a notice of appeal must be filed by the defendant within ten days of the "judgment," aka sentencing. An appeal is *not* a new trial (although a new trial may be the result of an appeal), and no new evidence can be presented during an appeal. An appeal consists of a brief filed by the defendant's attorney that outlines the problematic issues that occurred during trial/sentencing, along with excerpts from the record. The prosecution files a response to this brief, and then the defense has the option of filing a reply. After this, a panel of judges from the appeals court will review the briefs and anything from the record that has been submitted. Oral arguments may be heard, but they are very brief and usually focused on legal details. After everything has been submitted and oral arguments have been heard, it can take the court over a year to issue their decision. It is not uncommon for the entire appeals process to take two to four years or more.

There are various possible outcomes from an appeal. The appeals court could find that errors were made during trial and order that a new trial be conducted. They could order a new sentence be issued. In extremely rare cases, they could decide that there was insufficient evidence to convict (or another significant error was made) and they could then direct the district court to vacate the verdict. Or, they could decide that no errors were made (or that the errors were "insignificant") and the lower court's ruling should stand.

Final Thoughts

Reading about this system that is somehow billed as the "justice" system and experiencing it are two dramatically different things. The steps above seem logical and straightforward, but the reality is that they are anything but. Both defense attorneys and prosecutors are notorious for filing for extensions of time, dragging out the pre-trial timeline. Dates will be moved repeatedly. Things always take longer than they are supposed to and planning for anything can be incredibly difficult. This is especially true if you are trying to keep supporters informed and involved. Getting supporters to come to court dates can be inspiring and powerful, but it can be complicated when those dates change at the very last minute (often even the night before or the day of). Additionally, the procedural intricacies of the system are often more important in determining the outcome at trial than all of the so-called facts and evidence in the case.

Remember that often some of the most important decisions are made out of the presence of the jury during the trial, or well before the jury is ever selected. It is important for people in the wider community to know about these decisions, as they may affect our friends and movements in the future. Also, bear in mind how much is left up to the judge in a criminal case. They control what evidence is admitted and what is excluded. They decide who can testify, what defense strategies can be used and how they can be used (the extent of their say in these matters can be limited at times, though), and what legal definitions will be presented to the jury. Unfortunately, a bad judge can be worse than a bad jury, a bad prosecutor, and a bad attorney combined.

Perhaps most importantly, remember that this process is long, tedious and full of surprises. Things can take forever…but they can also change in an instant. Try to be ready for anything and remember that you do not have to do this alone. There are people ready and willing to support you and to help guide you through this process, as many have been here before.

Appendix B
SAMPLE JOINT DEFENSE AGREEMENT

JOINT DEFENSE/WAIVER OF CONFLICTS OF INTEREST

We, ___(Defendant Names)___ hereby agree as follows:

1. We understand that attorney, ___(Attorney One)___, currently represents ___(Defendant One)___ in the matter, ___(Case Number/Name)___, in ___(Court District)___; ___(Attorney Two)___ represents ___(Defendant Two)___ in that same case; and ___(Attorney Three)___ represents ___(Defendant Three)___. The criminal charges pending arise out of the incident that occurred on ___(Brief Description of Alleged Incident)___.

2. We understand that there is a possible conflict of interest between ___(Defendant Names)___ in that we may have claims against each other, including possible claims for the injuries received, and possible joint liability both civil and criminal.

3. We understand that due to the possibility of these claims, Attorneys __(Attorney One)__ , __(Attorney Two)__ and __(Attorney Three)__ (hereinafter "Attorneys") would have a conflict of interest, and would not be permitted to represent co-ordinate and cooperate unless all three of us waive any conflict of interests we have with each other arising out of the __(Alleged Incident)__ and regarding any and all issues and claims related to __(Alleged Incident)__ , and the actions of any and all protesters participating in any of those events.

4. We further understand that we individually hold the privilege of attorney client privilege, in that __(Attorney One)__ , __(Attorney Two)__ and __(Attorney Three)__ are not permitted to divulge any matters which are confidential between her and each of us, unless each of us so agree.

5. We understand that we have the right to consult another attorney with regard to these rights and claims. We hereby waive our right to consult another attorney.

6. By agreement of the parties and waiver of any conflicts or potential conflicts, we consent to the Attorneys cooperating and coordinating legal defense, information and legal strategies.

II. MUTUALITY OF INTEREST

We believe that there is a mutuality of interest between __(Defendant Names)__ in a common and joint defense or any and all criminal claims in regard to these matters and

any related civil, or administrative proceedings. In this regard, we wish to retain the respective Attorneys to represent
ourselves in our separate but common interests and to avoid
any suggestions of waiver of the confidentiality of privileged
communications, memoranda and documents. Accordingly,
it is our intention and understanding that communications
among them, either through the various Attorneys and their
firms, or otherwise, and any joint interviews of prospec-
tive witnesses, are confidential and are protected from disclosure to any third party by attorney-client and attorneys'
work-product privileges.

III. MAINTENANCE OF PRIVILEGE

In order to pursue our joint defense and joint claims effectively, we have also concluded that, from time to time, my
mutual interests will be best served by sharing documents,
factual material, mental impressions, strategies, legal theo-
ries, memoranda, interview reports, and other information,
including their confidences, all of which will hereinafter be
referred to as "Clients Materials." In the absence of such sharing, these Plaintiffs and Defense Materials would be privileged from disclosure to adverse or other parties as a result
of the attorney-client privilege, the attorney work-product
privilege or other applicable privileges. It is the purpose of
this Agreement to ensure that the exchanges and disclosures
of Clients Materials contemplated herein do not diminish in
any way the confidentiality of the Clients Materials and do
not constitute a waiver of any privilege otherwise available.

IV. CONSENT AND OTHER RIGHTS

To this end, it is understood and agreed that information obtained by Attorneys either from ___(Defendant Names)___ shall remain confidential and shall be protected from disclosure to any third party except as provided herein. It is further understood and agreed that any documents exchanged between us, either through Attorneys or otherwise, and the information contained therein, and any other confidences exchanged between ___(Defendant Names)___ shall be used solely in connection with the any and all Lawsuits, the Investigation, and any related civil, and criminal or administrative proceedings arising out of the incident of ___(Alleged Incident)___. We further agree that we will not disclose any Materials received from ___(Defendant Names)___ or through Attorneys or the contents thereof, to anyone without first obtaining the consent of all parties who may be entitled to claim any privilege with respect to such materials.

V. DEMAND OR SUBPOENA OF MATERIAL

If any other person or entity requests or demands, by subpoena or otherwise, any Defense Materials received from the other, directly or through Attorneys or jointly obtained on behalf of both parties, the party receiving the request or demand will immediately notify the other party. The person or entity seeking such Defense Materials will be informed that these materials are only on loan and that demand should be made on the appropriate party. Each party will take all steps necessary to permit the assertion of all application rights and privileges with respect to said Defense Materials and shall cooperate fully with the other in any judicial proceeding relating to disclosure of the Defense Materials.

VI. JOINT DEFENSE DOCTRINE

It is understood that all work performed by The Attorneys, their respective law firms attorneys, employees and agents with regard to its representations and communicated to either ___(Defendant Names)___ or all of them in connection with these representations shall be accomplished pursuant to the work product and the attorney-client privilege and to the "joint defense doctrine" (joint representation doctrine) and all other applicable rights and privileges, including those recognized in Continental Oil Company v. United States, 220 F.2d 347 (9th Cir.1964); Hunydee v. United States, 355 F.2d 183 (9th Cir.1965), In the Matter of a Grand Jury Subpoena Dated November 16, 1974, 406 F.Supp. 381 (S.D.N.Y.1975), and United States v. McPartlin, 595 F.2d 1321 (7th Cir.1979).

VII. CHANGED CIRCUMSTANCES

In the event any party decides to withdraw from this Agreement for any reason, that party shall immediately notify each named Attorney herein of that parties' withdrawal from this Agreement, which will thereupon be terminated as to that party; provided, however, that no such termination shall effect or impair the obligations of confidentiality with respect to materials previously furnished pursuant to this Agreement. Further, any party, upon withdrawal, shall return all materials provided by the other parties hereto, including any copies of Defense Materials.

VIII. CONFLICT OF INTEREST AND DISQUALIFICATION

We hereby further agree that in the event that if we withdraw from this Agreement, nothing in this Agreement shall create a conflict of interest so as to require the disqualification of the Law Offices of ___(Attorney One)___ from the representation of the other and we hereby waive any such conflict of interest.

It is agreed, however, that each named Attorney herein, shall not be disqualified based upon said firm's participation in this Agreement, from examining or cross-examining either ___(Defendant Names)___ if any testifies at any proceeding, whether under grant of immunity or otherwise.

IX. LIMITATION OF DUTIES AND CONFLICTS

We have been advised, and have agreed, that each Attorney will be acting only as the attorney for its client in each action and will owe a duty of loyalty only to its client. ___(Attorney One)___ represents ___(Defendant One)___, ___(Attorney Two)___ represents ___(Defendant Two)___ and ___(Attorney Three)___ represents ___(Defendant Three)___. Each client has agreed to knowingly and intelligently waive any conflict of interest that may arise from the Attorneys examining them at any proceeding.

X. INJUNCTIVE RELIEF

We acknowledge that disclosure of any communication in violation of this Agreement will cause the parties hereto to suffer irreparable harm for which there is no adequate legal remedy. Each party hereto acknowledges that immediate injunctive relief is an appropriate and necessary remedy for any violation or threatened violation of the Agreement.

XI. CONTINUANCE OF AGREEMENT

This Agreement shall continue in effect notwithstanding any conclusion or resolution as to either the criminal or civil Lawsuits or the Investigations or any administrative, civil, or criminal proceedings arising from or relating to any of them. I agree that I will continue to be bound by this Agreement following any such conclusion or resolution.

XII. NON WAIVER

Any waiver in any particular instance of the rights and limitations contained herein shall not be deemed, and is not intended to be, a general waiver of any rights or limitations contained herein and shall not operate as a waiver beyond the particular instance.

XIII. EXPLANATION AND MODIFICATION

By signing this Agreement, I (we) certify that the contents of this Joint Defense Agreement have been explained to us (me), and that I (we) agree to abide by the understandings reflected in the Agreement. Any modifications of the Agreement must be in writing and signed by all parties.

The foregoing is agreed to by the following parties as of the date first written below.

Date: ____(Insert Date)____ By ____(Defendant One Signature)____

Date: ____(Insert Date)____ By ____(Defendant Two Signature)____

Date: ____(Insert Date)____ By ____(Defendant Three Signature)____

APPROVED: ____(Attorney One Signature)____

_____(Attorney One Name), Esq.____

APPROVED: ____(Attorney Two Signature)____

_____(Attorney Two Name), Esq.____

APPROVED: ____(Attorney Three Signature)____

_____(Attorney Three Name), Esq.____

Appendix C

SAMPLE ATTORNEY RETAINER AGREEMENT

RETAINER AGREEMENT

This Agreement is entered into by and between _____("Client") and _____("Attorney").

1. On execution of this agreement, Client shall pay Attorney $ __2000.00__ as a retainer to assure Attorney's availability for: __WITNESS REPRESENTATION__ .

2. SCOPE AND DUTIES. Client hires Attorney to provide legal services in connection with __FBI INVESTIGATION UNKNOWN CASE NUMBER__ . Attorney shall provide those legal services reasonably required to represent Client, and shall take reasonable steps to keep Client informed of progress and to respond to Client's inquiries. Client shall be truthful with Attorney, cooperate with Attorney, keep Attorney informed of developments, abide by this Contract, pay Attorney's bills on time, and keep Attorney advised of Client's address, telephone number, and whereabouts.

3. TRUST, FEES, AND RETAINER AMOUNT. Client understands that the retainer shall be held in trust by Attorney for payment of costs, fees, and expenses. Attorney's time in this matter shall be billed at the regular rate of __$80.00__ per hour. Client further understands and agrees that __$1,000.00__ of the retainer amount shall be deemed non-refundable upon execution of this agreement; any other retainer amount in trust at the conclusion of services or termination of this agreement shall be returned to Client.

4. EXTRAORDINARY SERVICES. Extraordinary services are subject to Attorney's regular hourly fee of $150.00. Attorney will notify Client of any proceedings not covered by this contract. If Client wishes Attorney to provide additional legal services a separate written agreement will be required.

5. COSTS AND EXPENSES. In addition to legal fees, Client shall reimburse Attorney for all costs and expenses incurred by Attorney, including but not limited to process servers' fees, fees fixed by law or assessed by courts or other agencies, court reporters' fees, long distance telephone calls, messenger and other delivery fees, postage, photocopying, investigation expenses, consultants' fees, expert witness fees, and other similar items. Client authorizes Attorney to incur all reasonable costs and to hire any investigators, consultants, or expert witnesses reasonably necessary in Attorney's judgment. Attorney shall obtain Client's consent before incurring any cost in excess of $100. Attorney shall obtain Client's consent

before retaining outside investigators, consultants, or expert witnesses.

6. STATEMENTS. Attorney shall send Client periodic statements for fees and costs incurred. Payment for costs and fees will be withdrawn from the Client trust account. Client may request a statement at intervals of no less than 30 days. On Client's request Attorney will provide a statement within 10 days.

7. DISCHARGE AND WITHDRAWAL. Client may discharge Attorney at any time. Attorney may withdraw with Client's consent or for good cause. Good cause includes Client's breach of this Contract, Client's refusal to cooperate with Attorney or to follow Attorney's advice on a material matter, or any other fact or circumstance that would render Attorney's continuing representation unlawful or unethical.

8. CONCLUSION OF SERVICES. When Attorney's services conclude, all unpaid charges shall become immediately due and payable. After Attorney's services conclude, Attorney will, on client's request, deliver Client's file to Client, along with any client funds or property in Attorney's possession.

9. DISCLAIMER OF GUARANTEE. Nothing in this Contract and nothing in Attorney's statements to Client will be construed as a promise or guarantee about the outcome of Client's matter. Attorney makes no such promises or guarantees. Attorney's comments

about the outcome of Client's matter are expressions of opinion only.

10. CLIENT RIGHTS AND RESPONSIBILITIES. The Client has the right to be informed of all developments as they occur and to copies of all pertinent documents. The Client file and all its contents are the property of the client and will be made available upon request. It is the responsibility of the client to inform the attorney of reliable and current contact information.

Executed on _____(date)_____ by:

_____
(Attorney Signature)
_____
(Attorney Name)
Attorney at Law

_____
(Client Signature)
_____
(Client Name)
Client

ENDNOTES

1   Nelson Mandela, *Long Walk to Freedom: The Autobiography of Nelson Mandela* (New York: Little, Brown and Company, 1994), 341.

2   See *Lafler v. Cooper*, 132 S. Ct. 1376, 182 L. Ed. 2D 398 (2012).

3   See John William Sayer, *Ghost Dancing the Law: The Wounded Knee Trials* (Cambridge, MA: Harvard University Press, 1997).

4   This analysis is not to discount or ignore the realities of social harm, as people hurt, injure, assault, murder, wrong, and oppress other people every minute of every day. These social harms are serious and should be treated as such. Many times, the criminal legal system criminalizes these harms and provides those who have been harmed with some measure of redress for what they have suffered. While the state presents this system as the sole means of receiving justice after suffering harm, it also uses this system in inherently oppressive ways to benefit those with power. Thus it is by design and not by chance that people with money and power more often avoid arrest and criminal charges, receive lighter sentences, or get acquitted of charges than poor people, people of color, trans / intersex / gender non-conforming / queer people, or other oppressed

people. This reality shows that this system is not designed to address social harm and in fact prevents most people from receiving justice after being harmed.

5 Michael Deutsch, "The National Lawyer's Guild Work Defending Independentistas in the U.S.," *Claridad*, 21 October 2013, This article by Michael Deutsch of the National Lawyers Guild, written with assistance from Guild attorney Jan Susler, is a good source of information on the Puerto Rican independence fighters. Other independence fighters indicted on seditious conspiracy include Oscar López Rivera, who was sentenced to seventy years and is still incarcerated at the time of this writing, and Maria Haydée Torres, who was sentenced to life but was released after serving thirty years. As explained in the article, "In April of 1980, 11 Puerto Ricans were arrested in Evanston, Illinois and accused of being part of the FALN. They were first tried in state court and sentenced to terms of 8 to 30 years. The US then indicted them for seditious conspiracy, the same charge lodged against Albizu Campos and other Nationalist Party members in the 1930s and in the 1950s. Like Morales, the accused FALN prisoners, Carlos Alberto Torres, Carmen Valentin, Dylcia Pagan, Alicia Rodriguez, Lucy Rodriguez, Elizam Escobar, Ricardo Jimenez, Luis Rosa, Adolfo Matos, and Alfredo Mendez also asserted their right to be treated as POWs. Assisted by Guild lawyers who acted as legal advisers, since the accused refused to participate in what they considered an illegal trial, the accused filed an extensive document supporting their claim under international law. The lawyers also filed a petition with the UN Human Rights Commission and raised their case in international fora in Malta, Barcelona and Cuba. The federal prosecution resulted in grossly disproportionate sentences ranging from 55 to 90 years, with the judge lamenting that he could not give them the death penalty."

6   The BLA formed after a rift within the Black Panther Party (BPP). Assata Shakur's website offers this short overview: "Q: What is the Black Liberation Army (BLA)? A: The year was 1971. The FBI, CIA, and local police department's Counter-Intelligence Program planted degenerative seeds to increase tensions and factionalism within the Black Panther Party for Self-Defense (BPP). Their efforts culminated in the split between Huey P. Newton and Eldridge Cleaver. While Newton continued leadership of the broken BPP, Cleaver went on to lead what came to be known as the Black Liberation Army (BLA), which had previously existed as the underground faction and "fighting apparatus" of the BPP. The BLA is notorious for allegedly waging war against local police department oppressors through police car bombings. Q: What are the principles of the Black Liberation Army? A: The BLA, as a result of realizing the economical nature of the system under which we are forced to live, maintains the following principles: 1. That we are anti-capitalist, anti-imperialist, anti-racist, and anti-sexist. 2. That we must of necessity strive for the abolishment of these systems and for the institution of Socialistic relationships in which Black people have total and absolute control over their own destiny as a people. 3. That in order to abolish our systems of oppression, we must utilize the science of class struggle, develop this science as it relates to our unique national condition." WWW.ASSATASHAKUR. ORG/FORUM/RBG-STREET-SCHOLARS-THINK-TANK/23010-WHAT-BLACK-LIBERATION-ARMY-BLA.HTML.

7   To learn more about the Palmer raids, see Robert Murray, *Red Scare: A Study in National Hysteria, 1919–1920* (Westport, Conn.: Greenwood Press, 1980). To learn more about COINTELPRO (the Counter Intelligence Program), one good book is Ward Churchill and Jim Vander Wall, *Agents of Repression: The FBI's Secret Wars Against the Black Panther Party and the American Indian*

Movement (Cambridge, MA: South End Press, 2002). A good documentary is The Freedom Archives, "COINTELPRO 101," 2010 (available at www.freedomarchives.org/Cointelpro. html). To learn more about the Green Scare, a good place to start is Will Potter, *Green is the New Red: An Insider's Account of a Social Movement Under Siege* (San Francisco: City Lights Books, 2011).

8   To learn more about the FBI's use of entrapment in Muslim communities, see Trevor Aaronson, *The Terror Factory: Inside the FBI's Manufactured War on Terrorism* (Brooklyn, New York: Ig Publishing, 2013).

9   Even the Supreme Court of the United States has acknowledged that about 95% of all criminal cases are resolved through plea agreements. The idea of a "fair trial by a jury of your peers" is a myth that only becomes a reality for a few—and those few are likely to have the money and power needed to make that myth a reality.

10   *Black's Law Dictionary* defines "habeas corpus" as "Lat. (You have the body.) The name given to a variety of writs (of which these were anciently the emphatic words) having for their object to bring a party before a court or judge. In common usage, and whenever these words are used alone, they are understood to mean the habeas corpus *ad subjiciendum* (see infra.)." Translated from legalese, this is basically a legal concept that allows for a range of challenges to a prison sentence. Available at thelawdictionary.org/ habeas-corpus.

11   In 2015, Joseph was indicted under the AETA once again, this time with Nicole Kissane. At the time of this writing, Joseph was serving a two-year federal sentence and Nicole was awaiting trial. From supportnicoleandjoseph.com/: "On July 24th, 2015, Nicole Kissane and Joseph Buddenberg were arrested and federally indicted for alleged Conspiracy to Violate the Animal Enterprise Terrorism Act—Title 18, U.S.C., Section 43 (a) (1),

(2) (c) and (b) (3) (A). A FEDERAL GRAND JURY INDICTMENT alleges that Nicole and Joseph conspired to 'travel in interstate and foreign commerce for the purpose of causing physical disruption to the functioning of animal enterprises, to intentionally damage and cause the loss of real and personal property, including, but not limited to, animals and records used by the animal enterprises, and caused economic damage in an amount exceeding $100,000' by allegedly releasing thousands of animals from fur farms and destroying breeding records in Idaho, Iowa, Minnesota, Montana, Wisconsin, and Pennsylvania. The indictment also alleges that they caused economic damage to various retail and distribution businesses and individuals associated with the fur industry."

12   In-depth reporting by Will Potter on the case of the AETA 4, as well as copies of legal documents from this case, can be found at WWW.GREENISTHENEWRED.COM.

13   Information about Dhoruba Bin Wahad taken from a Democracy Now! Interview on December 7, 2000, available at WWW.DEMOCRACYNOW.ORG/2000/12/7/COINTELPRO_25_YEARS_LATER_NEW_YORK# and another one on December 8, 2000, available at WWW.DEMOCRACYNOW.ORG/2000/12/8/COINTEL_PRO_25_YEARS_LATER_NEW#.

14   For more information about Marilyn Buck and to read some of her poetry and other writings, see MARILYNBUCK.COM/INDEX.HTML.

15   For more information about Herman Wallace and the Angola 3, see ANGOLA3NEWS.BLOGSPOT.COM. Robert was released in 2001 after his conviction was overturned, and Albert was released in February 2016, on his birthday, after signing a no-contest plea to lesser charges.

16   Not everyone has the same level of support, unfortunately, and long-term prisoners may experience ebbs and flows in the support

they receive. People involved in revolutionary struggle and social movements outside of prison certainly have the responsibility of supporting their prisoners and reaching out to them, so hopefully they will be there should you need to reach out to them from the inside.

17   Attorney-client privilege is a legal term that describes the protections that defendants and their attorneys are supposed to have in their communications and trial preparations (often referred to as "work product"). Much of your communications with your attorney should be confidential, although some things your attorney will be required to share with the prosecution (i.e., these materials will be "discoverable"). Asking your attorney to lay out what is and is not protected by attorney-client privilege is a necessity for all defendants, particularly those facing charges for the first time.

18   A caveat is that new prisoners are often asked about their charges as soon as they enter the jail or prison (or are transferred to new areas within the facility) because the other prisoners want to make sure they are not a snitch or a child molester. Telling other prisoners the charges you are facing or pleading guilty to may be the safest move, but this is not the same as discussing the details or facts of your case.

19   Some exceptions exist. In some jurisdictions, a defendant can withdraw a guilty plea when an agreement was negotiated with the prosecutor but the judge decides to vary from it, such as by increasing the length of incarceration. This option can be more of a technical possibility than an actual move that can be made, however, as the judge generally needs to approve the withdrawal of the plea.

20   One of the clearest examples of this comes from Marius Mason's case. Marius is serving twenty-two years for a number of Earth Liberation Front actions. He had been a long-time environmental activist and member of the Industrial Workers of the World

(IWW) before he was betrayed by his ex-husband, Frank Ambrose, who cooperated with the FBI to tape record him and others talking about their previous actions in exchange for a lighter sentence for himself. During the sentencing phase of his case, postings from his MySpace page were used against him, as was an article he had written for *Fifth Estate* magazine about his arrest. The prosecution also used the fact of his widespread support network against him in their sentencing memo. Formerly known as Marie Mason, Marius came out as trans in July 2014 and announced that he wanted to be referred to as Marius Jacob Mason and use he/him/ his pronouns. From SUPPORTMARIUSMASON.ORG/ABOUT/: "Marius Mason is an anarchist, an environmental and animal rights prisoner serving nearly 22 years in federal prison for acts of sabotage carried out in defense of the planet. No one was injured in any of these actions. After being threatened with a life sentence in 2009, he pleaded guilty to charges of arson at a Michigan State University lab researching Genetically Modified Organisms for Monsanto, and admitted to 12 other acts of property damage. The sentencing judge applied a so-called 'terrorism enhancement' to his term which added almost two more years than the maximum requested by the prosecution. This is the harshest punishment of anyone convicted of environmental sabotage to date."

21   The "discovery" in your case is the evidence against you that you receive from the prosecutor, as well as the materials your attorney is required to provide to the prosecutor. The prosecutor is required to share all the evidence with you and your lawyer, although getting them to comply with this requirement is often an uphill battle.

22   CeCe McDonald gained international recognition and support as a result of the political organizing undertaken by her supporters. She was released from prison in January 2014, having spent the entirety of it in men's facilities, to serve the remainder of her sentence on

parole. For more on CeCe, visit SUPPORTCECE.WORDPRESS.COM.
There is also a documentary about her case: "Free CeCe!," directed
by Jac Gares (Jac Gares Media, Inc., 2016). WWW.FREECECEDOCU-
MENTARY.NET.

23   The Symbionese Liberation Army operated in California from
      1973 to 1975. The group grew out of prison organizing between
      an African-American activist and radical white supporters on the
      outside. They proposed to move the African-American freedom
      struggle forward through urban guerrilla warfare. One notable
      action was the kidnapping of millionaire heiress Patty Hearst.
      Kathleen Soliah apparently participated in robbing a bank in
      1975 (in which a customer accidentally was murdered), and in
      making and placing two pipe bombs under police cars. After her
      indictment for the bombing attempt and before she could be
      arrested, she fled California for Minnesota. There she assumed the
      name Sarah Jane Olson, married a doctor, raised three daughters,
      participated in community theater productions, and worked on
      progressive political causes. An episode of *America's Most Wanted* (a
      TV show) profiled her in 1999, and a tipster phoned the FBI with
      an identification. See EN.WIKIPEDIA.ORG/WIKI/SARA_JANE_OLSON.

24   The Cleveland 4 are four anarchists who had been involved in
      Occupy Cleveland when they were targeted and entrapped by an
      FBI informant by the name of Shaquille Azir. Azir orchestrated a
      plot to bomb a bridge outside of Cleveland with C4, arranging the
      purchase of explosives from an undercover FBI agent and pushing
      some of the defendants to meet with and strike a deal with this
      "arms dealer." Azir provided some of the defendants with free
      housing, paid work, alcohol, and drugs throughout his operation.
      Three of the defendants—Brandon Baxter, Connor Stevens, Doug
      Wright—took plea agreements early on. Connor was sentenced to
      eight years, Brandon to ten, Skelly to ten, and Doug to eleven and

a half, and all of them were given life-time supervised release after serving their sentences. Joshua "Skelly" Stafford took his case to trial, representing himself, and was convicted to ten years plus life-time supervised release. They all appealed the life-time supervised release and all of these appeals were denied. More information can be found at CLEVELAND4SOLIDARITY.ORG.

25 The Lucasville 5 are Siddique Abdullah Hasan (aka Carlos Sanders), Jason Robb, Bomani Shakur, George Skatzes, and James Were. There is a documentary film about the Lucasville prison uprising: "The Great Incarcerator, Part 2: The Shadow of Lucasville," directed by D Jones. DARKLITTLESECRETMOVIE.COM/ THE-GREAT-INCARCERATOR-PART-2-THE-SHADOW-OF-LUCASVILLE. See also Staughton Lynd, *Lucasville: The Untold Story of a Prison Uprising* (Oakland, CA: PM Press, 2011). More information can be found at WWW.LUCASVILLEAMNESTY.ORG. Additionally, Bomani has published a memoir under his legal name of Keith LaMar. See Keith LaMar, *Condemned: The Whole Story* (KEITHLAMAR.ORG/). The transcript of Bomani's sentencing statement was taken from the video posted at KEITHLAMAR.ORG.

26 Leslie James Pickering, ed., *Conspiracy to Riot in Furtherance of Terrorism: The Collective Autobiography of the RNC 8* (South Wales, NY: Arissa Media Group, LLC, 2011), 376. The RNC 8 were eight anarchists who were pre-emptively arrested and charged with conspiracy and terrorism under the Minnesota version of the USA Patriot Act in the lead up to the 2008 Republican National Convention in St. Paul, Minnesota. The eight were Monica Bicking, Rob Czernik, Garrett Fitzgerald, Luce Guillén-Givens, Erik Oseland, Nathanael Secor, Max Specktor, and Eryn Trimmer. All of the defendants except for Erik had organized together as part of the RNC Welcoming Committee, which was directly infiltrated by at least one FBI informant and two undercover

cops. The defendants were initially all charged with conspiracy
to riot in the furtherance of terrorism and conspiracy to commit
criminal damage to property in the furtherance of terrorism.
The prosecutor later added those conspiracy charges without the
terrorism enhancements, totaling four counts for each defendant,
and subsequently was forced to drop the terrorism enhancement
charges due to a successful political pressure campaign waged by
the RNC 8 Defense Committee. After nearly two years of pre-trial
proceedings, Erik severed his case and took a non-cooperating plea
deal with a sentence of two months in county jail without probation afterwards. Three weeks later, the prosecutors dropped all
charges against Eryn, Luce, and Monica. The remaining defendants
ended up taking non-cooperating plea agreements to lower-level
gross misdemeanors and receiving probation of one to two years
with no additional prison time. For more information on this case,
visit RNC8.ORG.

27   See Paul LeBlanc, "Smith Act Trial, 1943," in *Encyclopedia of the
      American Left*, eds. Mari Jo Buhle, Paul Budle, and Dan Georgakas
      (New York: Oxford University Press, 1998). Also see EN.WIKOPE-
      DIA.ORG/WIKI/SMITH_ACT_TRIALS_OF_COMMUNIST_PARTY_LEAD-
      ERS. The *Yates* decision has been eroded significantly in the years
      since, so that people accused of conspiracy can now be convicted
      based on the most insignificant actions that might threaten the
      state or a corporation.

28   An inspiring example is Kuwasi Balagoon, who was a member of
      the Black Liberation Army. Kuwasi was radicalized while fighting
      in Vietnam. After returning to the United States, he joined the
      Black Panthers and was one of the defendants in the Panther 21
      case. He later went underground with the Black Liberation Army
      and was arrested with other revolutionaries in December 1981. He
      died in prison of AIDS in 1986. Many revolutionaries who loved

him came together to pay tribute to him shortly after his death. The program they put together states: "Black revolutionary soldier Kuwasi Balagoon died on Dec. 13 at the Erica County Medical Center in upstate New York. He had been moved there from the New York State penitentiary at Auburn where he was incarcerated for his political-military work in behalf of Black Liberation. Information on Balagoon and quote taken from "A Soldier's Story: The Making of a Revolutionary New Afrikan Freedom Fighter: A Memorial and Tribute to Kuwasi Balagoon," WWW. FREEDOMARCHIVES.ORG/DOCUMENTS/FINDER/DOC513_SCANS/ KUWASI_BALAGOON/513.KUWASI.MEMORIAL.TRIBUTE.PDF. To learn more about Kuwasi and to read his trial statements, see Kuwasi Balagoon, *Kuwasi Balagoon: A Soldier's Story: Writings by a Revolutionary New Afrikan Anarchist* (Montreal: Kersplebedeb Publishing, 2003).

29 Again, see Deutsch, "The National Lawyer's Guild Work Defending Independentistas in the U.S."

30 A common assumption is that one can avoid answering questions by simply pleading the Fifth Amendment privilege against self-incrimination. The reality is that this privilege is quite limited and it is often up to the judge to determine what risk of self-incrimination is present in the case at hand, and thus whether the Fifth Amendment applies. For example, someone subpoenaed to testify against an activist facing charges may not be at any risk of facing charges themselves, but may have information that will help the prosecutors win a conviction against the activist. The judge would likely not allow the person subpoenaed to invoke the Fifth Amendment, so that person would either have to answer the questions or risk being held in contempt of court for refusing to talk. The bottom line? The criminal legal system writes their laws in ways that benefit the state, not radicals who do not want to

cooperate with them. The American Bar Association published an informative article on the limitations of the Fifth Amendment and ways lawyers can sidestep it to get the information they want. See Nancy C. Wear, "Taking the 5th: How to Pierce the Testamonial Shield, *Business Law Today* (May/June 2000), APPS.AMERICANBAR. ORG/BUSLAW/BLT/BLT00MAY-SHIELD.HTML.

31   Nathan Block (aka Exile) and Joyanna Zacher (aka Sadie) were exposed as neo-fascists in August 2014 by NYC ANTIFA. Their article presents links to Block's blog and postings he has made on social media sites such as Tumblr. While the article mostly focuses on Block, it also specifies racist statements that Zacher has made: "Exile and Sadie's first post-sentencing statement ends with a reference to Charles Manson's racist ecological philosophy ATWA (meaning either 'Air Trees Water Animals' or 'All The Way Alive'). Sadie repeated this formulation as late as 2012 in a letter from prison to the Earth First! Journal. Both in prison and out, Sadie and Exile have repeatedly made disparaging remarks about people of color, and Exile has made statements supporting white separatism, which Sadie defended when Exile was rightfully called-out for making them." The authors identify themselves by writing, "*This article was written by longtime Green Scare prisoner supporters in consultation with anti-fascists in Olympia, WA.*" See NYCANTIFA. WORDPRESS.COM/2014/08/05/EXILE-IS-A-FASCIST.

32   Potter, *Green is the New Red*, 79. More information about Operation Backfire can be found in this book and the pamphlet "Operation Backfire" by the National Lawyers Guild, available at WWW.NLG.ORG/RESOURCE/KNOW-YOUR-RIGHTS/OPERATION-BACK-FIRE. Daniel's website also states, "The government made dropping the motion and abandoning the request for any kind of a response an absolute condition of resolving the case without a trial. We have no more information about the existence of NSA surveillance of

Daniel today than we did when we requested the information originally." www.supportdaniel.org/faq/#Anchor-What-37516.

33   For more on the Tinley Park 5, including open letters written
        from prison as well as after release, visit tinleyparkfive.word-
        press.com. All of the five were released on parole by late 2014.
        The investigation into this case may still be ongoing at the time
        of this writing. A Chicago-based activist named Jason Hammond
        (twin brother of Jeremy Hammond) was arrested in July 2013
        and charged with being involved in the same action. He was held
        for about a month before posting bond. He accepted a non-coop-
        erating plea agreement to 3.5 years in prison in November 2014
        and reported to prison in January 2015. He was released onto
        parole in April 2016. For more on Jason, see freejasonhammond.
        blogspot.com.

34   Information for this example comes from Sayer, *Ghost Dancing the
        Law*. The letter that some of the jurors sent to the attorney general
        read, in part: "We wish you to know we would not have voted to
        convict either of the two defendants on any of the charges and we
        would not have voted to convict because each of us concluded that
        there was not enough evidence to do so. In our view a govern-
        ment that cannot in an eight-month trial present enough evidence
        against the two leaders of the Wounded Knee siege to secure a
        conviction on any count should for moral and ethical reasons drop
        the criminal charges against all the other Indian people and their
        supporters" (Sayer, 201).

35   Eric McDavid was sentenced to nearly twenty years in federal
        prison for "thought crime," ultimately serving nearly nine years
        before being released in January 2015 as a result of filing a *habeas
        corpus* petition and successfully using a Freedom of Information
        Act (FOIA) request to expose how the FBI had withheld evi-
        dence at his trial. He was arrested in January 2006 as part of the

government's ongoing "Green Scare" campaign against environmental and animal rights activists after being targeted by an undercover FBI informant known as "Anna" who formulated a crime and entrapped him. Eric was arrested with two other activists, Zachary Jenson and Lauren Weiner, both of who quickly cooperated with the state and snitched on him in exchange for light sentences. All three activists were charged with "conspiracy to damage and destroy property by fire and an explosive." The informant "Anna" spent a year and a half drawing Eric in to the crime she orchestrated and was paid over $65,000 for her work with the FBI. After a trial riddled with errors, lies, and blunders on the part of the government, a jury found Eric guilty. Many of those same jurors later made damning statements about the FBI's handling of the case, and two of them submitted declarations to the court stating that they believed Eric deserved a new trial. For more information, visit SUPPORTERIC.ORG.

36 The NATO 3—Brent Betterly, Jared Chase, Brian Jacob Church— are three Occupy activists who were targeted and entrapped by undercover Chicago cops in the lead-up to the May 2012 North Atlantic Treaty Organization (NATO) summit in Chicago. The cops, Mehmet Uygun (aka "Mo") and Nadia Chikko (aka "Gloves") pushed the defendants to create Molotov cocktails and directed them in doing so, going so far as helping purchase gas for them and cutting up a bandanna to serve as wicks. The cops also provided the defendants with beer on multiple occasions and presented themselves as experienced militant activists to gain credibility with the defendants, who were all relatively new to activism. They were charged under the Illinois version of the USA Patriot Act. They took their conspiracy and terrorism charges to trial in January 2014 and were acquitted of all the terrorism charges, although they were each convicted of two counts of mob action (a

lesser-included charge for the original conspiracy to commit terrorism and material support for terrorism charges) and two counts of possession of an incendiary device. The latter charges carried a maximum of thirty years in prison. Brian was sentenced to five years in prison, Brent to six years, and Jared to eight years; they all received credit for two years served in jail while awaiting trial and were designated to serve their sentences at 50% (meaning Brian was to serve 2.5 years in prison with the rest spent on parole, and so on). Brian was released in summer 2014 and Brent in summer 2015. Jared was scheduled to be released in summer 2016 but was facing additional felony charges from an incident that occurred while in custody pre-trial. He pleaded guilty to these charges in April 2016 and was sentenced to an additional year in prison; he has also lost a lot of "good time" due to disciplinary infractions and will serve more than 50% of his sentence. More information on this case can be found at FREETHENATO3.WORDPRESS.COM.

37   A notable exception was in the case of Michael Brown in Ferguson, Missouri. Police officer Darren Wilson fatally shot Brown, who was an 18-year-old Black youth, in August 2014. Brown's murder led to massive riots and demonstrations in Ferguson, with solidarity demonstrations and actions around the country and world. The prosecutor made a public display of telling the world that he was presenting all the evidence to the grand jury so they could determine whether Wilson was guilty of any crime at all. The grand jury declined to indict Wilson and the prosecutor then released nearly 5,000 pages of grand jury transcripts to the public, claiming he was doing so in the interests of transparency. In reality, the prosecutor controlled the grand jury proceedings and was able to allow Wilson to present a narrative that justified his actions, thereby ensuring that no criminal action could be found and thus no indictment issued. The prosecutor presented the grand jury process as a trial

in which the jurors decided there was no guilt, whereas grand juries are ostensibly intended to determine if there is *probable cause* for an indictment, after which a judge or trial jury would ultimately weigh the evidence and determine guilt. Basically, the prosecutor shared the transcripts to dupe the public into thinking that justice had been served. A smart critique of this calculated move appeared in an interview on Democracy Now! on November 25, 2014. Available at www.democracynow.org/2014/11/25/ it_is_officially_open_season_on.

38   Talk with your lawyer to figure out which motions are appropriate in the jurisdiction your case is in.

39   Cops are the exception to this rule. If a grand jury even looks at whether a cop should be indicted for brutalizing or murdering someone, the result is usually that an indictment is not issued.

40   See Joyce L. Kornbluh, "Industrial Workers of the World," in *Encyclopedia of the American Left*, eds. Mari Jo Buhle, Paul Budle, and Dan Georgakas (New York: Oxford University Press, 1998).

41   When hiring an investigator, make sure you or your defense committee is able to interview them beforehand, even if they are recommended or suggested by your lawyer. Investigators can be crucial to a defense team. Unfortunately, they sometimes know little to nothing about doing actual investigatory work.

42   Kevin Van Meter, "A Curious Case: Long Island Radicals Confront the Green Scare," in *Life During Wartime: Resisting Counterinsurgency*, eds. Kristian Williams, Lara Messersmith-Glavin, William Munger (Oakland, CA: AK Press, 2013).

43   Let us never forget that the state defines legality. Just because something is "illegal" does not mean they will not do it with impunity.

44   Filing FOIA requests is a tricky, time-intensive, and often frustrating experience. Technically, FOIA is about requesting government documents on events, organizations, groups, and so

on. Requesting government information about people falls under the Privacy Act. Additionally, each state has its own process for requesting data collected by state agencies. There are some good guides to filing these requests available online. A radical attorney in California, Caitlin Kelly Henry, has produced a detailed video and slide show available at CAITLINKELLYHENRY.COM/FOIA-TRAINING-1. The Center for Constitutional Rights has also produced a detailed guide, available at CCRJUSTICE.ORG/SITES/DEFAULT/FILES/ASSETS/ CCR_FOIA_REQUEST_RESOURCE_GUIDE.PDF. Additionally, the Reporters Committee for Freedom of the Press has guides on filing FOIA requests, FOIA appeals, and state data requests available at WWW.IFOIA.ORG/#!/RESOURCES.

45   See George Orwell's classic novel *1984*.

46   See the cases against Eric McDavid and the NATO 3 (Brent Betterly, Brian Jacob Church, and Jared Chase—who is still in custody at the time of this writing).

47   This language was taken from jury instructions in Eric McDavid's case.

48   *United States v. Davis,* 36 F.3d 1424, 1430 (9th Cir. 1994).

49   Investigative journalist Trevor Aaronson has written extensively about the use of entrapment in the so-called War on Terror. In a 2015 article, he writes, "Entrapment has been argued in at least 12 trials following counterterrorism stings, and the defense has never been successful." Trevor Aaronson, "The Sting: How the FBI Created a Terrorist," *The Intercept*, March 16, 2015, THEINTERCEPT.COM/2015/03/16/HOWTHEFBICREATEDATERRORIST. See also Aaronson, *The Terror Factory*.

50   Bradley Crowder and David McKay, the Texas 2, served time for possessing Molotov cocktails during protests against the 2008 Republican National Convention. Brandon Darby, a bona fide activist who secretly switched sides and volunteered to inform for the

FBI, goaded them into creating the Molotovs and arranged for the FBI to arrest them during the convention. There is a documentary about this case: "Better This World," directed by Kelly Duane de la Vega and Kelly Galloway, *Point of View* (PBS, 2011).

51   See Sacramento Prisoner Support, "The Myth of Entrapment: The Eric McDavid Case as a Model for Government Misconduct in Green Scare Prosecutions," *Fifth Estate* no. 386 (Spring 2012), WWW.FIFTHESTATE.ORG/ARCHIVE/386-SPRING-2012/MYTH-ENTRAPMENT.

52   The Liberty City 7 were accused of plotting to blow up the Sears Tower in Chicago and various federal buildings in Miami. Even the Attorney General at the time, Eric Holder, admitted that their plans were "more aspirational than operational." FBI agents posed as operatives of al-Qaeda, provided equipment and encouragement, and then arrested the so-called conspirators. For basic information on this case, see EN.WIKIPEDIA.ORG/WIKI/LIBERTY_CITY_SEVEN.

53   For an eye-opening overview of US history, see Howard Zinn, *A People's History of the United States* (New York: HarperCollins, 2003).

54   The text of the AETA as it was passed into law can be found at WWW.GOVTRACK.US/CONGRESS/BILLS/109/S3880/TEXT. For the most up-to-date version, search for Title 18, Section 43 at USCODE.HOUSE.GOV/BROWSE.XHTML.

55   The SHAC 7 were indicted in 2006 under the AEPA for running a website that targeted Huntingdon Life Sciences. The defendants were Andrew Stepanian, Darius Fullmer, Jacob Conroy, Joshua Harper, Kevin Kjonaas, and Lauren Gazzola. Their support website states, "The SHAC 7 are 6 animal rights activists and the organization Stop Huntingdon Animal Cruelty USA (SHAC USA) who were convicted on March 2, 2006, under the controversial Federal Animal Enterprise Protection Act. The Act punishes anyone who

'physically disrupts' an animal enterprise. The charges stem from these activists' alleged participation in an international campaign to close the notorious product testing lab Huntingdon Life Sciences." See SHAC7.COM for more information.

56   Van Meter, "A Curious Case."

57   If you have a state case, keep in mind that the laws and rules regulating public defenders and appointed attorneys vary from state to state. As we have tried to generalize in ways that will apply to most cases, if you are uncertain about how something relates to your particular situation, be sure to do the proper research.

58   At times, public defenders (or private lawyers) might send an assistant (another attorney or a paralegal) to talk with you. This is not necessarily a bad sign about their representation, but is not necessarily a good one either. You will likely need to evaluate both your attorney of record and the assistant to make sure you are receiving the representation that you need.

59   The NLG can be reached at WWW.NLG.ORG or 132 Nassau Street, Rm. 922, New York, NY 10038, phone: (212) 679-5100, fax: (212) 679-2811.

60   The CLDC can be reached at WWW.CLDC.ORG or 259 E 5th Ave, Ste 300 A, Eugene, OR 97401, phone: (541) 687-9180, fax: (541) 686-2137.

61   The PLO can be reached at WWW.PEOPLESLAWOFFICE.COM or 1180 N. Milwaukee Ave., Chicago, IL 60642, phone: (773) 235-0070, fax: (773) 235-6699, email: peopleslaw@aol.com.

62   *Faretta v. California*, 422 U.S. 806 (1975).

63   Lynne Stewart was convicted of assisting one of her clients, Sheik Abdul Rahman, in sending instructions to his followers from his prison cell. From her support website: "Lynne has been falsely accused of helping terrorists in an obvious attempt by the U.S. government to silence dissent, curtail vigorous defense lawyers,

and install fear in those who would fight against the U.S. government's racism, seek to help Arabs and Muslims being prosecuted
for free speech and defend the rights of all oppressed people. She
was arrested in April 2002 and arraigned before Manhattan federal
Judge John Koeltl, who also presided over her trial in 2004. She
was convicted, and received a 28-month sentence in October 2006.
However she was free on bail until 2009, when the government
appealed the sentence. In late 2009 Lynne was re-sentenced to
10 years in federal prison. **Lynne was freed from prison on
December 31, 2013 and is now home with her family!"** More
about Lynne can be found at Lynnestewart.org.

64   William L. Switzer, "If I Had a Hammer—*United States v. Kabat*—
Sabotage and Nuclear Protesters," *Creighton Law Review* vol. 20
(1987): 1170.

65   Woodson served twenty-seven years in total because she continued
to conduct political protests immediately upon being paroled.
For more on Woodson's case and to read a letter she wrote shortly
before being released in September 2001, see "Longest-Serving
Nuclear Resister Due Out in Sept.." *Nuclear Resister* (September
2011), www.nukewatchinfo.org/Quarterly/Fall%202011/
page2.pdf. For more context on the anti-nuclear movement that
Woodson and other Plowshares activists at the time were part of,
see Sam Day, "Commitment to Nuclear Truthtelling," no-nukes.
org/nukewatch/spoosamday.html.

66   The United Freedom Front was a clandestine organization that
operated during the 1970s and 1980s. The members were Barbara
Curzi, Carole Manning, Jaan Laaman, Kazi Toure, Patricia
Gros, Raymond Luc Levasseur, Richard Williams, and Tom
Manning. (Information derived from en.wikipedia.org/wiki/
United_Freedom_Front.) The Anarchist Black Cross Federation
has a pamphlet about the members who remain incarcerated,

Jaan Laaman and Tom Manning. The pamphlet reads in part, "In 1985-86, members of [the United Freedom Front (UFF) and the Sam Melville-Jonathan Jackson Unit (SM-JJ)] were tried and convicted for conspiracy and bombing of unoccupied military and corporate facilities. For a decade these guerrilla units targeted governments and corporations who engaged in criminal activities in South Africa and Central America. Rather than verbally support the resistance movements in foreign lands, the UFF/SM-JJ Unit brought the war home to those who sponsored and facilitated these bloody wars against humanity. Sentences for the UFF/SM-JJ Unit prisoners ranged from 45 to 53 years in prison." Anarchist Black Cross Federation, "United Freedom Front Political Prisoners: Tom Manning, Jaan Laaman," WWW.ABCF.NET/ABC/PDFS/UFF.PDF.

67 Ray Luc Levasseur, "From the Shadows of the Mills: Trial Statement of Ray Luc Levasseur," HOME.EARTHLINK.NET/~NEO-LUDD/STATEMENT.HTML.

68 The Asheville 11 were eleven people swept up in the streets of downtown Asheville, North Carolina on May 1, 2010 and charged with felonies and misdemeanors for property destruction and conspiracy. They were held on exorbitant bails but all released pending trial. Their case dragged on for several years before the defendants worked out plea agreements to lesser charges. The defendants did not all know each other prior to being arrested, and a cop stated at one point that he had been instructed to arrest anyone who appeared to be out of breath or who had a bag or backpack. After the cases were resolved, some of the defendants outed one of them, Naomi Ullian, as a snitch for talking with the cops and prosecutors six months after their arrests. For more information on this case, visit ZINELIBRARY.INFO/FIVE-MYTHS-ABOUT-ASHEVILLE-11 and WWW.ANARCHISTNEWS.ORG/CONTENT/NAOMI-ULLIAN-OUTED-SNITCH-ASHEVILLE-11-CASE.

69　The Chicago 8 were Abbie Hoffman, David Dellinger, Jerry Rubin, John Froines, Lee Weiner, Rennie Davis, Tom Hayden, and Bobby Seale of the Black Panthers (who was later severed from the other defendants and proceeded to trial on his own). They were charged with conspiracy, inciting to riot, and similar charges for organizing in the lead-up to the 1968 Democratic National Convention. For a day-by-day description of this trial and its legal background, see *The Great Conspiracy Trial* by Jason Epstein, Random House, 1970. In the Chicago 7 joint trial, Abbie was often at the center of making fun of the trial, criminal legal system, and the judge himself. These defendants had clearly decided that their political goals were more important than any legal goals and were willing to receive whatever punishment was doled out. All seven defendants were convicted of inciting to riot, although these convictions were later overturned. Bobby was sentenced to four years and served that sentence. More basic information can be found at EN.WIKIPEDIA. ORG/WIKI/ABBIE_HOFFMAN#CHICAGO_EIGHT_CONSPIRACY_TRIAL.

70　David Gilbert is an anti-racist, anti-imperialist political prisoner serving a life sentence in New York state for his role in the Brink's expropriation. He had gone underground with the Weather Underground then briefly resurfaced before going back underground to act in solidarity with the Black Liberation Army. The Jericho Movement, an organization dedicated to supporting and working to free Black liberation and allied political prisoners, has posted a short autobiography that reads: "In 1970, responding to the murderous government assault on the Black Liberation Movement and on the unending, massive bombings of Vietnam, some of us [Students for a Democratic Society members] went underground to raise the level of resistance, forming the Weather Underground Organization, which functioned for 7 years. By the end of the 1970s, after the WUO dissolved, I tried to work more directly as an ally of the black liberation struggle. On 10/20/81 I was captured when a unit of the Black Liberation Army and allied white revolutionaries attempted to take funds from a Brinks truck, with the tragic results of a shoot-out in which a guard and two policemen were killed. Subsequently, Mtayari Shabaka Sundiata was killed by police, while many other comrades were captured and given long sentences. I was convicted under New York's 'Felony Murder' law. That means that even with no allegations of doing any shooting, any participant in a robbery bears full legal responsibility for all the deaths that occur. I was given 75 years to life and cannot even be considered for parole before 2056. Any hope for my eventual release is totally bound up with qualitative social change for all, advances big enough to lead to the recognition of PPs in the U.S. and/or major reform of draconian sentencing structures." THEJERICHOMOVEMENT.COM/PROFILE/GILBERT-DAVID. David has written extensively, including his memoir: David Gilbert, *Love and Struggle: My Life in SDS, the Weather Underground, and Beyond* (Oakland, CA: PM Press, 2011).

71   The case of radical lawyer Lynne Stewart is an example.

72   This case was referred to by the Canadian courts as "The G20 Main Conspiracy Group." The defendants were Adam Lewis, Alex Hundert, Bill Vandreil, David Prychitka, Erik Lankin, Joanna Adamiak, Julia Kerr, Leah Henderson, Mandy Hiscocks, Meghan Lankin, Monica Peters, Pat Cadorette, Paul Sauder, Peter Hopperton, SK Hussan, Sterling Stutz, and Terrance Luscombe. After negotiating plea agreements that entailed six of the defendants pleading guilty and the charges against the eleven others being dropped, the defendants wrote: "This alleged conspiracy is absurd. We were never all part of any one group, we didn't all organize together, and our political backgrounds are all different. Some of us met for the first time in jail. What we do have in

common is that we, like many others, are passionate about creating communities of resistance. Separately and together, we work with movements against colonialism, capitalism, borders, patriarchy, white supremacy, ableism, hetero/cis-normativity, and environmental destruction. These are movements for radical change, and they represent real alternatives to existing power structures. It is for this reason that we were targeted by the state….Of the 17 of us, six will be pleading and the 11 others will have their charges withdrawn. Alex Hundert, and Mandy Hiscocks are each pleading to one count of counselling mischief over $5,000 and one count of counselling to obstruct police, and Leah Henderson, Peter Hopperton, Erik Lankin, and Adam Lewis are each pleading to a single count of counselling mischief over $5,000. We are expecting sentences to range between six and 24 months, and all will get some credit for time already served in jail and on house arrest….Within this winless situation, we decided that the best course of action was to clearly identify our goals and needs and then to explore our options. Within our group, we faced different levels of risk if convicted, and so we began with the agreement that our top priority was to avoid any deportations. Other key goals we reached were to minimize the number of convictions, to honour people's individual needs, and to be mindful of how our decisions affect our broader movements. Although we are giving up some important things by not going to trial, this deal achieves specific goals that we weren't willing to gamble." Their full statement is available at RABBLE.CA/NEWS/2011/11/G20-CONSPIRACY-ARRESTEES-WE-EMERGE-UNITED-AND-SOLIDARITY.

73 Annette T. Rubenstein et al., "The Black Panther Party and the Case of the Panther 21," (Charter Group for a Pledge of Conscience, January 1970), 10, RBG-STREETSCHOLAR.WORDPRESS.COM/2014/08/08/

COINTELPRO-FRAMING-THE-PANTHERS-AND-THE-CASE-OF-DHORU-
BA-BIN-WAHAD-AND-PANTHER-21-CASE-READ.

74   Dhoruba Bin Wahad, "History 101: The Panther 21, Police
      Repression, The BLA and Cointel-Pro," December 14, 2015,
      HIPHOPANDPOLITICS.COM/2015/12/14/THE-PANTHER-21-CASE-A-
      GLIMPSE-INTOTHE-FUTURE-PAST-OF-RACIST-POLICE-REPRESSION.

75   For example, see an image of the first page of "Panther 21 Trial
      Bulletin 2" at WWW.DIVISIONLEAP.COM/PICTURES/23773.JPEG. *The
      Black Panther*, the newspaper of the Black Panther Party, published
      numerous articles about the defendants and the trial as well. See
      WWW.ITSABOUTTIMEBPP.COM/CHAPTER_HISTORY/PDF/NEW_YORK/
      NEW_YORK_21.PDF for a first-person account by one of the
      defendants, Roseland Bennitt. Another defendant, Lumumba
      Abdul Shakur, published an article on the history of the judge and
      prosecutor in this newspaper as well. Lumumba Abdul Shakur,
      "From NY 21 Black Community Information Center Bronx NY,"
      The Black Panther, February 28, 1970, WWW.ITSABOUTTIMEBPP.
      COM/CHAPTER_HISTORY/PDF/NEW_YORK/NY_CHAPTER_4.PDF.

76   KEYWIKI.ORG/COMMITTEE_TO_DEFEND_THE_PANTHER_21.

77   The Committee to Defend the Panther 21, "To Judge Murtagh
      from the Panther 21," in *What do the Panthers stand for*, ARCHIVE.
      LIB.MSU.EDU/DMC/AMRAD/WHATPANTHERSSTAND.PDF.

78   In the case of the Panther 21, the political context included
      COINTELPRO operations being in full effect and beginning to
      push Black radicals underground to avoid execution by the police
      or by other radicals who fell prey to the FBI's machinations. In
      "History 101," Bin Wahad writes: "In early January 1971, **Fred
      Bennett**, a BPP member affiliated with the New York chapter, was
      shot and killed, allegedly by Newton supporters. Newton came
      to believe that Bin Wahad was plotting to kill him. Bin Wahad,
      in turn, was told by **Connie Matthews**, Newton's secretary, that

Newton was planning to have Bin Wahad and Panther 21 codefendants **Edward Joseph** and **Michael Tabor** killed during Newton's upcoming East Coast speaking tour. As a result of the split and fearing for his life, Bin Wahad, along with Tabor and Joseph, were forced to flee during the Panther 21 trial. **Afeni Shakur**, a Panther 21 codefendant of Bin Wahad and pregnant with **Tupac Shakur** declined to go underground with her comrades" (bold in the original). Considering the political context these defendants were facing, publishing an irreverent and sharply worded letter to their judge was likely the least of the dangers they faced.

79   Scott DeMuth was indicted on a conspiracy charge under the Animal Enterprise Protection Act (AEPA) for an Animal Liberation Front lab raid at the University of Iowa in 2004. The government never indicted any co-conspirators, even though a video released after the raid showed multiple people present at the scene. His indictment was subsequently changed to include a fur farm raid in Minnesota in 2006, yet he still had no indicted co-conspirators. He ended up pleading guilty to the fur farm raid, which was a misdemeanor offense, and the felony conspiracy count for the lab raid was dropped. At the time of this writing, no one else has been indicted for either raid and the statute of limitations for the lab raid has run out. See DAVENPORTGRANDJURY.WORDPRESS.COM for more information.

80   In the government's motion to ask the court to put Scott back into custody pending trial, the prosecutor wrote: "Defendant's writings, literature, and conduct suggest that he is an anarchist and associated with the ALF movement. Therefore, he is a domestic terrorist." (Case 3:09-cr-00117-JAJ-TJS in the U.S. District Court for the Southern District of Iowa, Document 17, filed 11/25/2009, p. 6.)

81   See Leonard Peltier, "When the Truth Doesn't Matter," *Counterpunch*, January 9, 2007, WWW.COUNTERPUNCH. ORG/2007/01/09/WHEN-THE-TRUTH-DOESN-T-MATTER.

82   See Matt Stroud and Steve Horn, "Revealed: The Story Behind the
      'NATO 3' Domestic Terrorism Arrests," *Truthout*, June 21, 2013,
      WWW.TRUTH-OUT.ORG/NEWS/ITEM/17107-REVEALED-THE-STORY-
      BEHIND-THE-NATO-3-DOMESTIC-TERRORISM-ARRESTS.

83   For more information, see the Wikipedia entry, "Mumia Abu-
      Jamal": EN.WIKIPEDIA.ORG/WIKI/MUMIA_ABU-JAMAL.

84   You can access this manual online at WWW.RUCKUS.ORG/DOWN-
      LOADS/RUCKUSMEDIAMANUAL.PDF. According to their website,
      "The Ruckus Society provides environmental, human rights,
      and social justice organizers with the tools, training, and support
      needed to achieve their goals through the strategic use of creative,
      nonviolent direct action." To contact them, email RUCKUS@RUCK-
      US.ORG, call 510.931.6339, or write The Ruckus Society, PO Box
      28741, Oakland, CA 94604.

85   You can access this manual online at SPINACADEMY.ORG/WP-CON-
      TENT/UPLOADS/2012/04/SPIN-WORKS.PDF. According to their
      website, "The SPIN Academy strengthens non-profit organizations
      working for social change by teaching them to communicate
      effectively for themselves. The SPIN Academy provides accessi-
      ble and affordable strategic communications training, individual
      coaching, networking opportunities, and other concrete com-
      munications tools. Drawing on a dedicated network of nonprofit
      communications professionals, we build the communications skills
      of social change advocates and build the capacity of grassroots or-
      ganizations to accomplish their missions." To contact them, email
      INFO@SPINACADEMY.ORG, call 415.938.7506, or write The SPIN
      Academy, Community Initiatives, 354 Pine Street, Suite 700, San
      Francisco, CA 94104.

86   The Youth Media Council is now known as the Center for Media
      Justice. You can access this manual online at WWW.SCRIBD.COM/
      DOC/16596427/COMMUNICATE-JUSTICE-101 and can access other

resources they have produced at CENTERFORMEDIAJUSTICE.ORG/
TOOLBOX/STRATEGY-TOOLS. According to their website, "the Center
for Media Justice is a national movement building intermediary to
strengthen the communications effectiveness of grassroots racial
justice sectors, and sustain a powerful local-to-local movement
for media rights and access. Our mission is to create media and
cultural conditions that strengthen movements for racial justice,
economic equity, and human rights." To contact them, email
INFO@MEDIAJUSTICE.ORG, call 510.698.3800, or write The Center
for Media Justice, 436 14th Street, 5th Floor, Oakland, CA 94612.

87   Patrick Reinsborough and Doyle Canning, *Re:Imagining Change:
     How to Use Story-Based Strategy to Win Campaigns, Build
     Movements, and Change the World* (Oakland, CA: PM Press, 2010).
     More information can be found at WWW.STORYBASEDSTRATEGY.
     ORG. According to their website, "The Center for Story-based
     Strategy (CSS) is a national movement-building organization
     dedicated to harnessing the power of narrative for social change.
     We offer social justice networks, alliances and organizations the
     analysis, training and strategic support to change the story on the
     issues that matter most."

88   To access these handouts, visit SEEDSFORCHANGE.ORG.UK/RE-
     SOURCES#MEDIA. According to their website, "Seeds For Change
     Network is a network of non-profit training and support co-op-
     eratives which help people organize for action and positive social
     change. The network started in 2000 with informal co-operation
     between people who were doing workshops in their spare time.
     Providing training, workshops and support to grassroots campaign-
     ers is still the main focus of the work of the co-ops in the network,
     and this is financed by donations and working part time as trainers
     for NGOs, co-ops and charities. We concentrate on working
     with grassroots environmental and social justice activists to help

increase their effectiveness in campaigning and bringing about lasting positive change." You can contact either of the independent co-ops in their network. For the Lancaster one, email LANCASTER@ SEEDSFORCHANGE.ORG.UK, call 011+44+1524 509002, or write Seeds for Change Lancaster Co-operative Ltd., Storey Institute, Meeting House Lane, Lancaster LA1 1TH, United Kingdom. For the Oxford one, email OXFORD@SEEDSFORCHANGE.ORG.UK, call 011+44+1865 403134, or write Seeds for Change Oxford Collective Ltd., Old Music Hall, 106-108 Cowley Road, Oxford OX4 1JE, United Kingdom.

89   For more on PRISM, see EN.WIKIPEDIA.ORG/WIKI/ PRISM_%28SURVEILLANCE_PROGRAM%29.

90   The Electronic Frontier Foundation (EFF) produces an annual report entitled "Who Has Your Back?: Protecting Your Data from Government Requests" that rates various companies on their expressed policies for handling government requests for data and their transparency when responding to these requests. See, for example, WWW.EFF.ORG/WHO-HAS-YOUR-BACK-GOVERNMENT-DATA-REQUESTS-2015. In the 2015 report, Google and Facebook received star ratings in "Inform users about government data demands." But a recent Transparency Report on Google shows that they provided some or all of the information requested in 74% of the 7,032 subpoenas and 85% of the 3,588 search warrants they received between January and June 2015. See WWW.GOOGLE.COM/TRANS-PARENCYREPORT/USERDATAREQUESTS/US. While this data does not indicate why the other subpoenas and warrants were not responded to, Google clearly hands over data on the regular. It also bears remembering that subpoenas and search warrants are easy for the authorities to obtain.

91   The grand jury resisters were Kerry Cunneen, Matt Duran, Steve Jablonski, Katherine "Kteeo" Olejnik, Maddy Pfeiffer, and

Dennison Williams. Matt, Kteeo, and Maddy were all held on civil contempt, whereas Dennison's subpoena was dropped. Kerry refused to appear before the grand jury after being subpoenaed and successfully evaded apprehension to be forced to appear. Steve left the country rather than appearing before the grand jury after claiming that he received a call from the FBI saying that they had a subpoena they wanted to serve on him. (Sadly, former friends and comrades of Steve later wrote an open letter exposing his lies about being harassed by law enforcement and perhaps about being at risk of being subpoenaed at all. See ANARCHISTNEWS.ORG/ CONTENT/REGARDING-STEVEN-JABLONSKIS-DECEPTIONS-GRAND-JU- RIES-AND-SENSIBLE-SOLIDARITY.) At the time of this writing, no one subpoenaed to the grand jury is currently in custody. No one has been indicted at the federal level either, which suggests this case may be far from over (several people have been convicted of property damage at the Washington state level). For more on this case, visit NOPOLITICALREPRESSION.WORDPRESS.COM. A zine of statements from the resisters and their supporters was compiled by New York Year Zero and is available at YEARO.ORG/2012/10/22/ FOR-THE-PACIFIC-NORTHWEST-GRAND-JURY-RESISTERS. Kerry also did a radio interview after being subpoenaed that can be found at NOPOLITICALREPRESSION.WORDPRESS.COM/2013/01/24/ RADIO-INTERVIEW-WITH-KERRY-CUNNEEN.

92 Two notable exceptions are self-defense and necessity. For self-de- fense as a legal defense, defendants generally must admit guilt to at least some elements of the alleged offense (e.g., assault, murder) while claiming that engaging in these acts was necessary to defend their own lives. For a necessity defense, defendants must generally admit guilt to at least some elements of the alleged defense (e.g., trespassing or property destruction) while arguing that the moral imperative of doing so is more important than the fact that they

broke the law. The exact requirements of these defenses varies by jurisdiction and they may not be available or permitted in every jurisdiction for every alleged offense.

93 Information taken from Matt Sledge, "Bureau of Prisons Backtracks, Again, on Daniel McGowan," *The Huffington Post*, April 10, 2013, WWW.HUFFINGTONPOST.COM/2013/04/10/BU-REAU-OF-PRISONS-DANIEL-MCGOWAN_N_3054153.HTML.

94 The Supreme Court of the United States has acknowledged that about 95% of all criminal cases are resolved through plea agreements. See *Lafler v. Cooper*, 132 S. Ct. 1376, 182 L. Ed. 2D 398 (2012).

95 The Thirteenth Amendment reads: "Neither slavery nor involuntary servitude, except as a punishment for crime whereof the party shall have been duly convicted, shall exist within the United States, or any place subject to their jurisdiction." Available at MEMORY.LOC.GOV/CGI-BIN/AMPAGE?COLLID=LLSL&FILENAME=013/LLSL013.DB&RECNUM=596.

96 There is an increasing number of news articles, documentaries, and books about the prison-industrial complex—too many to list here. If you are incarcerated, ask your friends and supporters to find some of the latest books and articles to send to you. An organization that produces a lot of information about the current state of the prison-industrial complex, some of it written by prisoners, is Critical Resistance (CR). CR's focus is on prison abolition rather than reform; they produce a regular newspaper, *The Abolitionist*, that is free for prisoners. They can be contacted at *The Abolitionist*, 1904 Franklin St, Ste 504, Oakland, CA 94612. More information can be found at ABOLITIONISTPAPER.WORDPRESS.COM/ and CRITI-CALRESISTANCE.ORG.

97 See *Brandon Baxter v. The United States of America*, 1:12-cr-00238-PAG in the United States District Court, Northern District

of Ohio (Eastern Division), document number 355, filed on December 21, 2015, p. 13.

98   Ibid, p. 14 (citations removed).

99   Information on this trial taken from Sayer, *Ghost Dancing the Law*.

100   See the chart embedded in: Crimethinc Ex-Workers' Collective, "Green Scared? Preliminary Lessons of the Green Scare," *Rolling Thunder: An Anarchist Journal of Dangerous Living* no. 5 (Spring 2008): 28–42, THECLOUD.CRIMETHINC.COM/PDFS/ROLLING_THUN-DER_5.PDF. "Operation Backfire" was the name the FBI gave their 2004 investigation of Earth Liberation Front (ELF) arsons.

101   Note that the non-cooperating defendants (Nathan Block, Daniel McGowan, Jonathan Paul, Joyanna Zacher) all benefited from creative legal maneuvering that gave them leverage for plea agreement negotiations that are by no means guaranteed to all radical defendants. Their situation is explained in more detail in the "Gaining Leverage in the Negotiation Process" subsection be-low. As such, the data in this chart must be interpreted with this context in mind instead of being read as suggesting that all of the defendants, cooperating and non-cooperating, were in roughly the same legal situation prior to accepting plea agreements. Even so, the non-cooperating defendants were only able to benefit from legal maneuvers that forced the government's hand by fight-ing their charges and standing in solidarity with each other. The snitches never had a chance to figure out how to improve their situation because they caved in to the government's pressure and thus were at their mercy.

102   The Cleveland 4 all received a sentences ranging between 8 and 11.5 years plus *lifetime* supervised release, which means they will be under the thumb of the criminal legal system for the rest of their lives. Their attempts to appeal this aspect of their sentence were unsuccessful.

103 For more on the Weather Underground and Prairie Fire, see Dan
     Berger, *Outlaws of America: The Weather Underground and the
     Politics of Solidarity* (Oakland, CA: AK Press, 2006).

104 Balagoon, *Kuwasi Balagoon*, 72.

105 More about Jeremy can be found at FREEJEREMY.NET. His support
     crew writes, "Jeremy has been an anarchist communist organizer in
     the Chicago area for many years. His convictions have lead him to
     travel the country for many direct actions. At the time of his arrest
     in March, he was assisting in organizing protests against the NATO
     summit. He is accused of being part of OpAntiSec, a combined
     effort of Anonymous and Lulzsec targeting government servers as
     well as those of the military industrial complex. In particular, one
     of the many fruits of this operation has been released on Wikileaks
     as 'The Global Intelligence Files.' Consisting of thousands of emails
     from the private intelligence service Stratfor, the emails reveal
     the corruption rampant in the company; the flawed and biased
     information that helped determine U.S. Foreign policy, as well as
     government discussions on monitoring and infiltrating domestic
     organizations such as Occupy." Jeremy is the twin brother of Jason
     Hammond, who was one of the anti-fascists arrested after an attack
     on a fascist gathering in Tinley Park, Illinois in May 2012.

106 Available at FREEANONS.ORG/
     JEREMY-HAMMOND-SENTENCED-10-YEARS.

107 Not included in this excerpt is Jeremy's description of his first fed-
     eral prison sentence: "I have been arrested for numerous acts of civ-
     il disobedience on the streets of Chicago, but it wasn't until 2005
     that I used my computer skills to break the law in political protest.
     I was arrested by the FBI for hacking into the computer systems
     of a right-wing, pro-war group called Protest Warrior, an organiza-
     tion that sold racist t-shirts on their website and harassed anti-war
     groups. I was charged under the Computer Fraud and Abuse Act,

and the 'intended loss' in my case was arbitrarily calculated by multiplying the 5000 credit cards in Protest Warrior's database by $500, resulting in a total of $2.5 million. My sentencing guidelines were calculated on the basis of this 'loss,' even though not a single credit card was used or distributed—by me or anyone else. I was sentenced to two years in prison."

108   Chelsea Manning was sentenced to thirty-five years in military prison after going to trial on charges of leaking information about US military crimes. She was granted clemency by President Barack Obama in January 2017, shortly before his last day in office, with a slated release date in May 2017. Her support website reads,

"The trial of military whistle-blower and democracy advocate Chelsea Manning (known as Bradley Manning until her Aug 22, 2013 announcement) finished on August 21st. After a prosecution which starkly showcased US government officials' misplaced priorities when it comes to human rights, Army whistleblower PVT Manning was sentenced to 35 years in prison. The information that Manning gave to the public exposed the unjust detainment of innocent people at Guantanamo Bay, showed us the true human cost of our wars in Iraq and Afghanistan, and changed journalism forever. There is no evidence that anyone died as a result of the leaked information. **Through WikiLeaks Manning revealed:** the Collateral Murder video that exposed the killing of unarmed civilians and two Reuters journalists by a US Apache helicopter crew in Iraq; the Afghan War Diary that revealed uninvestigated civilian casualties and contractor abuse; the Iraq War Logs that revealed civilian casualties and uninvestigated reports of torture; and the US diplomatic cables that revealed the role that corporate interests and spying play in international diplomacy. On July 30, 2013, PVT Manning was found not guilty of the most serious charge against her, that of 'Aiding the Enemy.' However, she was convicted of 20 offenses, including 6 under the Espionage Act. On August 21, 2013 she was sentenced by military judge Col. Denise Lind to 35 years in prison—less than the 60 years requested by the government, yet still an unusually harsh sentence for a non-violent crime." Available at www.chelseamanning.org.

109 Josh Harper was sentenced to three years in prison as part of the SHAC 7 case and released from prison in 2009. His sections in this chapter are taken from Mike Klepfer, "Sometimes We Had a Brick: Interview with Former SHAC 7 Prisoners Jake Conroy and Josh Harper," *The Portland Radicle*, July 22, 2013, https://port-landradicle.wordpress.com/2013/07/22/sometimes-we-had-a-brick-an-interview-with-former-shac-7-prisoners-jake-con-roy-and-josh-harper.

110 Jake Conroy is an animal rights activist who was sentenced to four years in prison as part of the SHAC 7 case and released in November 2009. His sections in this chapter are taken from Kepler, "Sometimes We Had a Brick."

111 August Spies is a pseudonym for a present-day prisoner. We have chosen to use pseudonyms in place of current prisoner's names in this chapter in an effort to protect our comrades from further targeting and harassment by the state. They have acted courageous-ly in participating in this project and we would like to extend our sincerest thanks and solidarity to all of those who contributed. The real August Spies was an anarchist and radical labor activist. He was one of four people executed by the state in the aftermath of the Haymarket affair in 1887.

112 Emma Goldman is a pseudonym. The real Emma Goldman was an anarchist thinker, writer, and activist. She fought for women's rights, workers' rights, and other social issues. She also traveled to Spain to join the anarchist revolution during the Spanish Civil War.

113   Voltairine de Cleyre is a pseudonym. The real Voltairine de Cleyre was an anarchist writer and feminist whose writing often focused on opposition to both the state and marriage.

114   John Tucker is an anti-fascist activist who served a 3.5-year prison sentence in Illinois as one of the Tinley Park 5. The five were arrested after interrupting a meeting of white supremacists in Tinley Park, Illinois with hammers and other blunt objects. The ensuing altercation left ten injured fascists. John was released from prison in February 2014.

115   Lucy Parsons is a pseudonym. The real Lucy Parsons was an anarchist organizer who worked in the labor movement, for political prisoners, for women, and more. The Chicago Police Department is often quoted as once describing her as "more dangerous than a thousand rioters."

116   John Brown is a pseudonym. The real John Brown was an abolitionist who believed in armed insurrection as the means by which to end slavery. He led a raid on the armory at Harpers Ferry in 1859 and was subsequently hanged by the state for his actions.

117   The Central Intelligence Agency (CIA) wrote the KUBARK Counterintelligence Interrogation manual in 1963 and parts of it were declassified in 1966. This manual documents interrogation techniques ranging from manipulation to torture. The text of the manual can be found at HTTPS://EN.WIKISOURCE.ORG/WIKI/ KUBARK_COUNTERINTELLIGENCE_INTERROGATION.

118   Wopashitwe Mondo Eyen we Langa (known as Mondo we Langa or Mondo) was one of the Nebraska 2 (along with Ed Poindexter). He worked with the Black Panther Party against police brutality and helped set up community service programs. He was serving a life sentence in Nebraska and joined the ancestors on March 11, 2016.

119   Ricardo Flores Magón is a pseudonym. The real Ricardo Flores Magón was an anarchist who organized with the Industrial

Workers of the World (IWW) and edited the Mexican anarchist newspaper *Regeneración*. His words and actions contributed greatly to the movements that sparked the Mexican Revolution.

120 Eric McDavid is a green anarchist who was entrapped by a government informant in 2006 and charged with conspiracy to destroy property with fire or explosives. He was sentenced to almost twenty years in prison, but was released in 2015—almost ten years early— after filing a successful *habeas corpus* petition.

Made in the USA
San Bernardino,
CA